DUNBLANE UNBURIED

By

Sandra Uttley

BookPublishingWorld

A BookPublishingWorld Book

ISBN: 1-905553-05-6

Printed for BookPublishingWorld
by
The Cromwell Press
England

This book is dedicated to the memory of:

Gwen Mayor
Melissa Currie
Brett McKinnon
John Petrie
Joanna Ross
David Kerr
Ross Irvine
Victoria Clydesdale
Kevin Hasell
Emma Crozier
Megan Turner
Hannah Scott
Abigail McLennan
Mhairi MacBeath
Sophie North
Hannah Scott
Charlotte Dunn

Words, when Dunblane asks for silence, space to mourn, to rage, to try to understand the incomprehensible.

We assemble facts, names, lists, numbers.
We look for character traits, analogies, consequences.
But how much of that will enable us to solve the same impossible puzzle that assails the nation:
they were children, five-and six-year-olds, in a gym class, doing what five- and – six-year-olds do, laughing, playing, shouting, hoping, dreaming.
Children in a gym class.
How could it be?
How could anyone, in however twisted a mind,
turn children into creatures to be killed?
At times like this the modern world is so unfathomable.
A deranged man kills children in a violent slaughter.
Yet there is no calculus we can use to tell us whether or how our age is, in some grand moral scheme, any better or worse than previous ages.
What is sure is that, unlike those times, these days we know instantly almost as much as the people of Dunblane know about what happened to their children in that gym class.

As a result, Dunblane belongs to us all, at once, wherever we are….

(Editorial from The Independent, 14 March 1996)

Like other killers who seem to have passed beyond the boundaries of morality…
Thomas Hamilton's motives and values seem warped and distorted beyond recognition.
And yet the events at Dunblane come from somewhere.
Hamilton emerged from the backdrop against which he acted.
Hamilton's story, like the story of so much violence in our society, is a tale of men and weapons, sex and repression, power and revenge….
The events in Dunblane did not come from nowhere.
They emerged from a backdrop.

(The Independent, 16 March 1996)

In a very real sense, the surging water in an ocean does not move; rather, energy moves through it. In this same sense, the energy of violence moves through our culture. Some experience it as a light but unpleasant breeze, easy to tolerate.
Others are destroyed by it, as if by a hurricane.
But nobody – nobody – is untouched.

(Gavin de Becker, The Gift of Fear)

ACKNOWLEDGEMENTS

This was not a book I ever wanted to write. However, it has always been my aim to get the truth out about the circumstances surrounding the Dunblane Massacre and a book seemed to be the only way in the end. There are many people I must thank for helping me along this very bumpy road over the last three years. First and foremost, Doreen Hagger, who did more than anyone could possibly have done to try and stop Thomas Hamilton from continuing with his illegal activities. The odds were always stacked against her, as Hamilton was being protected by his friends. To my mind, Doreen is the true hero of this story. She really deserves a medal. And for all her help with the research for Chapter 2 of this book, and her contribution to Chapter 3, thank you hardly seems enough. Doreen, you did all you could. And thank you from the bottom of my heart.

Another big thank you has to go to William Scott, without whom the illegal one hundred year closure order on the Dunblane Inquiry documents would never have been written about and eventually overturned. William's friendship and steadfast support over the last three years have kept me going at times when I felt I couldn't continue any longer. You too deserve a medal William!

My thanks also go to Mike Wells, Richard Malbon and Joe Kelly of the Sportsman's Association who helped bring this book about. They have guided me around the maze of firearms and firearms legislation and considerably increased my understanding of guns and ballistics. When I first contacted them I felt I was betraying the children of Dunblane. The handgun ban was meant to be the great legacy of this horrendous mass murder and as a former Dunblane resident myself, I had supported the Snowdrop Petition to do away with handguns. However, the deeper and more involved I became in the background and true circumstances surrounding the Dunblane Massacre, the more I realised that the handgun ban was totally beside the point. Thomas Hamilton could have been stopped. The legislation in 1996 was strong enough to have disarmed him, and my initial fears about contacting shooting organisations have totally been dispelled. Mike and Richard have provided me with an education about firearms that I would otherwise never have had. They have also chivvied me along as my spirits have sagged, and increasingly so over the last six months. Thanks guys!

Being involved in campaigning for the truth about such a devastating incident has inevitably had serious emotional consequences for me. Believe me, I do NOT recommend taking on the establishment over a cover-up; it is the most demoralising, dispiriting experience anyone could ever enter into. So I must thank my parents for coming to the rescue and taking my little dog Jack into their care whilst I devoted my time to the campaign. My parents initially discouraged me from taking this on, but as time has gone on and I have persisted, they have encouraged me to see it through. For all the support you have offered me mum and dad, THANK YOU.

Another person I must express my gratitude to is my GP, Dr Stephen Johnson. He has never doubted what I've told him about the cover-up and also quickly realised the emotional devastation being involved in something like this causes, especially as a lone woman campaigner. Whenever I've just needed to talk, or cry, he has made time for me. I could appear to be doing okay at one appointment, then the next time he saw me I would be a wreck. Our chats have sustained me throughout this ordeal. Thank you Dr J!

A final thank you has to go to my friend in New York, Carlton Bright. Where do I begin thanking you Carlton? For all that we are thousands of miles of ocean apart, your regular email contact with me throughout the day – during the long tedious hours of sitting at my computer – has brought light and good cheer to what were otherwise very bleak days. Your critiques of my research and pieces I have written have always been invaluable. You are a wonderful friend and I can't thank you enough.

And last but not least, thank you to The Lord Burton for asking that crucial question in the House of Lords in 1999. Without that, none of what followed would probably ever have happened. Thank you Michael.

FOREWORD

On 22 March 2006, my petition to the Scottish Parliament was considered by the Public Petitions Committee. It read as follows:

Petition by Sandra Uttley calling on the Scottish Parliament to urge the Scottish Executive to instigate a New Inquiry into the shootings at Dunblane Primary School on 13 March 1996.

ADDITIONAL INFORMATION IN SUPPORT OF THE DUNBLANE PETITION OF MISS S UTTLEY. I AM NOT SATISFIED WITH THE FINDINGS OF LORD CULLEN FOR THE FOLLOWING REASONS:

- In a witness statement taken by police in the aftermath of the incident, Mrs Kerr, a neighbour of Hamilton's, stated that she saw him "getting out of or standing beside a grey saloon car, that he waved to the driver who then drove off, and that Hamilton was cheerful". I have made enquiries of both the Crown Office and Central Scotland Police about what measures were taken to identify the driver of this grey car, and was advised by the Crown Office that it was a neighbour of Hamilton's, a Mr Comrie Deuchars, who was apparently precognosed in detail by the procurator fiscal about this matter. However, in their reply, Central Scotland Police say a trace was done on this car and that it was NOT Mr Deuchars, as his car was gold.... I have since requested copies of all the documents relating to this trace, only now to be told by Central Scotland Police that Mrs Kerr gave a second statement suggesting that it WAS Mr Deuchars. I have requested a copy of this 'second statement' and made a further request for copies of all the documents relating to the trace of the car.

- the CID officer, DC Graham Capes, who gave evidence at the Dunblane Inquiry, gave wrong information about the CCTV sightings of Thomas Hamilton's van on the morning of 13 March 1996. In his original witness statement the times of the sightings are 08.44 and 08.46. On oath at the Inquiry DC Graham Capes said 09.12. After 3 years of writing to Lord Cullen and the Lord Advocate, and with the assistance of my MP, I eventually received an acknowledgement that DC Capes "made a mistake" in his evidence.

- I pursued this matter by then asking why DC Capes stated that Hamilton's van was seen "exiting on to the road to Dunblane" when in fact it did not. The Lord Advocate refuses to answer this question.

- DCS John Ogg, in his evidence at the Dunblane Inquiry said that the Headteacher's emergency call was an 'ordinary call' to the police, NOT a 999 call. The Headteacher himself was rather vague. However, DC Capes – who had already given wrong information about the CCTV sightings – say <u>he was told</u> by a sergeant that there was a tape of the 999 call by the Headteacher. Following investigation by the Scottish Information Commissioner on my behalf, Central Scotland Police "submitted that they are aware that the telephone call from Mr Taylor was recorded at the time and that the tape was registered as a production. However, it has not been located. The Police go on to state that there is no evidence that a transcript of the tape has been made. In its submissions (to the Information Commissioner), the Police indicated that a thorough examination was carried out of the area in which all the material relating to the Dunblane incident is held and this failed to locate the tape of the call made by Mr Taylor. The Police submitted that a search was also made of the database used by the Police in order to ascertain if a transcript of the call had been made, but again no transcript was found. I am satisfied that this tape is no longer held by the Police".

I always wondered how Central Scotland Police would get around this one. They claim not to have the tape, but nor is a transcript of the recording available at the National Archives of Scotland. It was inevitable that this tape would be spirited away. Who was the Sergeant who told DC Graham Capes that such a tape existed? Was it Sergeant Donald Cowan, friend of Hamilton's friend, former police officer William MacDonald?

• After making enquiries with the Freedom of Information Officer at Central Scotland Police, I received a copy of the witness statement of the off-duty police officer who was the first police officer to enter the gymnasium on 13 March 1996. For some reason this statement did not make it into the National Archives of Scotland. In Mr Brims accompanying letter, he writes:

• *Recently we wrote to you in relation to a FoI request concerning the identity of an off-duty police officer who entered DPS gymnasium shortly after the shootings there on 13th March 2005 (sic). At that time we understood that the statements of all those adults who were present at the gym and surrounding area in the immediate aftermath of the shootings there had been deposited in the NAS for the public to consult following redaction to protect personal information. It has now come to our attention that the statement of the off-duty police officer who was the subject of your request has not yet been deposited. I am hoping to arrange with the other parties for the deposit of this document in the near future, but in the meantime I enclose a redacted copy in the hope that you will find it of relevance and interest.*

- There are some interesting points in this statement: *I further observed the janitor who was standing to the left side of a black figure lying on the floor. I knew he was the gunman. I formed this opinion as he had shot himself in the head and together with other factors in my mind I took him to be as such. As I took all this in and formed my opinions I saw two pistols there. I saw that his head had been blown away and the contents were behind him (how did Professor Busuttil manage to retain the brain for neuropathological examination then?) I was focused on this image. I then saw the janitor bend down at the gunman's left side and saw him retrieve a pistol. It was dark coloured and was not a revolver. I cannot describe it further. I also saw a further pistol lying to the left side of the gunman's body. That was dark coloured as well and was not a revolver. I also said to the janitor as he stood up to put the pistol down on the floor. I saw him place it at his feet (where was the revolver Hamilton used to kill himself then?).... I also saw, at the same time as all this, that the gunman was gurgling and breathing heavily. I formed the opinion that he was still alive but obviously nearing death. He was wearing a black boiler suit and he had a tan coloured leather holster around his waist on his left side (note, ONE holster, not 4, as we were told at the Inquiry). I saw magazines, black coloured, lying about him. I did see spent cases of ammunition lying about his body too. I could not put a number on them. I didn't see ear defenders on the gunman at all (well who removed them?)*

- Did the Crown Office deliberately withhold this statement because it clearly states that the witness did not see a revolver, only two pistols? And that Hamilton only had one holster, not four? If Hamilton did not have a revolver with him, how on earth did he kill himself with a Smith & Wesson revolver? Did the Crown Office deliberately select the headteacher Ron Taylor to give evidence at the Inquiry, and not this police officer, because Ron Taylor didn't know a pistol from a revolver? In evidence Mr Taylor simply referred to two guns (NOTE, he didn't see four guns either – nor did the janitor John Currie). According to DCS Ogg, no-one spoke to moving the 4th gun. The Scottish Information Commissioner, on reviewing all the evidence, concluded that, "there is evidence in the witness statements of PC's Edward Goldie and James Sneddon which may address (this) request". Central Scotland Police, on the other hand, claim that "all endeavours on their part to establish who the person was who accounted for moving the fourth gun had failed, which was why the Senior Investigating Officer gave such evidence to the Inquiry. The Police submit that nothing has subsequently come to light to explain who could account for moving the fourth gun and that they are not aware of any evidence which would directly answer Ms Uttley's question". The Scottish Information Commissioner has instructed Central Scotland Police to release to me the name of the Police Officer who is recorded as removing the fourth gun in the witness statements of two Police Constables, within forty two days of the decision notice of 24 March 2006.

- In his report into the Shootings at Dunblane Primary School, Lord Cullen writes that Thomas Hamilton was wearing "black corduroy trousers" whereas the off-duty police officer states that Hamilton was wearing a "black boiler suit". Why was Hamilton's body partially unclothed at the locus, as Professor Busuttil in his evidence confirms? Why were Hamilton's clothes changed?

- Hamilton is said to have taken enough ammunition into the school to kill everyone there (over 700 pupils and teachers). It is claimed that he carried this ammunition into the school in a case, which was found immediately inside the gym. The Scene of Crime Officer says <u>he was told</u> that the case belonged to Hamilton. I have made a further FoI enquiry about this matter, as there are no witnesses who speak to Hamilton carrying such a large heavy case into the school, far less into the gym. Central Scotland Police refused to reveal to me who told the Scene of Crime Officer that the case of ammunition belonged to Hamilton, so I referred this matter to the Information Commissioner. I received their decision on 25 March 2006. In their submission to the Commissioner, Central Scotland Police state that they "are concerned that if they are ordered to release this individual's name, this would lead to his name being published by Ms Uttley in such a manner as to cause him distress". The Police spoke to the Officer in question and confirmed to the Commissioner that it was "the Officer's expectation that his details would not be disclosed to Ms Uttley".

Thankfully the Commissioner has adopted a more realistic assessment of the situation and concluded that, "I do not accept that disclosure of the information would breach the data protection principles. I am of this view as I would expect that where a Police Officer makes a statement in the course of his/her duties or attends an incident that he/she would have an expectation that any opinions or statements he/she makes may be included in any subsequent report that may be submitted. I am not satisfied that to release this information would be deemed to be unfair processing of the Officer's details". Central Scotland Police have to release this information to me within forty two days. What is the officer involved so concerned about?

- The parents of a child who was uninjured in the gym that day, say they saw two bullet holes in the south wall of the gym, about 2 inches apart and just 6 inches from the ground. Their statement

4

continues, "There were no other bullet holes in that wall and I noticed that there were quite a few bullet holes in the other walls which would confirm my (words are blanked out here..............) that he fired into the walls at the bottom end of the gym where Hamilton had entered the gym". WHO fired into the walls at the bottom end of the gym when Hamilton (re-entered) the gym through the fire exit door at the south end? Did Hamilton administer 2 (2!!) bullets to his head whilst lying down? It does not make sense. Lord Cullen does not even refer in his report to the bullet(s) used by Hamilton to kill himself. I made an FoI request to Central Scotland Police asking if the bullets retrieved from these 2 bullet holes came from his Browning pistol or his Smith and Wesson revolver. They declined to answer, so I referred this matter to the Information Commissioner. On 25 March 2006, the Information Commissioner advised me that all the information Central Scotland Police hold in respect of this request was lodged with the Cullen Inquiry and was made available to those represented at the Inquiry. The Police also advised that the evidence of the Scene of Crime Officer is available at the National Archives of Scotland (which I already knew). It will be very interesting indeed to see if the two bullets removed from the two holes in the wall where Hamilton's body was found are actually lodged as productions at the NAS...

- According to the Scene of Crime Officer, the gym was evacuated at midday due to fears that Hamilton's body – or the case – was booby-trapped. However, the bomb disposal unit were not alerted till 2.30pm and did not arrive till 3.20pm. When David Gould (bomb disposal) arrived, there were people present in the gym, despite it having been evacuated at midday.

- I asked Central Scotland Police if fingerprints were taken from all the doors that Hamilton possibly entered the school by. Astonishingly I discovered this was not done, yet Lord Cullen writes in his report that it was definitely ascertained that Hamilton entered the school by the boys toilet – how did Lord Cullen know this?

- Dr Jack Beattie, Consultant Paediatrician, arrived at the school at 10.15am to assist with the injured. Both on the day of the massacre (at a press conference), and several months later at the Inquiry, he stated that he did not see Hamilton's body in the gym. William Scott wrote to Dr Beattie about this matter and received a most aggressive reply. What is Dr Beattie afraid of?

- The time that scene of crime photos were taken on the day has also been concealed. Why? The Information Commissioner is making further enquiries about this matter for me. Central Scotland Police say it is not routine to record times of scene of crime photos, but I do not believe this to be true.

- The witness statement of Inspector Huskie has not been deposited at the National Archives of Scotland. In this statement, the officer says, "I was asked to search for firearms and photographs, or anything else I felt to be ambiguous". What does this mean? What could possibly be ambiguous? Hamilton was said to have all four of his firearms with him at Dunblane Primary School. Did Central Scotland Police know or suspect he might have had other firearms? And what of 'ambiguous' photographs?

- Insp. Huskie also states, "We attended at the locus of the search at 1800 hours same date and were met by Police witnesses_____ who informed me that they were there for the purposes of production gathering and logging". However, that was the task assigned to this officer and his team, so who were the other team? I have written again to the FoI officer at Central Scotland Police asking for a copy of the witness statements of the police officers who were already conducting a search at Hamilton's house when Inspector Huskie and his team arrived.

- Having obtained a copy of the Property Register of the various searches done on Thomas Hamilton's flat, apart from a jacket, there was no other clothing. I checked and double-checked with Central Scotland Police, and this is a complete list of the items taken from Hamilton's house. There was no other clothing.

- I have since made another request to ascertain what was found in the van that Hamilton hired the day before the massacre. Did he take all his clothes with him? Or did he bin all his clothes? However, all that would appear to have been found in his wheelie bin was a bag containing rags. He also left no money behind, just an empty wallet and four 10 pence pieces. So, did he take all his money aswell?

- Dr John Baird, Consultant Forensic Psychiatrist, gave evidence at the Dunblane Inquiry about Hamilton's mental state. He stated, "Had his (Hamilton's) intention been to engage in some sort of killing spree, he could have continued for longer. There was no reason, when he killed himself, to have done that". Despite many requests for information about the material he examined with regard to Hamilton's mental state, I have now used the FoI legislation to try and get some answers.

- Professor Busuttil, who carried out the post-mortem on Hamilton's body, refuses to answer the following questions: (1) how does a pathologist establish if a gunshot injury is self or other-inflicted; (2) how many exit wounds were there from Hamilton's head; (3) how did he manage to retain for neuropathological examination such a seriously damaged brain and also detect a tiny nodule when the brain was so damaged by gunshot injury; and (4) is Hamilton's brain still being stored, and if so, where?

- Busuttil said the bullet exited the <u>left side</u> of Hamilton's head. Scene of Crime Officer Malcolm Chisholm says the <u>top</u> of the head. Chisholm states that the bullet came out of the top of his head and impacted on the ceiling. However, surely if the exit wound was above the left ear, it would have hit a wall not the roof? Busuttil states, "The entry wound corresponding to <u>this</u> exit wound was located... ". ***This exit wound...***

- Busuttil is then asked about the internal parts of Hamilton's body. When asked questions about the digestive system, the Lord Advocate says, "leaving aside the gunshot injury again was it normal?" When asked questions about the genito-urinary, lymphatic and endocrine systems, he asks "and again they are all normal with the exception of the gunshot wound?" Leaving aside the gunshot injury? His post-mortem showed a parchmented yellow based abrasion in the region of his left hip. After Busuttil described this injury, the Lord Advocate intervenes with, "So if we pause there, as far as the recent injuries were concerned, leaving aside the post-mortem matter you have just mentioned, they are limited to signs of gunshot **wounds** where the entry point had been located within the mouth and exit point the area in your head that you pointed to a moment ago?" The Lord Advocate would appear to have attempted to divert attention from this matter, whilst also accidently referring to more than one head wound.

As I expected, my petition was 'closed', ie. thrown out. The Scottish Executive, Lord Advocate and Crown Office know only too well that they will be thoroughly shamed by a New Inquiry. It is in their interests to keep the truth hidden. The MSPs sitting on the Petitions Committee said the families of those killed at the town's primary school 10 years ago were looking for "dignity" rather than further investigations. The Convener, Michael McMahon, said: "If we continue to allow this to be taken forward, then we're not working in the best interests of those affected". He added that the families themselves had not called for a new inquiry during the publicity which surrounded the 10th anniversary of the shootings.

"I became concerned that these petitions were not being helpful to the parents. He said the petitioners had "suspicions but no information".

Scottish National Party MSP Sandra White said: "I would agree that the parents at no time have contacted this committee. What they are looking for now is not so much closure, but a bit of dignity."

It has long been understood that victims of crime must not influence public policy or crime sentencing. And yet what happened after Dunblane? The Government bowed to the wishes of the parents and despite no such recommendation from Lord Cullen, all handguns were banned. This was pointless and irrelevant legislation, given that the gun laws were already strong enough to have stopped Thomas Hamilton.

Now the Scottish Parliament bows to the parents' silence about the truth... Of course it is convenient for them to do so. They have perpetuated a scandalous cover-up and their words about 'dignity' etc do not disguise their obvious enormous relief that none of the parents are interested in the truth.

LET ME REPEAT: THIS IS THE REASON WE DO NOT ALLOW VICTIMS OF CRIME TO BE INVOLVED IN POLICY MAKING. THE LAW-MAKERS OF SCOTLAND FLOUTED THE TERMS OF THE 1921 TRIBUNALS OF INQUIRY (EVIDENCE) ACT, AND THAT IS WHAT THEY SHOULD HAVE BEEN ADDRESSING AT THE COMMITTEE HEARING.

Imagine if, after Dunblane, the parents had demanded to know more about why Central Scotland Police considered Thomas Hamilton fitted to own a gun? Imagine what might have happened if they had taken legal action against Central Scotland Police? Imagine how different things would be now. That is the terrible tragic irony of the parents lack of interest in the truth. The less they are interested, the more others are... And yet it is on the parents behalf, we are told, that the Dunblane Petitions were thrown out.

I emailed the First Minister, the Lord Advocate, the Scottish Information Commissioner, and all the members of the Public Petitions Committee: Michael McMahon, John Scott, Jackie Baillie, Helen Eadie, Charlie Gordon, Rosie Kane, Campbell Martin, John Munro and Sandra White:

"As John Gouriet wrote in his letter to the Lord Advocate on 24 February 2006, regarding your continued insistence on withholding the truth about Dunblane from the public, *it is a fact of life that eventually, sooner or later, the truth will always emerge. Nothing can ever be so wicked that those responsible for upholding the law, should seek to conceal the truth rather than fulfil their duty by bringing those accused of wrong-doing to justice. The longer this process is delayed, the more serious for all concerned and the deeper public suspicion becomes.*

My sincere thanks go to Rosie Kane for her attempts to undo the wrongdoing perpetrated by the Scottish Crown Office, the Lord Advocate and the First Minister in their handling of this matter over the last few years. Those of you who have now added your names to the long list of colluders in the cover-up of the truth about the murder of 16 schoolchildren and their teacher in a Scottish Primary School on 13 March 1996, should hang your heads in shame.

How you can consider the witness statement of the off-duty policeman, Grant McCutcheon, to be a mere 'suspicion' and not 'new information' is beyond me. This statement was never put before the Dunblane Inquiry, only vague mention was made of this officer at the Inquiry, Lord Cullen makes no mention of this man in his final Report, the statement was NOT released at the

National Archives of Scotland last October, and was only made available to me under the FOISA in November 2005, after repeated requests from me to Central Scotland Police for a copy. The fact that Mr McCutcheon's evidence directly contradicts the evidence of the janitor, John Currie, and the Scene of Crime Officer, Malcolm Chisholm, seems to be of little concern to you. Are you all just puppets?

I am offering you this opportunity to provide a comment about your actions - or should I say, lack of action - at yesterday's hearing of the Public Petitions Committee".

In reply to the above, MSP Helen Eadie responded as follows: "Evidence production - not hearsay - is the basis of our justice system. The message is clear provide evidence that can corroborate your suspicions. To do otherwise would mean that we have a justice system that does not uphold fundamental basics. The Procurator Fiscal is the person charged in Scotland with determining what is evidence and clearly he has done so in this case.

That is the way that our legal system operates in Scotland. Anything that you regard as being evidence should properly be placed before a Procurator Fiscal who is required to have regard to a whole set of legislation that governs what constitutes evidence and what does not".

This is a somewhat different response from the Committee's decision that the parents required 'dignity'. And despite pointing out to Ms Eadie that there wasn't one ounce of 'hearsay' in my petition, she refused to budge from her position. Clearly I cannot produce Thomas Hamilton's body for a second post-mortem. His body was hastily cremated. However, I had already requested to know about the two bullets found in the wall directly where his body was discovered and also made enquiries as to whether Hamilton's brain has still been retained. Ms Eadie's reply made me wonder if any of the MSPs, Rosie Kane excepted, had read the supporting information supplied with my petition.

Immediately after the petition hearing, Ms Kane emailed me: "I am sorry but petition was closed with others. Committee chair and all others expressed concerns about harm and pain for the parents and families concerned. I sensitively pointed out that that we are all concerned and that we do not wish to harm or hurt the families etc. It was pointed out by the chair that none of the families had asked for fresh inquiry - I said that this may be the case but others may have noticed issues, oversights and problems and it is their duty to pursue them. I also said that I am worried about many aspects of what was in front of us and feel it needs further investigation. The only route I could find to try to keep petition open is by seeking the views of information commissioner and I pointed out that he was already looking at some stuff for you.

Chair said there was no need and closed petition with full support of committee. John Smith of Tory party had some concerns also. Chair said that if Kevin Dunion throws up any questions or new info then new petition could come forward.

I am sorry about this. Take care and keep in touch. Rosie"

CHAPTER 1

It was a bitterly cold and icy morning as PC Grant McCutcheon rushed his two young children down the drive and into his red Vauxhall Astra. After putting the children into the back of his car, and securing them in their seats, he scraped ice off the windscreen before hastily driving to Dunblane Primary School. His daughter was to attend the nursery class which started at 9.30am and he was running late.

He drove along the Old Doune Road and entered the school yard via the main gates. After driving up the main drive, he had difficulty getting a parking space as there were lots of other vehicles parked there. He arrived at 9.32 am and was a few minutes late for the start of nursery. After taking his children from the car, he walked them into the school via the main entrance. He entered the main reception area, turned left and walked down a set of stairs. After turning left again, he entered the corridor of the nursery wing and entered the first classroom on the right. He left his daughter at the nursery class and walked off down the corridor with his son.

At another entrance to the school, local housewife Audrey McMillan was arriving to drop off her daughter at the same nursery class. She saw a white van driving very slowly between the two entrances to the school at about 9.27 am. It was moving at approximately 10 miles per hour. After passing the hotel, the driver put on his indicator about 20 yards before the school gates and drove into the school still driving very slowly. He appeared to be lost and unsure as to where he was going, but then turned into the access road leading into the Nursery playground where the Primary 1 and 2 infants were. The diesel van engine was noticeably loud. The van appeared to be very new and was very clean. It was a panel van and had only two doors with no markings on it. It also had 2 back doors.

Mrs McMillan was taking her daughter to Nursery class which started at 9.30am. As she walked her daughter into the playground she could still see the van moving slowly, but it was now travelling adjacent to the wall. It reversed hard against the wall, or possibly against a telegraph pole or lamp post. There was nothing else parked nearby. Mrs McMillan's daughter said, "What is that man doing there? He is not allowed to park there". The driver was by now out of the van and he looked across at them. They were just 50 yards from him. Mrs McMillan described him as middle aged, large build, if not fat, and was about 5 feet 10 inches in height. He was wearing dark framed glasses and the lenses were clear, like reading glasses. He was wearing a big heavy woollen hat level with his eyebrows – it was an extremely cold morning – so she couldn't see his face. He was wearing very dark clothing and the top was zipped just about to his mouth covering his neck. His trousers were dark coloured and he wore black steel toecap boots like Doc Martens. They were very clumpy with heavy soles.

He walked around the side of the van and to the drivers side and opened both rear doors. He then went into the van, but reappeared after a number of seconds, turned around and lay a silver grey plastic sheet on the ground which he unfolded. It appeared to be a tool rack and had objects in it but Mrs McMillan was unable to see what they were. After dropping off her child at nursery, she didn't see the man or the van, but she wasn't looking for either. Mrs McMillan then drove off.

Meanwhile, in the corridor of the nursery wing, Grant McCutcheon stopped so that his son could play with some toys and a Wendy House. After about three minutes, he saw a group of children, aged about seven or eight, being shooed along the corridor by their teacher. The teacher was middle aged with grey hair and wearing a shift. The children and teacher all passed him and entered the third room on the right, the GP room.

The corridor was then empty, except for Grant and his son and a young woman of about 30. She was quite tall, about 5 feet 8 inches, medium build, with long dark hair, wearing glasses, black leggings and a dark coloured top. As he stood watching his son play in the Wendy House, the Deputy Head of the school approached him. Mrs Awlson calmly said, "there is a man in the school – in the gymnasium – and he is shooting". His first thought was that she meant someone with an air pistol because he hadn't heard any gun shots. But then he realised that what she was telling him was something to be really concerned about. The man said "I am a policeman. Can I help?" Mrs Awlson replied "Yes please".

After handing his son over to the young dark haired woman, he ran up the corridor of the nursery wing to the main corridor with Mrs Awlson at his heels. He turned right and ran up a small set of stairs to where the janitor's office was located. A teacher, Grace Tweddle, was lying at the top of these stairs on the left, almost opposite the janitor's office. She had blood on her head and her hands, but was conscious and moving, so he continued to run towards the assembly hall area. There was no-one else around, and no-one in the assembly hall when he entered via the swing doors. At this point he was lost and didn't know where to go. Mrs Awlson told him to turn right. After going through another set of double doors, he turned left and ran along the corridor, up a flight of stairs half way along the corridor and then, on the left side of the corridor further on he saw a group of four children in gym kit sitting on the floor with their backs propped up against the wall on the left. They were all wearing blue T-shirts and dark shorts. All the children had gunshot wounds. They all had bloodstained clothing. One boy had what looked like pellet marks to his left leg. Another boy said to him, "He's got a gun mister".

As the children were all conscious and breathing, the policeman continued running towards the doors   leading to the gym. Both doors were ajar. He entered the gym.

This is what he saw (and this is taken from Grant McCutcheon's formal Witness Statement, made by him to Central Scotland Police but never even presented to Lord Cullen's Public Inquiry into the Dunblane Massacre):

"I saw carnage. A flurry of thoughts and feelings came on me and I was aware of a strong smell of gunsmoke. I also formed the opinion that all the children I saw were dead as all were motionless. I saw a group of bodies to my immediate right at the entrance doors where I stood. That was the group where the teacher Gwen Mayor was that died. I can recall that her body was on top of other children. I saw that they were dressed in gym kit, blue T-shirts and dark shorts. I formed the opinion that they were all dead. I also saw a group to my left, halfway up the left side of the hall. They consisted of about four or five further children, wearing exactly the same state of dress. I formed the opinion they were all dead also. I also saw another group of children half way up the gym hall on the right side. That group consisted of about four children who looked dead. I further observed the janitor (John Currie) who was standing to the left side of a black figure lying on the floor. I knew he was the gunman. I formed this opinion as he had shot himself in the head and together with other factors in my mind I took him to be as such. As I took all this in and formed my opinions I saw two pistols there. I saw that his head had been blown away and the contents were behind him. I was focused on this image. I then saw the janitor bend down at the gunman's left side and saw him retrieve a pistol. It was dark coloured and was not a revolver. I cannot describe it further. I also saw a further pistol lying to the left side of the gunman's body. That was dark coloured as well and wasn't a revolver. I also said to the janitor as he stood up to put the pistol down on the floor. I saw him place it as his feet. He was standing some 5-6 feet at the side of the gunman's feet. He told me he just wanted to get the gun away from him.

I also saw, at the same time as all this, that the gunman was gurgling and breathing heavily. I formed the opinion that he was still alive but obviously nearing death. He was wearing a black boiler suit and he had a tan coloured leather holster around his waist on the left side. He appeared to be wearing a dark coloured anorak which   had fallen open. I didn't notice his footwear. I saw magazines, black coloured, lying about him. I didn't know what number. I saw spent cases of ammunition lying about his body also. I couldn't put a number on them. I didn't see ear defenders on the gunman at all.

I saw the janitor walk towards me at that point. I also saw the headmaster (Ron Taylor) standing in the centre of the hall looking in the direction of the gunman. I saw that he appeared to be stunned and motionless. He then looked at me and asked me who I was. I told him I was a policeman. He ran up to me and started shouting at me "What can we do? What can we do?""

Thomas Hamilton had just shot dead 16 children and their teacher. He had also shot and injured a further twelve children and three teachers. The Dunblane Massacre had happened.

****

Thomas Watt Hamilton was born on 10 May 1952 to Agnes and Thomas Watt. The couple had married in December 1950 at Bridgeton Church in Glasgow. Agnes herself was born illegitimately, in 1931, to the widow Rachel Hamilton and was adopted by her aunt and uncle, Rachel's sister Kate and her husband James.

Thomas Hamilton's natural father, bus driver Thomas Watt, left Agnes for another woman, bus conductress Margaret McGill, before Hamilton was born. Well that is one story. Another version says that Thomas Watt stayed with Agnes till Thomas was 18 months old and by then they had a second child, a daughter named Sharon. Sharon has managed to continue living in obscurity, despite the atrocity committed by her brother. Thomas Hamilton also had 2 half sisters and 2 half brothers, from his father's second marriage to Margaret. He never knew them.

Born in Glasgow's Rottenrow Maternity Hospital, Hamilton spent his early years living in Glasgow. When Thomas Watt left his wife Agnes for Margaret, Agnes moved back to the home of her adoptive parents in Stirling. She was just 21, distraught at her broken marriage and unable to cope. In the spring of 1956, when Thomas was four, the grandparents adoped both children, Thomas and Sharon. Thomas Watt became Thomas Watt Hamilton and his life started again, with his grandparents masquerading as his mother and father. Agnes was reinvented as her son's older sister, deprived of all responsibility for Hamilton's well-being. Former neighbours say she was treated little better than a skivvy. And there seemed to be few friends.

The family lived in part of an old spacious elegant manse in Upper Bridge Street, Stirling. It was let to Hamilton's grandparents at a nominal rent. There was a large well-tended garden and this further estranged him from local boys. One fellow pupil, only identified as William, said "People used to think he was a bit of a snob because he lived in a fancy house when we all lived in council houses. He was different from us, a mummy's boy, or so we thought".

Hamilton went to Stirling's Territorial School. In 1965, at the age of 13, Hamilton moved to the 600-pupil Riverside Secondary School on the banks of the Forth. A former classmate at this school, Paul Cameron, remarked "No one liked him at school because he would take a delight in frightening them. He was only about 12 when I remember him threatening some of the younger girls unless they played with him". So, having few – if any – friends, he was already the outsider. In actual fact, Tommy Hamilton's best friend was a ghost. He told fellow pupils at Riverside Secondary School that he could hear spooks in the attic at night. But he wasn't scared. Ghosts were just dead people who wanted to talk. Shortly before committing the atrocity at Dunblane, he talked to his neighbour Grace Ogilvie about these ghosts. They obviously still played on his mind.

Nobody wanted to be Tommy's friend. At school, he was simply ignored, or bullied. There was nothing you might call friendship. Tommy Hamilton endured it all. He wasn't a cry-baby, but, somewhat ironically, he was considered a "mummy's boy". Thomas Hamilton had a soft, well-spoken voice. He was ostracised for not being one of the lads. He was labelled a snob and a poof, and he was probably both.

Some reports suggest that Hamilton was a hard working and dedicated pupil who excelled at technical drawing. His work was frequently pinned up for the supposed benefit of others. The other children were more than likely irritated by this however. Hamilton was also good at maths, and appeared to enjoy the challenge of solving complicated sums. Understanding the mechanics of things appealed to Hamilton, whether it was a design of a house drawn to scale, a wooden joist for a cupboard, or the workings of a gun. On the whole though, Hamilton paid little attention in class and frequently spent his time drawing on his books whilst he was supposed to be writing essays. He did however form a close rapport with the school's technical teacher, George Morrison.

In 1967 at the age of 15, Thomas Hamilton left school with few qualifications. One thing we know for certain is that he had poor literacy skills. Ina Mack, a departmental secretary at Stirling University, was employed by Hamilton to do typing. In her Witness Statement given to Central Scotland Police, she states that, "His letters were not of a good construction. I felt he knew what he wanted to say in the letters but he was unable to express this properly in a literal sense. His general construction was poor, with spelling mistakes, punctuation mistakes and they generally required tidying up with regard to the grammar. I typed his letters and without changing the content, constructed them and laid them out into a more acceptable grammatical literal standard of English. I always returned to him his original letters along with the letter I had typed for him and he was very appreciative of the help I had given him in this respect". When Hamilton wrote to Her Majesty The Queen shortly before 13 March 1996, he sent a letter through the post to Ina Mack for typing. She says of this letter, "I did not change the content of this letter from what he had written but corrected the grammar errors and the layout into better all round construction. There is only one omission which I can recollect in that where I have added to the letter "for fear of embarrassing ridicule", Hamilton had written "for people shouting poof, poof, poof at me".

On leaving school, Hamilton considered going into the Army, but chose instead to work in the old Stirling Burgh Council's architecture department. Here he was well-liked and highly regarded. Colleagues found him well-mannered and keen to work, demonstrating a burgeoning talent for design. At the same time Hamilton perfected one of his other great hobbies, woodwork. Taking up an evening job at a DIY store in Cowane Street, near to his home, he sold wood to the public and developed his own skills in carving. About this time, his enthusiasm for young boys was becoming increasingly apparent.

"He used to recruit boys of about 12 or 13 for the shop" his fellow pupil William said. "He used to get some sort of satisfaction from ordering young people about". Hamilton joined the Venture Scouts, for older teenagers, and pestered the District Scout Commissioner, Comrie Deuchars, to allow him to lead a troop. At the age of 21 he was invited to lead the Stirling 4/6 group, a new branch that had just opened in Bannockburn. Deuchars said, "He was very keen. There didn't seem any reason to doubt his enthusiasm". However, Deuchars regularly visited the new troop to see how they were getting on and he was not happy. Hamilton seemed to be more interested in getting the boys changed into their PE gear to play football or handball than doing badge work such as map reading and bird-watching, which did not involve getting changed. Forensic psychologist Paul Britton, remarked after the massacre, "Somewhere in his background I expect he was drawn into a relationship with another boy or someone slightly older. As he matured, the impact of this experience will have remained".

In 1970 he opened his own Woodcraft DIY Shop at the relatively young age of 18. From the very beginning, he offered discounts to police officers with Central Scotland Police.

In 1974 he was dismissed from The Scout Association. His Scout warrant was withdrawn and he lost his authority to act as a Scout Leader (see Notes 1). In 1978 he operated a boys' club from Territorial Army premises in Dunblane. Activities included pistol and rifle shooting. Hamilton trained boys to kill using live ammunition at a secret boot camp. Ten handpicked youngsters – known as his Sea Rovers Patrol – were taught to use rifles and handguns by day. At night Thomas Hamilton whipped them with a steel rod then rubbed lotion into their wounds. At the end of the weekends on Inchmoan Island, he paid the boys £5 each to keep quiet. Keith McGowan was recruited for the group when he was just 11. He referred to Hamilton as "big Tommy". He said that Hamilton had a Luger pistol, at least 6 rifles, and a couple of handguns. Days were spent cruising the loch on Hamilton's boat Tropical Linda. Then the boys, wearing only swimming trunks and armed with rifles, would be dropped onto the island in a military-style operation.

Keith said "We would hunt rabbit for dinner. But Tommy encouraged us to shoot any animal or bird we saw". In the evening, Thomas Hamilton would pick out two boys at a time and take them to his punishment tent. There they would be made to freeze in the press-up position and whipped with a steel rod. "He said it was part of the programme to make us as fit as we could possibly be. It was like he was training us to be his personal army. It makes us sick to think how he whipped us for hours then rubbed lotion on our wounds.

That's the only time he touched us but he would rub the lotion on us really hard. It wasn't until I grew up that I realised he was a pervert".

In 1981 Hamilton started up the Dunblane Rover Group. It met at Dunblane High School and is believed to be the first group operated within educational premises (according to Inquiry documents), although several witnesses at the Dunblane Inquiry refer to Hamilton having a boys' club at Stirling High School in the late 1970s. The first complaints were made to Central Regional Council and investigated by the Youth & Community Section. Enquiries were made with the Scout Association who indicated that Thomas Hamilton had been dismissed for homosexual tendencies. A memo was sent to the Director of Education outlining their concerns. On 15 August 1983, Central Regional Council discussed their previous concerns from 1981. A recommendation was made to terminate Hamilton's lets. This led to a large volume of correspondence by Hamilton to the authorities (see Notes 2).

Hamilton had shown an interest in guns from the age of 16. He was a member of a Rifle Club that met in Princes Street Hall in Stirling. His membership of the Club ended when the Hall was pulled down. By the time he was 20, Hamilton was frequenting the Scout Hall in Queen Street in Stirling. In 1978 Hamilton operated a boys' club from Territorial Army premises in Dunblane. His activities included pistol and rifle shooting, at a .22 rifle range which belonged to the Queen Victoria School. The range was located about half a mile from the school, near what is now the Duckburn Industrial Estate. Ewan Anderson sometimes went along to the Friday night gun club to help. One witness, Bruce Carruthers, reports an act of indecency at this club when Hamilton placed a hand on his thigh whilst speaking to him. This was attended by about 12 boys who were allowed to shoot weapons. During this time, he casually employed some of the teenage boys from the Queen Street Scout Group, including Thomas Hughes and Francis Cullen. Hamilton practised firing a crossbow and air rifles at targets at the back of his shop.

During the mid 1970s, Hamilton started having Island Camps on Loch Lomond. Hughes attended these camps, along with other boys aged 14 and 15. Beer and spirits were provided by Hamilton which the boys were allowed to consume at night. Activities included use of air weapons and crossbows. The weapons were misused by Hamilton, who encouraged the boys to do the same.

Hughes was paid money to strip to the waist and suffer .22 air gun pellets fired at his bare back at a distance of over roughly 50 yards. This would sometimes cause injury but payment would be withheld if he yelled out. On the other hand, payment was increased depending on how close Hamilton was allowed to stand. One shot struck his spine, causing great pain. Thereafter the practice was not agreed to. At another camp Hamilton tried to get a boy to swallow a bullet.

At one particular camp in 1975, following an evening meal and some alcohol, Hughes retired to bed with Hamilton and another boy, Kieron McKenzie. Hughes woke during the night to find the light on and Hamilton seated on a box. Hamilton pointed a shotgun towards him. At that stage Hamilton did not have a firearms licence and no official ownership of this weapon is known of, according to Central Scotland Police. When he tried to sit up, Hughes saw that he and McKenzie had been chained together. McKenzie denies any knowledge of this, yet Hughes says that when he asked Hamilton for an explanation the following morning, he was told, "do you know how easy it would be to kills yous" *(Scots pronounce this yooz).* Hughes relates another incident when Hamilton lit a fire within some sort of depression in one of the Loch Lomond Islands, then placed 1.5 kilogramme gas canisters on to the fire and sailed off in his boat to await an explosion.

About this time, parents approached Central Scotland Police reporting strange or changed behaviour in their children following an attendance at one of Hamilton's clubs. Former Detective Sergeant Kindness recalls interviewing Hamilton during the mid to late 1970s. In evidence at the Dunblane Inquiry, he stated that complaints came from parents whose boys attended the Forth Valley Rover Scouts, a club operated by Hamilton at Stirling High School. The complaints related to possible indecency, however, no evidence was found to prove this. The parents concerns related to a change of behaviour pattern in the boys that the parents couldn't explain. The boys had previously been stable, but there was a sudden transition after having attended Hamilton's club. Kindness suggests that what came through from the interviews of the boys was "a form of subversion by Hamilton in terms of parental authority. There had been a gross display, for example, of affluence by Hamilton. There had been money – I think gifts of money, lending bicycles, canoe trips – this sort of thing. There was also evidence I believe, of allowing truants to frequent his shop in Cowane Street".

At the age of 25, Hamilton became friends with Robert Oliver Campbell. Campbell worked within the vicinity of the hardware shop owned by Hamilton. This was in the spring of 1977 and through the proximity of their work, they became friendly with one another. Campbell was involved in local politics, which Hamilton had no interest in, his sole interest being boys' clubs and camping. According to Campbell, Hamilton had boys at his shop at the weekends to wash his van or before they went away on camps. He liked the boys to call him 'Sir'. At this stage apparently, the boys did anything Hamilton asked, willingly and dutifully. Hamilton appeared to enjoy the company of the boys. Campbell visited one of Hamilton's camps where he saw three or four boys aged about ten or eleven. The boys had no shirts on. Campbell says that at no time did he see anything improper in relation to Hamilton or the boys, and only found out later that one boy had been unhappy at the camp and that the boys parents had complained about Hamilton. This complaint had gone to Central Regional Council and Hamilton was banned from using the Council premises. Based on what Hamilton told him, he assessed the situation as the boy not being the type who was suited to overnight camping. When Hamilton said he intended to appeal against the Council's decision to ban him from the premises, Campbell told him he needed a proper committee with women, a proper constitution, one which was open to scrutiny. Hamilton later showed him a list of committee members, and some of the names on the list were women. Campbell was also led to believe that some members of the committee were police officers, although he says he made no attempts to scrutinise these lists.

Although Campbell knew about Hamilton's fight with Central Regional Council through the Ombudsman, he did not get embroiled in this dispute. Whilst he was a District Councillor he did "not want to hear anything untoward about Hamilton".

Campbell knew about Hamilton's interest in shooting and that he was a member of the Dunblane Gun Club, although he never saw his guns and he himself had no interest in shooting.

Campbell was – at the time of the Dunblane massacre – a Justice of the Peace for the borough of Stirling. After three years of serving on the Council he became a bailiff and sat in the District Court. On local government reorganisation in 1992 he became a Justice of the Peace for life, for which he received two or three lectures at Stirling University on his role as a JP. These lectures lasted about six hours and were about signing passport photographs, gun licences and other forms that you would be a witness for, to sign Search Warrants under oath and other forms that were put before you. Apparently he was never given specific instructions about signing firearm renewals with regard to a person's suitability.

In early 1992, Hamilton went to Campbell's home and asked him to countersign a form for his firearms renewal and to sign his photograph. Although he hadn't seen much of Hamilton since his shop closed in 1984, Campbell obliged. He had known Hamilton since 1977, a full fifteen years, and he says he never heard anything untoward about him, nor had he read anything in the newspapers about him. Over the next few years, he says he only saw Hamilton in passing. However, in January 1995, Hamilton again turned up at his house and asked him to countersign his firearms renewal. Hamilton assured him that he had made the necessary security for the guns and seeing no reason not to sign his forms, Campbell again obliged.

Although he found Hamilton "a bit unusual", Campbell states that Hamilton appeared no different mentally than before. Hamilton "had always seemed a bit odd" and as he had always owned guns as long as he had known him, seeing no change in his manner in January 1995, he concluded that Hamilton was a fit and proper person to have a gun licence. That was the last time Campbell says he saw Hamilton.

At the age of 25, Hamilton owned a 40 foot motor cruiser. How he came to own this boat is unclear, but it would appear that he purchased it for the paltry sum of £5,000. A strong rumour persists that it was 'gifted' to Hamilton by a friend in Central Scotland Police. On three or four occasions, Campbell helped Hamilton to varnish the boat. And according to Campbell, within three years of Hamilton owning the boat, the boat was destroyed as a result of a gas cylinder exploding on board (was Hamilton rehearsing for this with his gas canister explosions on Loch Lomond?) Hamilton received an insurance payment of £36,000 after negotiations with the insurance company. Ewan and Katherine Anderson were friends of Hamilton about this time and together with their two daughters, they went sailing in his boat on several occasions. William MacDonald (a former police officer with CSP) and his wife Helen, together with their son David, also went sailing with Hamilton.

During the mid 1970s, Hamilton "met and formed relations of sorts with members of the Central Scotland Police Diving Team" (from an Inquiry document) at Loch Lomond, that is, police officers Michael Mill and Anthony Bushnell. Here is Michael Mill's evidence from the Dunblane Inquiry (Anthony Bushnell did not give evidence):

MICHAEL MILL – EX CHIEF INSPECTOR

Examined by Mr Bonomy: You are a former police officer with Central Scotland Police? – That is correct.

Now retired? – Yes, I am.

And you live in Stirling? – Yes, I do.

For how many years were you a serving police officer? – 21 and a half years.

When did you first encounter Thomas Hamilton? – I first encountered Thomas Hamilton when I was stationed at Stirling about 1981, 1980, 1981.

In what connection? – He had a Do It Yourself shop in Cowane Street, Stirling.

Were you a customer? – Yes, I was.

Now, you knew him as a customer to speak to, I suppose, if you met him in the street? – Yes, I did.

Did you know something of his ownership and use of boats on Loch Lomond? – Yes, I did.

How was it you came to know about that? – I was a member of Central Scotland Police Force Underwater Unit and we trained up at Loch Lomond on training exercises on a weekly basis.

Can you tell me how many boats over the years Hamilton had at Loch Lomond? – I was first aware he had one, a speed boat, it was a small boat and it was called The Lady Sheila and he then purchased another boat which was a large cabin cruiser and that was called Tropical Winter (sic).

What happened to it? – It caught fire and sank.

Do you know when that was? – About 1982, 1983, about that time, I am not quite sure.

As a result of that sinking of the boat did the underwater unit have to do something about it? – The boat caught fire on Loch Lomond, on the

Strathclyde side of Loch Lomond just opposite Luss; after the fire the boat drifted over towards Balmaha Bay and sank just off the island; it sank in shallow water and the boatyard or the boatman at the yard asked us if we would move the boat into deeper water because it was causing an obstruction.

Were you involved in doing that? – Yes, I was.

Were you aware that Hamilton had summer camps in that area? – Yes.

When were you first aware of this? – Probably about 1980, 1981; as I say we visited Loch Lomond on a weekly basis, we knew of the person at the boatyard and they knew Hamilton as well.

In 1988 there was a police investigation into one of the camps and then an investigation into the police officers. Is it a fair summary of the position that Hamilton on a number of occasions tried to plead with you to say something, I suppose in his favour, in the course of this investigation? – I don't know if he was pleading with me to say something in his favour, he certainly initially came to see me in relation to the procedural side of it, thereafter it then became a bit more than that.

Did he visit you regularly? – Yes, he did.

Was he pleading his case? – Yes, he was.

Did you get the impression he hoped it would filter through from you into other police officers' ears? – Yes.

In 1988 were you involved at all directly in the investigations, for example, going to the camp site and seeing the state of the camp? – No, in view of Hamilton's letters to the Chief Constable I was directed to do a preliminary investigation just into events but not to go to the camp.

Was that in connection with complaints against Gunn and Duncan? – Yes, it was.

Did you speak to Hamilton in that connection? – Yes, I did.

Now, following that particular camp did you in later years at all go to the site to see what the camp was like? – Yes, I did.

When did you first do that? – After the 1988 camp he made a point of coming to see me to inform me of where he was having the camp and inviting police officers, if they wanted, to visit his camp; I went, I think, to the 1990 camp at Milarrochy Bay which was on the site of the caravan club at Loch Lomond.

Is that the first time you had actually gone on to one of the camp sites? – Yes.

What did you make of the camp in 1990? – As far as I was aware it was quite well run, the boys were all happy; I spoke to quite a few boys, I spoke to the warden at the site and I spoke to Hamilton; he showed me the layout of the site and also the food that was available for the boys.

Did he have any adult assistance? – Yes, he did.

How many people were there? – As far as I was aware there was one male person.

How many boys were there? – I am not sure – possibly about a dozen.

Did you visit any other camp? – No, I didn't.

Was the visit you have just described the subject of any police intelligence input into the system? – Not that I am aware of; I probably would have spoken with my Chief Superintendent but on an informal basis.

In a document prepared for the Dunblane Inquiry, it states: "Little is known about this Summer Camp since only one piece of documentation exists. On 18th July 1990 a parental complaint was received by Fife Regional Council complaining about the Dunfermline Boys Club in a recent camp where an 8 year old boy had come home with a chest infection. It was also alleged that there was inadequate supervision.

Cross-examined by Mr Taylor (for Central Scotland Police): When you met with Hamilton as you have described were you able to form a view of him? – In the early years?

Yes? – He certainly was maybe I should say a bit unusual, possibly in appearance, but that was basically it.

Did you find him an interesting person? – Not possibly a very forthright person. When he spoke to you on occasions, and basically when he spoke to me, if I can use the word, a very boring person.

How did he speak? – It was always very monotone, with virtually no expression at all in it.

Did he appear a happy person? – No, he didn't, no.

Did you at some time move to Dunblane as the Sub-Divisional Officer there? – Yes, I did.

Can you say when that was? – I moved to Dunblane in 1987 – 1987 or the early part of 1988. I think it was 1987.

In 1988 did you become aware of a complaint against Mr Hamilton in relation to the running of the camp at Inchmoan Island? – Yes, I did.

And did you become aware that he was unhappy with the treatment that he had received at the hands of Central Scotland Police? – Yes, he was.

How did you come to have knowledge of his dissatisfaction? – He visited me at Dunblane Police Office about the middle of August when the camp had finished and made references to the officers who had visited his camp at Inchmoan.

Did you become aware that he had taken matters up with the Deputy Chief Constable? – Not at that particular time. That was the early stages. At that particular time I didn't think he had spoken with the Deputy Chief Constable or the Chief Constable.

And can you tell us just a little bit more of your dialogue with him at this early stage? – I was on leave and came back at the beginning of August, and because I was responsible for that particular area I was briefed by the officers, and my sergeants, and they informed me that there had been a complaint against Hamilton by boys at the camp. The complaint was generally just the living conditions at the camp, and there was nothing of a physical nature against Hamilton. He came to my office probably the week after that and asked me if I knew of the incident, and at that time I was only aware of just generalisations and I said no, I didn't know of it, and I would find out, which I then made more enquiry into.

And you eventually became aware of some communication from Hamilton to the Deputy Chief Constable; is that right? – Yes, I did. He started showing a lot of concern about the way the police officers had handled their visit to the island. He started off, and then sent letters to me, indicating the type of things that he was doing at the camp. He sent receipts to me to show the type of food that he was buying. In the initial times he said he was making no complaint at all other than the fact that he didn't feel the police officers were qualified to make a judgement. At that time I was aware also it was Strathclyde Police area, and the Strathclyde Police were dealing with the matter.

Did you have contact with anybody in Strathclyde Police? – Yes, I did. I spoke with the person who was in charge of the investigation. It was a Detective Chief Inspector Hay.

Can you tell the Inquiry the nature of any discussion you had with him? – I asked him if there was anything other than what I had heard in relation to the complaint of the conditions, the conditions of the clothing that the boys were wearing, and he informed me that there was nothing further other than that, other than the living conditions, there was no complaints of abuse of any nature.

Eventually the Fiscal at Dumbarton marked the papers with the comment "No Proceedings". From your own information did that surprise you or not? – No, it didn't surprise me at all. I think the Detective Chief Inspector prior to it going felt that there would be no proceedings taken.

Were you eventually asked by the Deputy Chief Constable to perform any form of enquiry in relation to Mr Hamilton? – Yes, I was.

Can you tell us about that please? – He had written a letter to the Chief Constable making complaints against the two officers. The letter in itself indicated that he was not making a complaint against the police officers, but the Deputy Chief Constable then directed me to make a preliminary investigation into the officers who had visited the island.

And did you have further cause to interview Hamilton in the course of that enquiry? – I spoke with the officers, I spoke with Chief Inspector Hay. I then spoke with Hamilton, who was visiting me almost on a daily basis and sending letters.

And I wonder if you could have before you document D11K, which is otherwise known as DCD11. I think this is a report dated 11 October 1988 and it appears to be from yourself to the Chief Superintendent of 'A' Division, is that right? – Yes, it was.

And I think you concluded that there was nothing amiss in the manner in which Constables Gunn and Duncan had gone about their enquiries? – That is correct.

Now, I don't think the explanation and your informal report were acceptable to Mr Hamilton, and he subsequently went on to make a formal complaint; isn't that correct? – The day before I put the report in I spoke to Hamilton again about the camp, the actions of the police officers involved, and he at that particular time again still wished to make no formal complaint, and I reported that as well, in my report.

I think also at some point you were shown some photographs by Hamilton; isn't that correct? – Yes.

Can you recall when that was? – Probably two or three years later, probably about 1992.

Do you know what prompted him to send these to you? – Since this particular camp in 1988 Hamilton started sending letters, and then there were copies of letters. He sent to me any particular letter he sent to any person, whether it was a Chief Constable or a Member of Parliament, he would send me a copy of it. Primarily they were informative letters. He also gave me photographs that he had taken of the camps.

I think you also became aware of an incident in 1992 at Dunblane High School, is that right? – Yes, that is correct.

And that was a situation where I think two or three children were found in Dunblane in the evening; is that correct? – That is correct, yes.

Were you aware of there having been complaints made about the manner in which Mr Hamilton took other photographs, apart from the ones which you have referred to? – I was aware that there was an investigation by the Family Unit – the Family Unit were investigating complaints with regard to photographs.

And I think your name also appeared at some point in a memorandum which was circulated by Mr Hamilton, is that right? – Yes it did.

Can you tell us the circumstances of that? – It was a circulation concerning the starting up of a boys' club, and apart from the normal invitation to parents, on the back he had put contacts of persons concerning his club, and my name, along with I think the House of Commons, appeared on it, also the Central Region.

And were you happy that your name appeared on that form? – I was unaware it was on that.

How did you learn it was appearing in such a way? – Mr Flett from the Legal and Admin at Central Region contacted me, phoned me up about it.

And once you found out what steps did you take? – It was to have it removed.

And did you speak to Mr Hamilton in that regard? – Yes, I did. I asked him why he had used it, and he said it was only meant as a contact, and it wasn't there to show approval of his camp, his boys' camp.

Over the period it would appear you have had quite a lot of contact with Mr Hamilton; is that fair to say? – Yes, I have.

Were you aware Mr Hamilton was the holder of a Firearms Certificate? – Yes, I was.

Did you at any time in the course of your conversations with Hamilton and your interaction with him have any grounds for concern that he should be the holder of a Firearms Certificate? – None at all.

No re-examination.
Day 11 Wed 12 June 1996
MICHAEL MILL (Recalled)

Mill was reminded by Lord Cullen that he was still on oath. Mr Bonomy then asked Mr Mill: "Would you remind me of your present position in the Police Force?" to which Mill replied, "I retired from the Police Force as a Chief Inspector in charge of Callander Local Command Unit in April, 1994".

I want to ask you about one of Hamilton's renewal applications which you dealt with. Could you have various documents in front of you. First of all D51A which is an application dated 3rd January 1986, the RL2a which goes with it which is D52, and the AD2a form which is D53. If we start with the last of these, the AD2a form, you will see this is from Acting Chief Inspector Mill at Stirling to the Chief Superintendent of A Division on 29th January 1986. Is that from you to the Chief Superintendent? – Yes, it is.

That relates to what is headed up "Variation of firearms certificate 4588". It was actually a renewal with a variation built into it? – That is correct.

If you look at the application form you will see that? – That is correct.

And it relates to Thomas Hamilton? – Yes.

We have heard a little evidence of your involvement before in the Inquiry when you dealt with some of Hamilton's complaints about the police investigation at Inchmoan Island? – That is correct.

And we heard that you were the person he did from time to time come to try to plead his case, as it were? – Yes.

You became involved somehow or other in this particular renewal variation application. Can you explain to us how that came to be? – Yes. In January 1986 I was Inspector at Stirling and Chief Inspector Reid was my immediate supervising officer. He initially processed this RL3a form, and he went off ill, and in that interim I took over from him, at that particular stage of the variation and renewal.

Are you in the chain of command which would normally, as a result of that – that would normally deal with applications? – Yes.

Had you come in only because a query is raised? – With the processing of the application, the firearms application, the renewal application, as Inspector I would check the officer who is actually dealing with the application themselves. It would go through the chain of command through the officer who actually is doing the application, go through the Sergeant, through the Inspector, and then the Chief Inspector or Sub-Divisional Officer would then put his remark with "no objection" and it would then go to the Superintendent.

If you look at the RL3a, the Inspector has initialled it under the word "Station". You see that? – Yes.

I don't think that is your initials? – No. Yes, that would be Inspector Marshall. He would be the Inspector who initialled the renewal.

You would come in because you were deputising for the Sub-Divisional Officer?- Yes.

We don't see your signature anywhere on that document? – That one would have went through to the Superintendent with no objection at all to the firearms – well, the Deputy Chief Constable's office, who would then have seen something in the application and would have returned it. At that particular stage then I would have been deputising for the Chief Inspector.

Attached to AD2 is a note addressed to Sergeant Binning? – Yes.

Is that Marshall's written note? – Yes, it is.

He is asking him – well, he is saying it is unlikely a second 9mm pistol will be granted. "See Mr Hamilton and obtain full details of his reasons for requiring two pistols of the same calibre". Did you actually make that enquiry yourself of Hamilton? – No, I didn't. That would have been returned to the officer who was dealing with the application.

So that is Bell, is it, or Lesley Johnston? – Yes it would be Constable Johnston. Sergeant Binning would be her immediate supervisor.

Why would she not simply complete the AD2 form herself? – Well, she would normally do that. I don't understand why she hasn't done it. I just can't remember as to why I would have done it. It may have been to expedite the variation and the application. It may have been she was off, she went off ill or whatever.

Are you sure you didn't speak to Hamilton? – I didn't speak to Hamilton.

Were you yourself aware of the information in this AD2a from what you knew of Hamilton or is this information that could only have come from the enquiring officer? – This could only have come from the enquiring officer. I wouldn't have made any investigation into this particular variation.

No cross-examination.

In the preparatory material for the Inquiry, Mr Mill is not only referred to as a serving officer, but as an Acting Chief Inspector. On Day 11 of the Inquiry, Mill was reminded by Lord Cullen that he was still on oath. Mr Bonomy then asked Mr Mill: "Would you remind me of your present position in the Police Force?" to which Mill replied, "I retired from the Police Force as a Chief Inspector in charge of Callander Local Command Unit in April, 1994".

I wrote to Central Scotland Police to ask the date Mill retired and my letter was passed on to Stirling Council's legal department. Principal solicitor Peter Farquhar wrote, "I can advise you that under the terms of the Data Protection Act 1998, you are not entitled to information which you request in relation to ex Chief Inspector Mill". However, since then Mr Farquhar has confirmed for me that Mill left the force in April 1994. Understandably, I have had difficulty believing this and subsequently submitted a formal request for a copy of the relevant documentation. In December 2005, a redacted photocopy of the Chief Constable's Orders was sent to me that suggests Mill did indeed retire from the service in 1994. I referred this matter to the Scottish Information Commissioner only to be told that my application was "frivolous". And there the matter must rest.

In the same material it states that Mill "submitted a report in the papers at D/53/L explaining that Hamilton was active in competition shooting and the additional weapon had a more advanced design". This was not true of course, and had to be concealed at the Inquiry as Hamilton was NOT active in competition shooting.

In his evidence at the Inquiry, Michael Mill states that he first knew of Thomas Hamilton around 1980-81, when he was stationed at Stirling. Asked in what connection he knew him, he replies, "He had a Do It Yourself shop in Cowane Street, Stirling". Mill says he was a customer. Mill is also asked, "Did you know something of his ownership and use of boats on Loch Lomond?" – Yes I did. "How was it you came to know about that?" – I was a member of Central Scotland Police Force Underwater Unit and we trained up at Loch Lomond on training exercises on a weekly basis". Michael Mill was not prepared to admit at the Inquiry that this is how he first came into contact with Hamilton – 5 years earlier than he states, in 1976 in fact.

When asked about Hamilton's boats, Mill provides a very detailed reply: "I was first aware he had one, a speed boat, it was a small boat and it was called Lady Sheila and he then purchased another boat which was a large cabin cruiser and that was called Tropical Winter" (sic). Mill was also aware that Hamilton had summer camps in the area. He is asked "When were you first aware of this?" – Probably about 1980, 1981; as I say we visited Loch Lomond on a weekly basis, we knew of the person at the boatyard and they knew Hamilton as well. He says his first contact with Hamilton was in 1980, 1981 – *as a customer*, not through his police work, yet in the answer above he implies Hamilton was already well known to him at Loch Lomond by 1980/81.

Mill is then asked about the 1988 police investigation into one of Hamilton's camps. By 1988, Mill was sub-divisional officer at Dunblane Police Office. He is asked, "Is it a fair summary of the position that Hamilton on a number of occasions tried to plead with you to say something, I suppose in his favour, in the course of this investigation?" – I don't know if he was pleading with me…. "Did he visit you regularly?" – Yes, he did. "Was he pleading his case?" – Yes he was. "Did you get the impression he hoped it would filter through from you into other police officers' ears?" – Yes. Why did Hamilton consider Mill the best person to plead his case to?

Mill is then asked if he was directly involved in the investigations. He replies, "No, in view of Hamilton's letters to the Chief Constable I was directed to do a preliminary investigation just into events but not to go to the camp". Mill spoke to Hamilton about his complaints against police officers George Gunn and Donna Duncan. Under cross-examination by Mr Taylor, the solicitor for Central Scotland Police, he is later asked, "Did you become aware that he had taken matters up with the Deputy Chief Constable?" Mill says he was not aware of this at that particular time. "I didn't think he had spoken with the Deputy Chief Constable or the Chief Constable". But Mill had already said he knew that Hamilton had written letters to the Chief Constable...

Mill is asked if following that camp (in 1988) he went in later years to see what the camp was like. He replies yes. However, Hamilton never got the use of Inchmoan Island again after 1988. Mill states that he went to the Milarrochy Bay camp in 1990 and that this was the first time he had gone on to one of the sites. His answer is confusing. The question had been asked about him visiting the Inchmoan camp. Mill is asked if the visit he made to the camp was the subject of any police intelligence input into the system. He replies, "Not that I am aware of; I probably would have spoken with my Chief Superintendent but on an informal basis". Why was he at the camp then?

Hamilton had extended an invitation to the police to visit his camps in response to the Gunn and Duncan investigation – that investigation had ended by 1989 – so why was Mill visiting Hamilton's camp in 1990? Asked how he came to have knowledge of Hamilton's dissatisfaction, Mill says that he visited him at Dunblane Police Office about the middle of August when the camp had finished. Mill himself was just back from leave at the beginning of August. He states that because he was "responsible for that particular area" he was briefed by his officers. Mill confuses matters however by saying, "At that time I was aware also it was Strathclyde Police area, and the Strathclyde Police were dealing with the matter".

This is a very grey area at the Inquiry. One witness believes that Inchmoan Island is within Strathclyde Police area (George Gunn, Balfron station) whilst Mill says Central. At the beginning of his evidence, Mill states that he had been involved in moving Hamilton's boat that caught fire and sank. It caught fire on the Strathclyde side of Loch Lomond. After the fire the boat drifted over towards Balmaha Bay and sank just off the island. Presumably he is implying that Balmaha Bay is in Central Scotland Police area and that is why he was asked to help remove the boat.

Hamilton visited Mill the week after his return from camp (the camp finished on 14 August, so this would have been approximately 21 August). He started sending him letters, indicating the type of things that he was doing at the camp. He sent receipts to show the type of food he was buying.

Mill had already been briefed by his officers at the beginning of August, when he returned from leave. He knew about the problem long before Hamilton turned up in his office the last week of August. Did Hamilton send letters from the camp to Mill?

Police Constable George Gunn (Balfron) had received a complaint of assault on 17 July 1988. He visited the island on 20 July with Donna Duncan. The next he heard was when his inspector told him an informal complaint had been made against him. He is asked, "Who was your Inspector?" – Michael Mill. Gunn was required to give an explanation to Mill. Hamilton had not just made an oral complaint. He was writing letters to Mill and other officers. It would appear that Mill was aware of the whole situation from the very beginning.

Gunn states that he received a phone call from a parent whose child had been at the camp. Bonomy, unhappy with this response, says "Well, was it a parent on the phone to Balfron or was it another policeman?" His new answer is, "I believe it was actually another policeman. The parents had called at Drymen Police Office and he was relaying the message to ask us to call over at Drymen Police Office". This does not make sense. Balfron is further away from Loch Lomond than Drymen. Why didn't the Drymen officer investigate the child's complaint?

At the Inquiry, Mill is asked if he contacted anyone in Strathclyde Police. He replies yes, Detective Chief Inspector Hay. He contacted Hay at the end of August. He asked Hay for information about conditions, clothing of the boys, etc. Hay said there were no complaints of abuse. This is not true. George Gunn states in his evidence that he had received complaints from children. He was asked if he considered this as assault and he states yes. He also confirms that he reported this to DCI Hay.

So far then we have two investigations into Hamilton's complaints. The last one ended 11 October 1988. Both investigations were carried out by Mill – the first investigation for the Chief Constable was during Hamilton's camp, according to Mill, although he says he didn't actually go to the camp. Enter James Keenan, who was called in to investigate an informal complaint that had already been investigated for the Deputy Chief Constable and the Chief Constable by Mill. The result of Keenan's investigation was that there were no grounds established for disciplining either of the two officers. This decision was taken by DCC McMurdo. Yet DCC McMurdo had already made that judgement on Mill's report, so why bother with another investigation? If Hamilton originally sent letters to the Chief Constable on this matter, surely that suggests he made a "formal" complaint from the outset? We are told that Hamilton only made his complaint "formal" in the first week of December. The informal investigation by the Chief Constable (carried out by Mill in July) and the informal investigation carried out by Mill in August, were then superceded by a formal investigation carried out by Keenan.

Hamilton visited Mill the week after the camp finished (anywhere between 15 and 21 August). He made references about the officers who went to his camp. These were Mill's officers. He was their Inspector. Mill spoke to Hay before McBain's report was sent to the procurator fiscal at Dumbarton. McBain sent summonses and full statements to the Procurator Fiscal (a summons specifically means "an official order to appear in court"). The complaints specifically included allegations of physical assault. However, Mill in his evidence at the Inquiry states that Hay told him there was no report of abuse of any nature. But Gunn said there were complaints. Who is telling the truth?

Doreen Hagger was present at the 1988 summer camp for approximately three weeks. Her time at the camp came after the visit by Gunn and Duncan. Mrs Hagger had constant arguments with Hamilton about providing food for the children. She did two or 3 shops during the time she was at the camp, and handed over the receipts to Hamilton. Her final fall-out with Hamilton was regarding food for the children. Doreen believes that the receipts she gave to Hamilton were forwarded to Mill. She also believes that Mill got the letters and receipts whilst Hamilton was still on the island. Mill was on holiday at that point. Doreen suggests that Mill might have tipped off Hamilton about the Chief Constable's investigation. She also states that there was a visitor to the island one evening – a tall man – who did not wish to be seen. However, Steven Williams, David Smith and Sam Davie knew who this man was. Who was he?

Hamilton's friendships appear to have spanned a good two decades. His connections and friendships within Central Scotland Police also spanned a good two decades: Michael Mill, Anthony Bushnell, William MacDonald and John Wilson.

Another long-standing friend of Hamilton's was Clive Wood. Eight years Hamilton's senior, the two met in 1981, at Callander Gun Club (according to Wood), which Hamilton started attending at the same time. At the end of 1986 and into early 1987, Hamilton began attending the Stirling Rifle and Pistol Club *as a guest of and in the company of Clive Wood.* However, in his evidence at the Inquiry, when asked if he had anything to do with Hamilton becoming a member, Wood states "he may have introduced himself to me. I don't recollect actually specifically sponsoring him. I think he sort of turned up and we knew each other". In November 1990, Clive Wood bought a 9mm Beretta pistol from Hamilton for £200.00.

Two witnesses at the Dunblane Inquiry – Gordon Crawford and John Moffat – speak to always seeing Hamilton and Clive Wood together at shoots, and Ewan Anderson also knew of Hamilton's friendship with "a man called Clive". Hamilton and Wood usually travelled to shoots together in Wood's car, however one of the last people to transport Hamilton to a shoot – in March 1996 – was an Alex Wood, not Clive Wood.

According to Hamilton's neighbours, Grace and Jim Ogilvie, Clive Wood was one of the three most regular visitors to Hamilton's flat in Stirling, and they told me that he continued visiting right up to 13 March 1996. Wood himself said that he hadn't seen Hamilton since the January. The Ogilvies only knew him through his car, which had the STV logo on it. As an STV cameraman, Clive Wood was involved in media coverage of the events at Dunblane Primary School on 13 March 1996.

CHAPTER 2 :

THE EVENTS OF 13 MARCH 1996

The following is what Lord Cullen had to say about Thomas Hamilton's movements and actions on the morning of 13 March 1996:

About 8.15am Thomas Hamilton was seen by a neighbour to be scraping ice off a white van outside his home at 7 Kent Road, Stirling. They had a normal conversation. Some time later he drove off in the van in the direction of Dunblane *(writer's note: this is not true)*. At about 9.30am he parked the van beside a telegraph pole in the lower car park of Dunblane Primary School. He took out a pair of pliers from a toolwrap and used them to cut the telephone wires at the foot of the telegraph pole. These did not serve the school but a number of adjoining houses. He then crossed the car park, carrying the weapons, ammunition and other equipment which I will describe later, and entered the school by way of a door on its north west side which was next to the toilets beside the gym *(this was never definitely ascertained at the Inquiry, but Cullen writes it as a certainty. I have since written to the Freedom of Information Officer at Central Scotland Police asking if fingerprint samples were taken from the doors where Hamilton might have entered the school. Amazingly, they were not)*. Had he used the main entrance to the school it was more likely that he would have been seen as there were many persons in the vicinity of the entrance at that time. The main school building has six entrances and two doors controlled by push bars for emergency exit. In addition to the main school building there were six hutted classrooms in the playground. Most of the huts had two doors, not including fire exits.

The school day had started at 9am for all primary classes. Morning assemblies were held in the school's Assembly Hall which was situated between the dining area and the gymnasium. The school had 640 pupils, making it one of the largest primary schools in Scotland. The Assembly Hall was not large enough to accommodate the whole school at one time, with the consequence that assemblies were limited to certain year groups in rotation *(there is conflicting evidence about this which is detailed later)*. On 13 March all primary 1, 2 and 3 classes had attended assembly from 9.10 am to 9.30 am. They consisted of a total of about 250 pupils, together with their teachers and the school chaplain. They included Primary 1/13 which was a class of 28 pupils, along with their teacher Gwen Mayor. This class had already changed for their gym lesson before attending assembly. Twenty five members of the class were 5 years of age, and three were 6 years of age. Mrs Mayor was 47 years of age.

At the conclusion of assembly all those present had dispersed to their respective classrooms, with the exception of Primary 1/13 who with Mrs Mayor had made their way to the gymnasium, passing the entrance which *(it is assumed)* Thomas Hamilton used to gain access to the school, and entering the gymnasium by the doorway at its north end. A physical education teacher, Mrs Eileen Harrild, had already arrived there along with Mrs Mary Blake, a supervisory assistant, who was to relieve Mrs Mayor in order to enable her to attend a meeting. The children had been instructed to go to the centre and away from the equipment which was at the south end. Mrs Harrild had been talking to Mrs Mayor for a few minutes. As she was about to attend to the waiting class she heard a noise behind her that caused her to turn round. This was probably the sound of Thomas Hamilton firing two *(he only fired one)* shots into the stage of the Assembly Hall and the girls toilet outside the gym. He then entered the gym. He was wearing a dark jacket, black corduroy trousers *(Grant McCutcheon, the off-duty police officer who was first on the scene, said Hamilton was wearing a black boilersuit)* and a woolly hat with ear defenders *(McCutcheon said Hamilton did NOT have ear defenders on)*. He had a pistol in his hand. He advanced a couple of steps into the gym and fired indiscriminately and in rapid succession. Mrs Harrild was hit in both forearms, the right hand and left breast. She stumbled into the open-plan store area which adjoined the gym, followed by a number of the children. Mrs Mayor was also shot several times and died instantly. Mrs Blake was then shot but also managed to reach the store, ushering some children in ahead of her.

From his position near the entrance doorway of the gym Hamilton fired a total of 29 shots in rapid succession. From that position he killed one child and injured others. During this shooting four injured children made their way to the store. In the store Mrs Blake and Mrs Harrild tried to console and calm the terrified children who had taken refuge there. The children cowered on the floor, lying helplessly in pools of blood hearing the screams and moans of their classmates in the gym, and waiting for the end or for help. Thomas Hamilton walked up the east side of the gym firing six shots. At a point midway along it he discharged 8 shots in the direction of the opposite side of the gym. He then advanced to the middle of the gym and walked in a semi-circle systematically firing 16 shots at a group of children who had either been disabled by the firing or who had been thrown to the floor. He stood over them and fired at point-blank range.

Meanwhile a child from Primary 7 class who had been sent on an errand by his teacher, and was walking along the west side of the gym heard loud banging and screaming. He looked in and saw Thomas Hamilton shooting. Thomas Hamilton shot at him. The child was struck by flying glass and ran off. It appears that Thomas Hamilton then advanced to the south end of the gym. From that position he fired 24 rounds in various directions. He shot through the window adjacent to the fire escape door at the south-east end of the gym. This may have been at an adult who was walking across the playground. Thomas Hamilton opened the fire escape door and discharged 4 shots in the same direction from within the gym.

He then went outside the doorway and fired 4 more shots towards the library cloakroom, striking Mrs Grace Tweddle, a member of the staff, a glancing blow on the head. A teacher, Mrs Catherine Gordon, and her Primary 7 class who were using hut number 7 which was the classroom closest to the fire escape door saw and heard Thomas Hamilton firing from that direction. She immediately instructed her class to get down on the floor, just in time before he discharged 9 shots into her classroom. Most became embedded in books and equipment. One passed through a chair which seconds before had been used by a child.

Thomas Hamilton then re-entered the gym where he shot again. He then released the pistol and drew a revolver *(no witness said this)*. He placed the muzzle of the revolver in his mouth *(nor is there any witness who said this)*, pointing upwards and pulled the trigger. His death followed quickly *(no witness said this)*.

Mrs Mayor and 15 children lay dead in the gym and one further child was close to death. They had sustained a total of 58 gun shot wounds. Twenty six of these wounds were of such a nature that individually they would have proved fatal.

Response to the incident

Mrs Agnes Awlson, the Assistant Headmistress, was making her way across the playground from her classroom when she heard several sharp metallic noises and screaming coming from the gym. She ran along a corridor and saw what she thought were cartridges lying outside its doorway. Realising that something dreadful was happening she ran back to the office of the Headmaster, Mr Ronald Taylor, who was making a telephone call. The call began at 9.38am. He was conscious of hearing noises like indistinct bangs. This puzzled him and his reaction was to think that there were builders on the premises about whom he had not been informed. Mrs Awlson entered his office in a crouched position saying that there was a man in the school with a gun. Mr Taylor cut short his call and made an emergency call to the police *(we don't know if this was an ordinary call, or a 999 call – and it would appear that we are never going to know. For Ron Taylor, the former Headteacher, this must be a bit like having the Not Proven verdict hanging over your head, with all the shadow of doubt that such a verdict brings)*, which was received at 9.41 am. He then ran along the corridor to the gym. On the way he heard no further noises. A student teacher told him that he had seen the gunman shooting himself. Mr Taylor's estimate was that some 3 minutes had lapsed between his first hearing the noises and being told this by the student teacher.

Mr Taylor burst into the gym. He was met by what he described in evidence as "a scene of unimaginable carnage, one's worst nightmare". He saw a group of children on the right hand side of the gym who were crying and obviously less injured than the others. He asked the student teacher to take them out of the gym and give them comfort. He then ran back to his office and instructed the Deputy Headmistress, Mrs Fiona Eadington, to telephone for ambulances. That call was made at 9.43am. He then ran back to the gym calling for adults, and in particular the kitchen staff, to come and help. He moved through the gym along with the janitor Mr John Currie. He noticed Thomas Hamilton lying at the south end of the gym. He seemed to be moving. He noticed a gun on the floor beside him and told Mr Currie to kick it away, which he did. He also removed the revolver *(note, Grant McCutcheon says it was a pistol, not a revolver)* from Thomas Hamilton's hand and threw that aside. By this time the Assistant Headmaster, Mr Stuart McCombie, and members of the kitchen staff were in the gym endeavouring to help the injured children until the arrival of the police. When Mr Taylor went to the store area he discovered the injured who were there. Other members of staff arrived and endeavoured to attend to the injured, who were taken to the Assembly Hall.

Another version of the events of 13 March 1996:

Around 8.30 on the morning of 13 March 1996, Thomas Hamilton was standing outside his house in Stirling talking to a man who has so far remained unidentified. The man he was talking to was driving a large grey saloon car and Hamilton waved and smiled at him as he drove away. In just over an hour, Thomas Hamilton became the most horrific child killer in history. He calmly walked over to the white van he had hired the day before, and started to scrape ice off the windscreen. If this man was planning to commit suicide that day, he must have wished for less inclement weather, involving far less effort than this. However, he seemed cheerful, according to his neighbours.

Forty five minutes later, having taken an unexplained detour via the road to Braehead Primary School in Bannockburn, Hamilton pulled up at Dunblane Primary School. He clearly did not try to make himself inconspicuous because he took out a grey bag from the back of the van, and proceeded to cut the telephone wires in full view of a local woman dropping off her child at the school.

It is impossible to know with any certainty what happened next. The version of events put forward at the Cullen Inquiry is certainly plausible, but when so many witnesses lied and altered their testimony, it is perfectly reasonable to assume that any other scenario is possible too. The official version of events is that Hamilton entered the school at a corridor near the boys toilets, and was thus not seen entering the building. Other versions suggest that Hamilton walked in through the main entrance and was confronted by various adults on his way to the assembly hall. And yet another story goes that he first started firing in the playground.

In the investigation following the incident, Police Constable No. 552, Margaret Dick, from the Traffic Department at Stirling Police Headquarters, did a timed run to see how long it would have taken Hamilton to get from his home to Dunblane Primary School. She timed the journey from 7 Kent Road at 7.2 miles and 8.1 miles. Her first run commenced at 0844 hours and concluded at 0900 hours, taking exactly 16 minutes. The total distance of the run was 7.2 miles. Her second run commenced at 0916 hours and concluded at 0933 hours, taking exactly 17 minutes. The total distance of the run was 8.1 miles. DC Capes, who gave evidence at the Inquiry, was extremely vague about this matter.

In his original Witness Statement, Acting Detective Constable Graham Capes said CCTV cameras picked up Hamilton's van leaving Stirling on the morning of March 13, 1996 at 08.44 and 08.46. The journey to Dunblane Primary School would normally take about 15 minutes but Hamilton did not arrive there until 09.30. At the Inquiry, DC Capes – on oath – said there were sightings of Hamilton's van leaving Stirling at 09.12 (the above CCTV times from his original statement were ignored). Why?

In Lord Cullen's report, he ignores all of the above and simply refers to a sighting of Hamilton scraping ice off the van outside his house at about 08.15. I have written to Lord Cullen three times asking if he or anyone else enquired into what Hamilton did in the missing half hour on the morning of 13 March 1996. Lord Cullen's answer to this question – via his secretary Glynis McKeand – is that he did not read any of the preparatory material, including police statements. That is some admission, given that there were over 1,000 witness statements taken, yet less than 200 witnesses gave evidence at the Inquiry. So I wrote to the Lord Advocate, asking the same question. Nearly two years later he conceded that DC Capes had "made a mistake" in his evidence, but that this did not constitute perjury. When I wrote again asking why DC Capes stated that Hamilton took the exit road off the Burghmuir Roundabout that "led on to the road to Dunblane" (when he in fact took the Kerse Road exit), the Lord Advocate refused to reply.

In Chapter C of the productions given to **all the counsel** at the Inquiry, Statement 701/C states the following:

Acting Detective Constable, no. 605, Graham Capes, Criminal Investigation Department, Stirling – aged 26 – service 5 and a half years.

The witness finally viewed tape number 000346 dated 3rd March (this is a typing mistake – it should read 13th March 1996 of course). At 0844 hours, camera number 6 shows a white van fitting description Ford Escort motor van, registration number M394 KB0 travelling on Burghmuir Road, Stirling heading north west towards Burghmuir Roundabout, Camera number 4 at 0846 hours shows the vehicle travelling round the roundabout and appearing to exit towards Kerse Road, Stirling.

The police, in their evidence at the inquiry, said they were on scene at 9.50am. Police witness Edward Goldie stated that his best estimate of when he and Constable Sneddon – both of Dunblane Police Office – arrived at the primary school was approximately 9.50am. Ambulancewoman Alison Irvine says there were **no** uniformed police officers or police cars there when she arrived at 9.57. The first ambulance on the scene arrived at 9.57am. The crew came from Callander Ambulance Station. They were met at the main entrance to the school by Grant McCutcheon, the off-duty police officer. He told them they were the first there and that about 12 children were dead and a similar number injured.

As already stated, at the Inquiry there was a difference of opinion between the headteacher Mr Taylor and a police officer, DCS John Ogg, about whether Mr Taylor actually made a 999 call, or phoned a direct number at Stirling Police HQ. DCS John Ogg stated that the police log showed it was not a 999 call. This piece of evidence was not even asked to be seen. None of the counsel asked for the tape of the call to be played.

In his evidence on the first day of The Cullen Inquiry, DCS John Ogg was asked: "…I think you have done your best on the basis of all the information available to estimate the time at which the first shot was fired?" – That is correct. "What is your conclusion about that?" – About 9.37. "And why do you reach that conclusion?" – The Headmaster, Mr Taylor, was on the telephone. The itemised calling shows that that call was made at 9.38 and 52 seconds, just shortly before 9.39. The phone call to the police was at 9.31 (sic) and that's when a witness came in and told the Headmaster to contact the police, that someone was in the school with a gun. The ballistics evidence indicated that the shots that were fired could be discharged in 10.2 seconds, so it is working from these calculations. "I think the ballistics information was it could be discharged in 50 seconds?" – Sorry – 50.2 seconds.

"But what we do have is a fixed time for Mr Taylor's telephone call to a colleague at 9.38 and 51 seconds?" – That is correct. "And that is confirmed by telephone record?" – It is. "And we have the call to the police by Mr Taylor, a 999 call?" – It wasn't a treble 9 call. "From the school at 9.41?" – Yes, but it wasn't a treble 9. It was an ordinary call. "An ordinary call at 9.41?" – (No answer).

On Day 2, Mr Stephen, the solicitor representing Ron Taylor, asked DCS Ogg: "Yesterday you said that the call which Mr Taylor had made to report the incident was an ordinary call and not a 999 call?" – That is correct.

"I think the reference is page 98 of yesterday's notes. Do you know for sure that it was indeed an ordinary call or could it perhaps have been a 999 call?" – No, I am almost 100 per cent certain, because it came into our switchboard and not into our control room, and all 999 calls come into the control room.

"And is there any log of that?" – Yes, we checked on that.

"Could I ask you to look at Production R28, in particular the second page of that? This is headed up "Major Incident at Dunblane Primary School Log, 13th March, 1996?" – That is right.

"Could you read the first entry from that?" – That is a 999 call to the Ambulance Service, which I think was made by Mrs Eadington or Mrs Awlson.

"That wouldn't be a reference to Mr Taylor's call?" – No. That was a telephone call that was made to the Ambulance Service.

Although DCS Ogg appeared to lie about the time that parents were told their children had been killed, he is emphatic about the emergency call being an ordinary, not 999 call.

The next witness was Mr Taylor. He was asked: "What did you do?" – From the look in her eyes I realised immediately that something was seriously amiss and I cut off my call to Mr Livingston. "What did you do then?" – I then dialled 999.

"There has been some evidence about who you dialled at that point and there is no doubt it was the police; are you clear in your mind it was a 999 call?" – In my own mind I am clear about that because I have never dialled a 999 call before and I didn't have the number of the local police station to dial". Mr Taylor fudged the issue by saying he didn't know the number of the local police station. However, the call was made to the switchboard at Stirling Police Station, where DCS Ogg was based. Dunblane Police were radioed from Stirling to attend the scene. Remember, DCS Ogg had seen the "telephone record".

The parents of a child who was uninjured in the gym that day, say they saw two bullet holes in the south wall of the gym, about 2 inches apart and just 6 inches from the ground. Their statement continues, "There were no other bullet holes in that wall and I noticed that there were quite a few bullet holes in the other walls which would confirm my (words are blanked out here..............) that he fired into the walls at the bottom end of the gym where Hamilton had entered the gym". WHO fired into the walls at the bottom end of the gym when Hamilton (re-entered) the gym through the fire exit door at the south end? Did Hamilton administer 2 (2!!) bullets to his head whilst lying down? It does not make sense. Lord Cullen does not even refer in his report to the bullet(s) used by Hamilton to kill himself. It may seem an insignificant detail, considering what had happened, but if any of the facts of that morning have been altered, then it is reasonable to ask, Why?

So, mystery still surrounds the death of Thomas Hamilton on 13 March 1996. We have always been led to believe that after a three minute rampage in which he shot dead 16 children and their teacher and injured 12 other children and 2 teachers, he then turned the gun on himself. Questions are still being asked about whether this was really the case.

I have written several times to Professor Anthony Busuttil, the pathologist who conducted Hamilton's post-mortem, asking how a pathologist establishes if a gunshot wound is self or other-inflicted, how many exit wounds there were from Hamilton's head, how it was that Hamilton's brain was retained for neuropathological examination when by all accounts the skull's contents had been blown out, therefore how did he manage to detect a tiny nodule on Hamilton's brain when the weapon he used to 'kill himself' resulted in serious damage to the brain? Professor Busuttil has refused to answer any of my questions, referring me instead to the Crown Office (who refuse to answer my questions). The matter is now with the Scottish Information Commissioner.

Those who knew Hamilton know for certain he didn't kill himself. Doreen Hagger says "he was far too much of a coward". At the 1988 camp on Inchmoan Island she did all she could to protect the boys from Hamilton's sadistic cowardly bullying. One day she encouraged the boys to collect spiders and other creepy crawlies to put in his sleeping bag. He was terrified. Then when the island was 'invaded' by geese, Hamilton sought protection from Mrs Hagger.

Immediately after the massacre at Dunblane, Doreen said: *When I heard his name on the TV and heard he'd shot himself, I said 'That creep wouldn't have the guts'* (Daily Record 15 March 1996). It is a myth that those who take their own life are cowards. Cowards take the life of others, whilst wishing to preserve their own.

Professor David Cooke told the inquiry in Stirling: "I would speculate that he formed the suicide intention before he killed the other people but that is *purely speculation* based on the fact that he changed weapons before killing himself. It seems ritualistic." And Dr John Baird told the inquiry: "Had his intention been to engage in some sort of killing spree, he could have continued for longer. There was no reason, when he killed himself, to have done that".

Hamilton was not the loner that Lord Cullen and sections of the press made out. He actually had many "friends", although they preferred to describe themselves as acquaintances when giving evidence at the inquiry in 1996. His most regular visitors continued coming right until the end, say Grace and Jim Ogilvie, Hamilton's immediate neighbours. Yet nearly all those who knew Hamilton claimed, at the inquiry, that they hadn't seen him for several months. Mr and Mrs Ogilvie know for certain that the men who regularly turned up in large flashy cars to visit Hamilton continued doing so well beyond the dates they claimed. Two other neighbours, Mrs Kerr and Mr Deuchars, saw no apparent change in Hamilton's demeanour. He certainly did not seem depressed. Quite the opposite. Mrs Kerr says he was actually more cheerful and chatty in those last few days.

Did Hamilton plan to escape? Is that why he hired a van the day before and offered to pay the full cost upfront, when he was only expected to pay a deposit? Is that why he purchased several new shirts in the weeks beforehand? Shirts that weren't even found in his house when a search was done on 13 March 1996. The only item of clothing found was a jacket. Were all his letters to the Queen, and the press, and his MP during that last week really a signal that he at last intended to leave the small town where rumours about him were rife? It was a source of amazement to some that Hamilton continued to live in a place where there was so much rumour and gossip about him. Was he conned – by an accomplice – into believing that after carrying out his act of revenge against the people of Dunblane that a new life beckoned?

Other questions point to doubt about whether financial difficulties were a motivating factor in Hamilton's actions on 13 March 1996. Were we told the truth about Hamilton's finances at the Inquiry? Some sources suggest that he obtained two credit cards and apparently spent freely at the end of 1995 and early 1996, despite being unemployed. What enquiries were made to ascertain whether Hamilton was blackmailing or being blackmailed?

Hamilton had links with the Queen Victoria boarding school in Dunblane, a Ministry of Defence establishment. There are suggestions from a former housemaster that boys there were abused. Who were Hamilton's contacts at this school? The Inquiry did not probe into this, despite three witnesses testifying to Hamilton's connections with the school.

Two days earlier, Bank video tapes of a male fitting the description of Hamilton showed him within the Clydesdale Bank in Murray Place, Stirling at between 9.52 am and 9.59am. Was he depositing or withdrawing money? The only money found in Hamilton's house in the search done on 13 March 1996 were four 10 pence pieces (and an empty wallet). Around 9am on that Monday, he was seen by his neighbour Helen Peters in Kent Road, carrying a wooden box.

On the same day, CCTV footage of a man fitting the description of Hamilton detailed his movements between 10.14pm and 10.21pm, going from Goosecroft Road in Stirling to the Linden Avenue Roundabout in Stirling, presumably from the train station to his home. By all accounts, he ran his club as usual that night at Thomas Muir High School in Bishopbriggs and must therefore have returned home by train.

The next day, Tuesday 12 March, CCTV footage of a man fitting the description of Hamilton, details his movements from Wellgreen, Stirling to Burghmuir Road, Stirling. This was between the early hours of 1205 and 1210. It is unclear if this is the very early hours of March 12th or March 13th. He bought a train ticket at 11.55am on 12 March – a ticket that was issued somewhere between Dunblane and Stirling. Should that be 11.55pm? If he was seen by a CCTV camera in the early hours of 13th March, that suggests he returned from somewhere by train the night before the massacre. Why, when he'd already hired a van? Who did he visit?

Earlier in the evening he ran his club as normal at Bannockburn High School. One boy at the club, William McFadyen, received a medal for gymnastics that night. About quarter to eight that evening he asked Hamilton if football would be on at the Thursday club in Dunblane. Hamilton replied that it would not. He said he had to go and "see a man in Dunblane". He didn't tell William who the man was or what he was going to see him for.

At 9pm that same evening Hamilton phoned his friend David MacDonald, whom he had known for about 15 years. Where did he make this phone call from? Hamilton's mother tried phoning her son at his home that evening but got no reply. In her evidence, Agnes Watt stated that she usually received a phone call from her son "every night", but after he left her house at 6pm on Tuesday 12 March, she didn't hear from him again. She tried calling him.

At the inquiry she was asked, "So you talked when you phoned him?" – No, she replied. I couldn't get anybody. Where did Thomas Hamilton spend his last evening, and in whose company? Hamilton spoke to his friend David MacDonald for roughly 45 minutes, initially talking about cameras and then later about his business, which he said was not going too well (Hamilton was unemployed at this point, and certainly had no official business). Earlier in the day, at 9.08am, Hamilton phoned another long-standing friend, David's father, William MacDonald, an ex police officer with Central Scotland Police. Their evidence is detailed in full later in the book.

TO SUM UP THEN: Some time between 8am and 8.40am on 13 March 1996, Thomas Hamilton was seen standing beside, or having just got out of a large grey saloon car parked outside his house. He waved to the driver who drove off. He then went over to a white van. Hamilton was in a cheerful mood according to witness Cathleen Boswell Kerr (who was not called to give evidence at the Inquiry).

According to CCTV cameras examined by police witness Graham Capes (Graham Kate at inquiry), Hamilton's van was seen driving out of Stirling at 08.44 and 08.46, travelling on Burghmuir Road, heading north west towards Burghmuir Roundabout. His vehicle is seen travelling round the roundabout and appearing to exit towards Kerse Road, Stirling. At the inquiry he said the van was seen at 09.12. Why were these times changed? When pressed to say how long it would take to drive from Stirling to Dunblane, Graham Capes/Kate replied "15 minutes". This would be about right. The times have obviously been altered for a reason. It would NOT have taken 45 minutes for Hamilton to drive from Stirling to Dunblane. So, where did he go? Did he meet with someone?

In his final report, Lord Cullen ignores all the above times – and time alterations – and refers instead to Hamilton being seen at 08.15 scraping ice off the van. Hamilton is more likely to have scraped ice off the van immediately before setting off, at approximately 8.40am.

DCS John Ogg clearly states in his evidence that the Headteacher made an ordinary call, not a treble 9 call. Mr Taylor said he did not know the number of the local police station, so it would have had to be a 999 call. How remiss of a Primary Headteacher not to know the number of the local police station. It is a number I have always found easy to remember (822222). Police witness Capes/Kate, who had already given wrong information about the CCTV times, was asked, "one of the items which you at one stage handled in the course of this Inquiry was an audio cassette tape recording of a telephone call?" – Yes. "And that was given to you by a sergeant in the course of the investigation?" – Yes. "Now, what did that audio recording relate to?" – I was told by the sergeant that it related to a treble 9 call received at the control room – by Mr Taylor. "This is a call from Mr Taylor?" – Yes. "So that was actually a recording made which the police do have of the call Mr Taylor made to the police on the 999 Emergency Service system?" – That is what I was informed, yes. Graham Capes/Kate did not listen to the recording himself then.

Witness Eileen Harrild, the first teacher to be shot by Hamilton, was asked at the inquiry, "Are you able to put any estimate on the number of minutes between the shooting stopping and the arrival of the first member of staff?" – *I think possibly it was more towards the end of the shooting....* So, someone – not necessarily a member of staff at all – turned up before Hamilton finished shooting. Who was this person? Mrs Harrild did not see who it was because she had taken refuge in a storeroom. So who entered the gym whilst Hamilton was still firing?

Ron Taylor was asked similar questions. Asked, "Was there still a noise?" he answered, I didn't hear any noise until I arrived at the gym door. "Was there still a noise?" – He repeats: I didn't hear any noise until I arrived at the gym door *(what noise did he hear at the gym door?)*

"I am concerned about the banging noises?" – No, I heard no further banging noises. "When you got to the gym door I take it there were still no banging noises?" – There were still no banging noises. "So the shooting was over?" – Yes, the shooting was over, Mr Scott had told me at that point that he had shot himself. "He had seen that?" – He had seen that. "Can you give us a rough estimate of the time lapse from when you first heard these noises when you were outside and the time Mr Scott told you that he had shot himself?" – About 3 minutes. Mr Taylor was told by Mr Scott that Hamilton shot himself. Mr Scott did not give evidence at the inquiry. Mr Taylor merely repeats what Mr Bonomy asks.

David Scott – the only eye witness to Hamilton's suicide – is said to have seen into the gym from the art class. But the location of the art class was not shown in the aerial view photograph of Dunblane Primary School at the back of the Cullen Report. So it is not possible to work out where David Scott would have been in relation to the gym and whether he would have had a clear view. Why is this detail missing?

Why did Lord Cullen write in his report that Hamilton placed the muzzle of the revolver in his mouth, pointing upwards and pulled the trigger? David Scott is only reported as saying that he saw the gun "close to his face". He did not say he saw Hamilton put the revolver in his mouth.

We know that Hamilton's body was given a full dissection. Professor Anthony Busuttil simply said the cause of death was "gunshot injury". But this does not explain the manner of his death, whether or not it was self-inflicted and if there were were other gunshot injuries that were not fatal. If it was a simple suicide, what is there to hide? Were there other injuries? What wounds did Hamilton's body show?

Ron Taylor states that he saw two guns, as did Grant McCutcheon and John Currie. Yet by 11.30am there were four guns on the scene. Scene of Crime Officer Malcolm Chisholm said that there were four guns next to Hamilton, two on each side. John Currie, janitor, removed a gun from Hamilton's hand (a revolver he says, but Grant McCutcheon says it was a pistol) and threw it away from Hamilton's body. He kicked away another gun, to the left-hand side of Hamilton's body.

According to Malcolm Chisholm, Hamilton's ear muffs, woolly-type hat and spectacles were lying to the left of the body. The hat had damage to the top of it. Did Hamilton remove these items after committing suicide? If he removed them before shooting himself, the hat would have been undamaged.

Hamilton's revolver was lying at a "funny angle", according to Chisholm – the butt propped up in the air against a bench. It was fully loaded. The janitor kicked the first gun away and it landed beside the bench. He then removed the second gun from Hamilton's left hand and threw it away. It landed beside the fire exit door. Yet Chisholm states the guns were "next" to Hamilton.

Chisholm was asked if there was a camera bag near the door of the gym. Chisholm states, yes, it was rather a large case, it was quite obvious as we came into the gymnasium. "From the information available at that time did it appear to belong to Hamilton?" – I was told it belonged to Hamilton, yes.

Yet David Gould, army bomb disposal officer, describes the bag as 15cm by 35cm, in other words, quite a small bag.

In his evidence, DCS John Ogg referred to a bag – not a case – being found in the gym. He states that the pliers used by Hamilton to cut the telephone wires were found in the "bag" in the gym. Neither Chisholm nor Gould referred to pliers being found in the "case" they examined. In fact, a Freedom of Information request by William Scott has revealed that the only item in the bag was a personal stereo. David Gould's incident report says the same. This bag/case was said to contain further ammunition. Hamilton was not seen entering the school with any such case. He was armed with two loaded handguns and shoulder pouches containing ammunition.

It has always been claimed that Hamilton had enough ammunition with him to shoot ALL the children in the school, over 700 of them. However, at a press conference on the day of the massacre, Chief Constable William Wilson stated that Hamilton might have run out of ammunition....

Malcolm Chisholm ordered the gym to be evacuated at 12 o'clock. David Gould, ammunitions technician/bomb disposal, only received the instruction at 2.30pm and didn't arrive at the school until 3.20pm. The gym was then evacuated (NOT at 12 o'clock as Chisholm states). Gould was asked to check the case, the body of Hamilton, his firearms, and the hire van. He states he was there about 15 to 20 minutes. He then informed the Chief Superintendent that the officers could resume their investigations.

Gould asked the police if he was to unload the guns and they indicated he should. He unloaded the guns and informed the police officers what he had done. He did not know who the people were in the gym. He assumed they were part of the investigation, but he did not ask who they were.

David Gould unloaded the guns. Malcolm Chisholm states that he did not touch anything until Gould had checked for a booby-trap. At this stage, Chisholm says all he did was "observe" the scene and that he did not touch anything, whilst also stating that the case/bag was locked. So how did he know this?

Only after Gould had been and gone did Chisholm check the guns, according to his evidence at the inquiry. Yet he says that when he examined the guns he could tell how many bullets there were in each gun and which ones had a bullet in the chamber. But Gould had <u>already</u> unloaded the guns. Did Chisholm check them earlier? When asked how long it was before people came back into the gym after evacuation, Chisholm doesn't immediately answer. He is asked again and says he can't answer that – it seemed ages. Gould says he was only in there for 15 to 20 minutes.

Ron Taylor said that after telling David Scott to take some children outside the gym, he went back to the office area and asked for someone to phone for ambulances. Ron Taylor then went back to the gym. As he was going through the gym he became aware that the janitor, John Currie, was to his left. They both moved slowly through the gym, although Currie was further ahead than Taylor. Taylor noticed Hamilton at the top of the gym and said he seemed to be "moved". On first reading, it is easy to assume he meant "moving" – that Hamilton's body was still moving. But Taylor had already been in the gym and seen the bodies, including Hamilton's. So when he went back in, did he think that Hamilton's body had been moved?

Hamilton went out of the fire exit door firing. Steven Hopper, aged 11, was only yards from the gymnasium in a converted hut when the massacre began. Steven said, "I looked over and saw the gunman. He seemed to come out of the gymnasium and was <u>just firing at something</u>. He was coming towards me so I dived under my desk when he turned and fired at us. It was very fast, like someone hitting a hammer quickly. It was pretty scary when he started shooting at our window because all the glass smashed in and I got hit by a piece".

Hamilton may have been shooting at a woman who was walking across the playground. In her Witness Statement, Alison Currie says, "I walked across the playground then thinking that the noise I heard was in fact, a gun. As I was about to enter the alcove, which allows entry to the school at the library, I was only a few steps away, I became aware of a man on the raised veranda at the fire exit door to the gym. I thought it unusual that this door was opened because I only ever recall it being opened for fetes held at the school. I think this man was coming out of the gym, he was dressed in black clothing... This man was standing upright in a funny way although I can't remember seeing his hands or a gun or anything.... At the same time, I heard and felt something whizzed past my left arm and right side of my face. I realised he was a gunman and he was shooting at me. I think he fired at me more than twice, not more than five, although at that time I didn't hear any gunshots".

According to the student teacher David Scott, Hamilton went in and out of the fire exit door on two separate occasions and was holding the gun in his left hand when he wasn't using both hands. Hamilton fired 4 more shots towards the library cloakroom, striking Mrs Grace Tweddle, a member of the staff, a glancing blow on the head. This was directly outside the janitor's office. According to Alison Currie's statement, on fleeing into the school for her safety, she saw the janitor standing in the middle of the steps just outside his office, looking dazed. She asked if the police had been called and was told yes.

The bullets Hamilton fired entered the cloakroom at the end of Hut 7. The windows in Hut 7 gave a clear view through from one side to the other. Hamilton went to the far side of Hut 7 and fired a further 9 bullets. He then returned to the gym and, according to Chisholm, fired a lot of shots in all directions. The injured teachers say there were just a few shots when Hamilton came back in the gym. Both injured teachers testified to the rapid-fire shooting in the first instance, the shooting then ceasing, and then starting up again, this time just a few shots and not rapid.

Shots fired: 1 shot at stage floor (not 2, as Lord Cullen states in his Report); 1 fired in hallway; 29 fired to all parts of gym on entering; 6 fired while walking up left side of gym; 8 across the gym from the left; 16 fired in middle of gym; 30 at the top of the gym; 1 through window next to fire door; 4 shot at cloakroom from fire door; 4 fired when he stepped outside; 9 fired at Hut 7 from far side; Total 109 – NOT 105, as claimed by Cullen; Hamilton re-entered the gym and directed a "large number" of shots towards all parts of the gym including the games equipment room. Why are the spent cartridges not accounted for in the total above? Were they fired by Hamilton or by a person unknown?

Chisholm states that 105 bullets could be fired in 50.4 seconds. Hamilton was said to have killed himself after 3 minutes. What happened in those remaining 2 minutes? Where is the evidence of the single shell used by Hamilton to shoot himself?

In his evidence DCS John Ogg said that in the statement taken from the janitor, the fire doors were locked. Yet we are told that Hamilton went out of the firedoor. Why was this firedoor open, and all the others locked? The firedoor out of the store area of the gym was locked, thus preventing the injured teachers and children being able to escape from the building. As a consequence of this firedoor being locked, they had to "hide" in the store-room.

The pathologists are repeatedly warned by the Lord Advocate to refer only to Hamilton's head injury and not to other areas of his body. Pathologist Anthony Busuttil said the bullet exited the left side of Hamilton's head. Chisholm says the top of the head. Chisholm states that the bullet came out of the top of his head and impacted on the ceiling. However, surely if the exit wound was above the left ear, it would have hit a wall, not the roof? Busuttil states, "The entry wound corresponding to this exit wound was located... ". *This exit wound...* This suggests there was more than one exit wound from Hamilton's head. There was a hole 155mm above the bridge of Hamilton's nose. This was 70mm to the left of midline. This was on the top of his head, not near his left ear. Busuttil is then asked about the internal parts of Hamilton's body. The cardiovascular and respiratory systems were fairly normal for a man of his age. When asked questions about the digestive system, the Lord Advocate says, "leaving aside the gunshot injury again was it normal?" When asked questions about the genito-urinary, lymphatic and endocrine systems, he asks "and again they are all normal with the exception of the gunshot wound?" Leaving aside the gunshot injury?

Furthermore, his post-mortem showed a parchmented yellow based abrasion measuring 3mm x 5mm. This was in the region of his left hip. After Busuttil described this injury, the Lord Advocate intervenes with, "So if we pause there, as far as the recent injuries were concerned, leaving aside the post-mortem matter you have just mentioned, they are limited to signs of gunshot **wounds** (plural) where the entry point had been located within the mouth and exit point the area in your head that you pointed to a moment ago?" The Lord Advocate clearly attempts to divert attention from this matter, whilst also referring to more than one head wound.

Chisholm states that there were four right-handed holsters. Grant McCutcheon refers to just **one** holster. Hamilton had only marked the ammunition for the Browning pistols. It is likely that the Browning he fired the shots with was the only gun he intended to use. The second Browning was his back-up. The Browning he used was honed to perfection and balanced. At the gun club he only practised with these two guns. At the gun club he was said to have one holster on the left and one on the right.

After the shootings, DCS John Ogg went to Hamilton's house. He was asked what he saw in the lounge. Ogg states that there were "cases" of bullets and some cartridges. Hamilton had applied coloured sticky tape to the front and back of the bullets for easy loading. Why would Hamilton go to such lengths but then leave this labelled ammunition at home?

Why was the muzzle-weight missing from Hamilton's gun according to Scene of Crime Officer Malcolm Chisholm? (Day 1 of the Inquiry). According to Chisholm, a custom-built foresight had been attached instead. Yet according to firearms examiner Alistair Paton (Day 18 of the Inquiry), when he examined the gun used by Hamilton, it had a muzzle-weight attached to the end of the barrel. Was the custom-built foresight accidently replaced with a muzzle-weight?

Hamilton's body was partially unclothed at the locus, according to Professor Busuttil. Who took these clothes? A body should not be touched or anything removed from the body. This should be done by the pathologist carrying out the post-mortem. This would appear to go against standard procedure. Hamilton started out wearing a black boiler suit. After his death he was said to be wearing black corduroy trousers. Were Hamilton's clothes removed to prevent them being tested for D.N.A, or to conceal an injury to his body? Hamilton's hands were bagged and swabbed for firearms discharge. DCS Ogg believes that Hamilton went in the door to the school at the boys toilet. If so, finger prints would have been present on that door. However, fingerprint samples were not taken. This should have been done to ascertain if Hamilton definitely entered the school at the boys toilet. The fire exit door could also have been tested for fingerprints. By process of elimination they would have found out which door he went through. Hamilton's fingerprints would also have been on the guns. Were these checked?

When David Gould, bomb disposal officer, arrived at Dunblane Primary School at 3.20pm, he was asked to do a search of Hamilton's hire van. In his Incident Report, which I obtained under the Freedom of Information Act, Gould states that the van had already been searched by the police before he arrived. Who searched the van and what items were removed by Central Scotland Police?

Why did police photographer Ian McDiarmid (Day 3 of the Inquiry) state that there were boxes full of ammunition in the **rear bedroom** of Hamilton's house, when DCS John Ogg (Day 2) stated that the ammunition was found in the **lounge**? According to McDiarmid, all he found in the living room was an open briefcase, some paper and a magazine. Mr Bonomy says "otherwise nothing unusual about the room?" McDiarmid replies "No".

Why did Police Constable Stephen Connell (Day 3) say in his evidence that he took part in a search at Hamilton's home in Kent Road on 20 March 1996 (when he found a railway ticket), when in his original witness statement he says he took part in a search at Hamilton's home on **both** 13 March **under the command of (non-witness) Inspector Huskie** (5.30pm – 9pm) and then **again** on 20 March from 2pm-6pm?

Why did Detective Sergeant Andrew Lawless (Day 3) and "colleagues" (nameless) remove certain items from Hamilton's house on the afternoon of 13 March 1996? Why haven't these items been named? Were these items the rounds of ammunition that were placed in the gym to create the impression that Hamilton entered the school intent on killing everyone?

The ammunition found in Hamilton's house consisted of the following, according to Lawless: 280 rounds of .357; 715 rounds of 9mm and 11 rounds of .38 Special.

These are remarkably similar amounts to what Chisholm says he found in the gym: 242 rounds of .357 and 501 rounds of 9mm, totalling 743 rounds of ammunition, enough to kill everyone in the school. How convenient.

Headteacher Ron Taylor (Day 2) said that Assembly alternated from week to week, with the younger children going to Assembly one Wednesday and the older children the next week. Was the statement of the boy (see below) that was read out at the Inquiry intended to give the impression that Hamilton's plan was to kill everyone in assembly? The myth that has now been established about Hamilton intending to kill everyone in the school is just too convenient. This myth was established in order to diminish the actual scale of the massacre. What were 17 deaths when there could easily have been over 700?

Witness Jamie Cook – whose evidence was read out at the Inquiry (Day 3) – says in his original witness statement that Assembly was on a Wednesday morning and "the younger ones went after the older ones". When asked by Hamilton what time Assembly started, Jamie Cook (then aged 9) told him 9.30am. Hamilton clarified with Jamie that the younger children from Primary 1 to 4 went to Assembly at a different time from Primary 5 to 7. Jamie stated that Hamilton asked what time the assembly started and was told 9.30am. Hamilton asked him if the younger children, like the primary 1s to 4s went to the assembly at a different time to the primary 5s to 7s. The pupil told him the Assembly was on a Wednesday morning and that "the younger ones went after us."

In his evidence at the Inquiry, headmaster Ron Taylor said the following: "The assemblies take place at the moment on a Wednesday morning, but they are rotational, because we cannot get all the children into the hall at the one time, so we rotate them. On one Wednesday there would be the infants' assembly, which is Primaries 1, 2, 3 and 4, followed by a senior assembly Primaries 5, 6 and 7. These dates would be rotated in relation to when was the best time for the assembly. On one Wednesday there would be the infants' assembly, that is Primaries 1, 2 and 3, then an assembly for Primaries 4, 5 and 6, and a senior assembly for Primary 7. These dates would be rotated in relation to when was the best time for assemblies". When he was asked later if this had been a senior assembly what time would it normally have finished his reply was "It varied. It would normally have finished about 9.40."

Hamilton however, appeared to believe Jamie Cook about Primary 5s to 7s having assembly at 9.30am every week not every other week as Ron Taylor is suggesting. Jamie's father, Andrew Cook, a nearby neighbour of mine at the time, stated that his son Jamie attended a boys club of Hamilton's that was held at Dunblane High School. This had been going on for two years, on Thursday nights, between 6 and 8pm. Mr Cook – having spoken with Hamilton a few times – was satisfied that Hamilton was capable of running the club. His son Jamie joined Hamilton's club in 1994, by which time not only the parents of boys in Dunblane were alarmed about Hamilton, but many other parents throughout Central Scotland were too. Mr Cook had heard rumours and had made tentative enquiries, but found he could not come up with any specific complaints against Hamilton. He said he monitored the club quite closely and was satisfied that it was run properly.

On Thursday 7 March 1996, Jamie Cook attended Hamilton's club as usual. There were about six other boys present. Halfway through playing football, Hamilton took Jamie to one side and sat him down on a bench to speak to him. He asked him the way to the gym at the Primary School and the way to the hall. However, Hamilton already knew Dunblane Primary School through having run his Rovers Club there in 1977. He used the gym for this club, according to Inquiry Witness Garry McDonald. Hamilton did not need to ask one of his boys for directions in the school. He already knew the layout of the school.

Under a section headed **Preparation**, Lord Cullen writes about Jamie Cook's evidence as follows:

The Inquiry heard the statement of a boy of 9 years of age who attended Dunblane Primary School and was a member of the Dunblane Boys Club. He stated that on 7 March when he had been playing football at the club Thomas Hamilton took him out and sat him on a bench in order to speak to him. He then continued: "He asked me the way to the gym and the main way into the school. He asked directions about once he was in the main hall, how to get to the gym and where the stage was. He asked how to get to the Assembly Hall, and I told him to turn right after the main entrance. He said what day do all people go on the stage to do the play. I didn't know and he said to ask the P7s to find out. He asked if the younger children, like the primary 1s to 4s go to the assembly at a different time to the primary 5s to 7s. I told him that the assembly was on a Wednesday morning and that the younger ones went after us. He asked me what time did assembly start and gym, I said 9.30 for assembly. I didn't tell him the time for gym..... The other question was something to do with the gym fire exit. I think it was how many fire exits there were to get out of the gym. Mr Hamilton asked me these questions every single week. He had been asking me these questions for a long time, about two years. He didn't ask me any more questions and said I could go back to playing football". It is hard to avoid the conclusion that this evidence points to a degree of pre-planning by Hamilton, but why the difference between the Headteacher's statement and Jamie Cook's?

So why was there no assembly for the older children on 13 March 1996? And why did teacher Mrs McLeod not know that her class should have been at assembly that morning? Teaching assistant Mary Blake had to remind Mrs McLeod to take her class to assembly. She was ten minutes late. Was this because of the sudden time change?

Clearly there are differing versions of which group of children would normally have been in assembly at the time Hamilton arrived. Why was this issue not cleared up at the inquiry? Why wasn't the class register taken on the morning of 13 March 1996 for Primary One Class 1/13? Why did the class change for gym in their classroom and not in the changing rooms? What was the rush?

In the end, there were two vital witnesses who did not give evidence at the Inquiry: David Duke Scott, the student teacher who says he saw Hamilton shoot himself, and Grant McCutcheon, the off-duty police officer who was first on the scene. The former, even now, refuses to speak about what he saw and the evidence that he gave. In 2003, John Ogg, former DCS with Central Scotland Police, said he didn't recall the name of the off-duty police officer. Deputy headmistress Agnes Awlson said in her evidence at the Inquiry, that she was aware of "some sort of police officer" being present. Fortunately, after several years of private enquiries, I found this man and got a copy of his statement. To put it mildly, this did not please Central Scotland Police.

CHAPTER 3 :

THE BACKDROP

We aren't meant to say Thomas Hamilton's name. After the Dunblane Massacre it was decided that mentioning the murderer's name only served to glorify him. What rubbish. We mustn't forget Thomas Hamilton. If we do, we forget one of the worst examples of murderous paedophilia we have ever seen in this country. I know Dunblane was a one-off tragedy. I know it is unlikely to ever be repeated (in that form). But there was a background to what happened that has been conveniently wiped out...

Before 13 March 1996, Thomas Hamilton had a lifelong career as a paedophile. Starting in his teens, he found ways to have young boys around him, wherever, whenever. He was the Fagin of our times.

Hamilton always kept himself on the right side of the law... just. When the Children Act of 1989 was introduced – requiring that only club leaders for **under-eights** needed to be checked out in advance by local councils to see if they are 'fit persons' – Hamilton took to recruiting **over-eights**. If Hamilton had continued running clubs for under-eights, the following checks would have had to be made. An examination of: 1/ his personal qualities as a leader, including his ability to foster children's development and learning; 2/ his ability to provide warm and consistent care; 3/ his mental stability; 4/ his integrity, and 5/ his flexibility. Hamilton would have failed on all counts.

Seven years later, government policy regarding the care of children under the supervision of others, was heading in the opposite direction. The Deputy Prime Minister Michael Heseltine, and Secretary of State for Scotland, Michael Forsyth, planned to scale down restrictions on those providing childcare. This was apparently part of the whole deregulation initiative of that time. Again, using the arbitary cut-off age of eight, the Conservative Government in office at the time of the Dunblane massacre had planned to extend the exemption period for groups providing child care for under-8s from council and police checks, from **6 days to 60 days!** Quite rightly, welfare organisations at the time branded this a Molester's Charter. Think of it another way. It was Hamilton's Charter. It was designed for Thomas Hamilton....

Inevitably, in the aftermath of Hamilton's Massacre, these measures were put on hold, and ultimately disappeared. Can you imagine a similar circumstance where a man with the reputation of someone like Thomas Hamilton was allowed, year after year, to take young boys away to a remote island, allowed no contact with their parents, and forced to wear swimming trunks no matter what the weather? We have become so numbed to the circumstances surrounding Dunblane, that we have lost sight of the fact that

Hamilton was – as everyone knew – living on the wrong side of the law and had been doing so for a long time. He was flouting the law on technicalities time and time again.

Although Hamilton had no convictions for any sexual offences, 18 months before the Dunblane massacre he was cautioned by Lothian and Borders Police who found him with his trousers down in a compromising position with a 'young man' (age not specified) in Edinburgh's Calton Hill area. Immediately following the massacre, quantities of computer software and photographs of half-dressed boys were said to have been removed from Hamilton's home in Stirling. It was thought that Hamilton had links to an international child sex ring. An Internet link of Hamilton's was being investigated, and then the media interest died down until the Inquiry began in May 1996. Any links that Hamilton might have had to an international paedophile network were not raised by Lord Cullen during the Inquiry.

As Alan Clark put it, in the News of the World (17 March 1996),

"Here was a situation where every single antenna that informs a community had signalled a warning. Children didn't like him but couldn't, or didn't want to, say why. Voluntary organisations expelled him or refused membership without giving reasons. Shops wouldn't accept his photos for development. Parents who visited him to remonstrate were threatened with the law......

In former times, or in more "primitive" communities where human recognition of natural justice has not been brainwashed out of the citizen's psyche; and where there are not a dozen agencies standing ready to make excuses for those who may be accounted "disturbed", it would never have got · this far".

What kind of influence did Thomas Hamilton have with his Conservative Member of Parliament, Michael Forsyth? As Secretary of State for Scotland in the years leading up to the massacre in 1996, Michael Forsyth was an important political player – a friend of Margaret Thatcher's even. Forsyth urged Thomas Hamilton to publicise having his name cleared by the Ombudsman in 1984. In a letter to Hamilton on 23 November 1984, Forsyth wrote, "Thank you for sending me the Commissioner's report and may I congratulate you on your success. I hope that you will take steps to ensure this is given proper publicity".

To be allowed access to children for 60 days without being subjected to council or police checks was exactly what Thomas Hamilton needed to run his summer camps without interference. His Loch Lomond Camps spanned a total of 8 weeks each summer, usually throughout the months of July and August. 8 weeks. That's 56 days. Which is just under 60 days. Which would have made Hamilton exempt from checks...

Hamilton lived under the best, most paedophile-friendly era this country has ever known, and will ever know. Not only did he destroy the 'hobby' that so many other men shared – shooting – he destroyed the easy-access to children that paedophiles were previously granted (for which we must be thankful). The internet has taken over with regard to child pornography, but how many men like Hamilton could you imagine being allowed to take a dozen or more 5 – 11 year old children away to a remote island where they would have no contact with their parents? It is mind-boggling.

Doreen Hagger knew Thomas Hamilton because of her son's involvement with one of his clubs/camps, so when the shootings happened at Dunblane Primary School and she heard who the perpetrator of the massacre was, her memories of that man came flooding back. In her own words, this is her experience:

In 1988 I had foolishly allowed my 10 year old son Andrew to attend Hamilton's summer camp on Loch Lomond. After a police raid on a cinema in Balloch, all the boys were returned home. Andrew came home without any of his belongings. Hamilton phoned me to say I could collect Andrew's belongings from Balmaha boatyard. When I got there I asked Hamilton what had been going on. He claimed that none of his helpers had turned up and that he needed someone to come to the next camp and cook for the boys. When I asked him where the chalets were that the boys were supposed to be staying in, he said he hadn't been able to get that particular island. What lies that man told.

Concerned about what was really going on, I agreed to help. I returned home to Bridgend, near Linlithgow, and enlisted the help of my friend, Janet Reilly, and a male friend, Sam Davie. Together with my daughter Vikki and son Andrew, we set sail for the island of Inchmoan. Janet's son William went to stay with his granny. He'd briefly attended one of Hamilton's clubs and refused to go back. He didn't like Hamilton touching his chest and told him so.

At the camp, I learned all about the real Thomas Hamilton. I did all I could to protect the boys from his sadistic treatment of them. I stood up to Hamilton, but Hamilton was unflinching. He was in charge of his own private little army of boys, and no mere woman was going to get in the way of that. I had many arguments with Thomas Hamilton, and when he threatened to burn my tent down, I decided for the safety of my children, to leave. Even that didn't prove easy. I had to bribe an older boy, Stephen Williams, to take Janet, Vikki, Andrew and myself off the island in the middle of the night – when Hamilton was asleep. Here is what led up to that moonlight flit.

The first night we were at the camp, Hamilton pointed out a box with meal and asked if I could make porridge. I remembered my son had told me about the oatmeal and water, so I told him "no, I can't make porridge". After he had gone to bed, I had a look through the so-called "supplies", and found a box with 2 packets of bacon and 2 dozen eggs. I had a good idea who they were for, and it wasn't the boys. I spent a very restless night. I was missing my home comforts and during the night it got incredibly cold, so I didn't sleep much. I got up very early, about 5.30am, and started the fire. Janet and I made a make-shift table and used sleepers as seats. We put cardboard on the ground beside the table, as my son said they had to kneel in the wet ground to eat.

I got out the frying pans and started cooking the bacon and eggs for the boys. We toasted bread on the metal grill over the fire. I had a box of cereal of my own and put it out for use. We collected all the plates, knives, forks and spoons which were scattered in the mud, washed them and set places for the boys.

Hamilton came down after the boys were seated and he went mad because I had used his bacon and eggs from his private box. I apologised and said I thought it was camp food, but I knew it was his private stash, along with biscuits, sweets and tins of food, which he used for himself, feeding the boys Smash with curry powder, and cooking in the same pot without washing it. The pots were all filthy. He made the boys drink water from the loch, but he had juice and two bottles of Martini in his box. That day I demanded he go to a shop and get fruit, vegetables, eggs, cereal, mince, pork chops, bacon and sausages, or I was leaving. He eventually agreed. It cost him £80+, which broke his heart. I gave him another list five days later, which he tried to argue about, but I insisted he got it so I could feed the boys properly. I had to demand that proper food be supplied. I had to steal plasters and cream from the first-aid kit, as he wouldn't hand them over. I stole the kids socks from his tent and had a stand-up argument with him about his behaviour. When he wouldn't let the boys have their socks, the kids and me started putting pebbles in HIS socks and throwing them into the loch. It helped reduce the boredom as well.

I remember in one instance he more or less demanded that the adults were fed first and he be handed his meal first. I turned and told him that I was here to provide meals for the boys and not for adults, who could feed themselves. And that I would feed the boys first, and adults last, as my main concern was the boys. He didn't like my answer… he said he disagreed, at which point I told him "I am not here to boost your ego or run after you. I'm here to provide a meal 3 times a day for the boys. Take it or leave it".

One day the kids were made to go and collect firewood. And I don't mean little sticks. It was massive logs and branches which it took two or 3 boys to carry. Hamilton never did any work himself. The kids were doing this from 8am, and at 10.30 they were tired and thirsty, but he kept at them. By 11am I thought 'enough is enough'. The boys had been asking for a drink but he wouldn't let them, so I said to Janet, let's make up some squash and as the boys come down, sit them down for a biscuit and a drink. So we did this. The boys were scared at what Hamilton might do and I assured them I would deal with it. After a while, no boys were going back as they were having a drink, so he started blowing his whistle. Blowing and blowing – so I got a whistle and kept blowing back. He came thundering down the hill. "Who's blowing a whistle?" he shouted. "I am" I said, "it was to draw your attention to the fact that I am giving the boys a drink". "On whose orders? I didn't give permission for them to have a drink". "Sorry, I must have misunderstood. I thought this was to be a holiday camp, not a prison camp". At which point he turned to the boys and said "hurry up and get back up for more wood", which was unnecessary, as there were two huge piles of it. Then he said, "can I have a glass of squash please Mrs H" and I said, "Certainly Mr H – there's the water and the squash, do it yourself".

He then put the boys back to work until I again blew the whistle at 12 o'clock for lunch. He came storming down. "Mrs H, as I'm the leader, I'm the only one allowed to blow a whistle" and he took the whistle I had from me. "It's not time for lunch" he said. I told him it was and it was going to be served in 5 minutes. I felt so sorry for the boys. They were tired and fed up. This was not an exciting holiday for them. Hamilton wanted them to bring more wood after lunch and I told him there was enough for four to 5 days already. So the children just sat about. They were tired, covered in scratches and miserable. I asked for antiseptic cream and plasters for some. He said, "you're too soft". I told him a couple of the boys had nasty cuts. He said, "let them toughen up". So I waited until he went for a walk with Sam Davie and went into his tent and took the things I needed for the boys' cuts. Sam Davie had a hold over Hamilton. I don't know what was going on there. Hamilton was paying for his drink and ciggies because Davie had no money. He tried to tap me for money but I told him to eff off.

At the camp I had started keeping notes of all the things that were wrong and his wrong-doings. He spotted me writing in it one day and asked me what I was writing. I told him I was making up menus and a list of food I would need, but I knew he didn't believe me and I was proved right. I kept my book with me all the time. When I returned from the store in Alexandria, one of the boys told me Mr Hamilton had been in my tent for a while and was looking through all our stuff. I think he was looking for my book and the camera spools, but I had taken them with me as I didn't trust him or Sam Davie by then.

I had bought two packets of crisps each for the boys, plus sweets and biscuits. I had to go through each item on the till receipt with him and he blew his top, because of the crisps, etc. He told me I had no right to buy that, so I told him to take it out of my son's pocket-money which he had taken from him, but never returned. He stormed off. He took all the kids' money. They never saw it again. He kept it.

One day Hamilton was playing a game where there were two teams. Janet, Vikki and I were asked to join in to make up numbers. One team had to hide and the other team find them. If you were spotted, you were grabbed and taken back to base. If you caught someone you had to hold them, but they could try to escape. I was caught by Hamilton and on the way back I started to struggle. As we got nearer to base he was being a pest and at the edge of a bank, I body checked him and he went flying. He didn't fall far, but what upset him most was the kids laughing. So that was the end of the game.

When we sat around the camp fire at night Hamilton would tell us about a club he went to. I asked him what kind of club and he said the freemasons club. Janet asked if that was a disco type place, but I knew what he meant.

Hamilton did not have any toilet facilities at the camp and it was not until two weeks later that a toilet tent was erected. But he rarely let the boys use it. He used to follow them to the woods when they went to the toilet. I asked him why and he said just to make sure they weren't messing about. I said I objected to that behaviour and that I did not think he should be doing it. There was one particular boy, a little blonde haired lad – Hamilton followed him everywhere. I dread to think what might have happened to that boy if I hadn't been at the camp.

I also stopped Hamilton from drawing one bucket of water and making the boys use it to clean their teeth. They would have to take one beaker with a little water, rinse their mouths, spit it back into the bucket, then the next boy and the next. So after two or 3 had done that, the remaining boys were rinsing their mouths with spit from the previous boys. I got the bucket and threw the contents out. I got water which had been boiled and cooled and gave the boys a cup each. He was fuming mad; said I was too soft. I told him it was a disgusting thing to do and I wasn't having it. At that he walked away from me.

Hamilton terrorised the kids in lots of ways – mentally more than physically. He made two little boys his target and I stood up to him on that. He had what he called a "punishment tent". And he kept it away on its own. On the second night I was there, I heard a boy crying and went into the tent. It was a very dark night and I had my lantern. I asked the boys what was wrong. One of them had refused to rub sun-tan oil on Hamilton, so he put the boy and his brother in this tent as a punishment, with no lights and away from the camp. They were very scared, so I chatted with them and told them I would leave my lantern with them. The youngest boy asked for a cuddle, which I gave him, and I told him I would sort this out. I was almost back at my own tent when I heard Hamilton shouting. It came from the tent I'd just left, so I ran up and asked what was wrong. He said they are not allowed this lantern. I pointed out to him it was my lantern and I gave it to the boys and it was going to stay there as he had no right to leave boys frightened in the dark. He strutted away and never looked at me. The boys were again very upset, so I stayed with them until they fell asleep. In the morning I told Hamilton that I found his attitude a disgrace and as I pulled the punishment tent down, he had no option but to let the boys back in the main tent. When Hamilton threatened to burn my tent down, I knew it was time to leave… After escaping the island in the middle of the night, we camped in my car until daylight then went straight to Alexandria Police Station to make a formal complaint against Hamilton. I felt awful leaving those boys behind and I imagined the police would go straight out to the island to rescue them. They did not. (see Notes 3 for police details of these camps).

For the next year I tried my utmost to get Hamilton stopped from having access to boys. This culminated in me breaking the law in May of 1989 when I threw a bucket of homemade swill – made of suntan lotion, fish fertiliser, flour and whatever else I could find – over him outside Linlithgow Academy. I wanted to get Hamilton into court. Despite the presence of police and journalist witnesses, I was not charged with breach of the peace, nor did Hamilton press charges against me. I wonder if I would get away with this criminal act in the presence of the police if I decided to use such tactics against anyone else? I somehow doubt it.

Thus, because of my dealings with Thomas Hamilton, I was called as a witness at the Dunblane Inquiry. It is only recently that I have discovered the lengths Lord Cullen and the Crown Office went to to destroy my character at that Inquiry. The day before I gave evidence, PC Derek Anderson of Lothian and Borders Police, was cross-examined by Mr Taylor, representing Central Scotland Police. He was asked, "You indicated that Mrs Hagger was a person who was known to you and also known to other officers in the Force. Can you indicate how it came about that you were aware of the involvement of her and other officers?" Anderson replied, "I really can't recall whether I am remembering this after the event or whether being aware of it at the time but thinking back there was something about an investigation with Mrs Hagger that involved Mr Hamilton. I am sorry, I can't be any more………."

Not satisfied by this response, Mr Taylor continued with, "Before that however I got the impression from the evidence which you gave in-chief that there was a certain knowledge of Mrs Hagger amongst your colleagues?" – Yes. "Can you tell us a little bit about the involvement which the police have had with Mrs Hagger prior to this incident which we are looking at today?" – In relation to this incident?

Mr Taylor, "No, prior to?" – Prior to? There was domestic matters. She stayed with, at one point….do you want the name?

LORD CULLEN: Mr Taylor, are we going into a string of events?

Mr Taylor: I don't wish to go into detail of any one occurrence. I would like the witness to tell me if he can generally comment.

LORD CULLEN: All right.

Anderson continues with, "Okay. She stayed with a male on and off who would be occasionally put out of the house or would cause bother round about the place, trying to get back with her. I can remember that. Well, at least I had a couple of incidents like that. There seemed to be a continual……. I have dealt with several calls where she along with Janet Reilly would complain about another family who stayed above Janet Reilly when Mrs Hagger used to visit Janet Reilly and also vice versa.

Mr Taylor, "When you say vice versa, does that mean complaints from the other family about Mrs Hagger and Mrs Reilly?" – Yes, they would complain about Mrs Reilly and Mrs Hagger causing an annoyance through drink, etc.

Mr Taylor, "Was that drink on the part of Mrs Hagger or drink on the part of the others?" – Both Mrs Hagger and Mrs Reilly was drink related.

Mr Taylor, "Are Mrs Reilly and Mrs Hagger reasonably well known to yourself and your colleagues?" – Yes.

Well, there you go then. I was damned before I even made it into the witness box. As a sufferer of multiple sclerosis, I did not drink alcohol and was therefore never drunk. Alcohol simply doesn't agree with me. As a result of my MS however, I have a hearing and a speech problem, which results in my words often sounding slurred. At the time of my giving evidence at the Dunblane Inquiry, I didn't know about this character assassination the day before.

The man referred to by PC Anderson was Sam Davie. Interestingly, although Mr Davie attended at the summer camp with myself and Janet Reilly, he wasn't called as a witness at the Dunblane Inquiry. Why was Sam Davie spared interrogation?

On the sixth day of the Inquiry, I gave evidence. My evidence runs to 40 pages of A4, so I will only give brief examples here. My son Andrew was thrown off a boat by Hamilton, despite an absolute terror of water, and with no life jacket on. On arrival at the camp, Hamilton made him take all his clothes off, took all his clothes from him and made him put shorts on. Hamilton also took all his money. I testified to seeing Hamilton thumping children, one boy having been punched between his shoulder blades because his fingernails were dirty. He slapped another boy over the face just for speaking.

Sam Davie, Steven Williams, Thomas Hamilton and friends of theirs who were visiting the island one night, had a drunken barbeque party. Sam Davie couldn't find his sleeping bag and tried to take Janet's. He threatened Janet that he would put an axe in her head. In different ways, Janet and I were threatened by both Hamilton and Davie.

During my evidence about what happened a few weeks after the camp, I explained that Hamilton came to my house and told me he didn't like people talking to the police about him. He said he had friends that didn't like people doing that. When I started to say that I thought his friends were his guns, Lord Cullen intervened to say that they couldn't understand what I was saying. Mr Bonomy, the Advocate Depute, said "I think that you do have an illness that makes it difficult for you to communicate, is that right?" I replied, yes, my hearing. Bonomy then said, "And also to speak very clearly?" – Yes.

My communication problem was now clearly explained, but this still didn't stop Mr Bonomy from not facing me so that I wasn't able to lip-read, nor stop him becoming very impatient with me. Still, I continued to answer all the questions as best I could. I explained that my son told Inspector Keenan about having to rub suntan lotion all over Hamilton's body. This had totally shocked and disgusted me. I described how Hamilton came to my house another time and threatened me with a gun. In the end Lord Cullen decided he didn't believe that, just because I didn't report it to the police. Yet when another witness, a friend of Thomas Hamilton's called James Gillespie gave evidence that Hamilton pointed a gun at him – an incident he didn't report to the police – Lord Cullen seems to have believed that.

The cross-examination then became more gruelling. Mr Hardie QC, Dean of Faculty, representing both the Scottish Police Federation and Lothian and Borders Police, asked me "Are you aware that your daughter said that she didn't remember ever seeing the incident in relation to the van but depended upon what you had told her?" – No.

"Well, did you tell your daughter about Mr Hamilton coming to the house in a van on the occasion you have spoken about?" – No.

So are you saying that at no time between 1989 and the present day did you tell your daughter that Mr Hamilton had come in a van and had had a gun?" – My daughter was there.

"Well, listen to the question and remember at the beginning you took a ……..?" – She would have heard me saying……

"Could you let me finish please; can you remember that you took an oath to tell the truth today; did you between 1989 and today at any stage tell your daughter about Mr Hamilton coming to the house in a van?" – My daughter was there when he came in the van, I didn't have to tell her.

Do you understand the question, Mrs Hagger? – No.

"Can I repeat it and could you answer it Yes or No please; did you at any stage between 1989 and today tell your daughter that Mr Hamilton had a gun when he was in the van?" – No.

Despite persistently answering "No", he asked me again, "Would you answer this question Yes or No please; did you at any stage between 1989 and today tell your daughter that Mr Hamilton had a gun when he was in the van?" – No.

I have now made a formal complaint to the Crown Office about this matter and the defamatory remarks made against me. I have also made a complaint to the Crown Office about Central Scotland Police taking a Witness Statement from my 15-year-old daughter Vikki – in April 1996 – when it was obvious she was high on drugs. The police ordered me out of my own living-room even though I was Vikki's mother and guardian. I objected to them taking a statement from her when she was in no fit state. This resulted in Vikki running away from home when she knew she was going to be called as a witness at the Inquiry. She couldn't remember what she had told the police in her statement. Vikki paid a heavy price for my getting involved in Thomas Hamilton's summer camp in 1988. What remains a mystery to me though is why Andrew and all the other boys from that summer camp – most of them in their late teens at the time of the Inquiry – weren't called to give evidence. Doreen's final words on the matter are, "I also can't bear to think about what the kids at all Hamilton's other camps must have suffered, when there was no-one there to defend them, or simply care for them."

And sure enough, Hamilton's abuse of boys continued. At the 1991 Summer Camp at Millarochy Bay, Loch Lomond, between 14th and 28th July, there were several incidents regarding the use of photographs, video cameras and assaults on boys. These were reported to the police. Hamilton slapped a boy in the face and on the back of the legs. He took the children to an unknown island on Loch Lomond and then insisted that the children play-act in a video film which he would direct and which had the theme of "Lord of the Flies". All the children were issued with small black swimming trunks and were made to wear them throughout the film and the weather was not good. Hamilton wouldn't let the boys put their clothes on. One child in particular was forced to lie in the cold water whilst he was being filmed. When the boys complained, Hamilton cursed and swore at them. Parents complained to Central Scotland Police and the Child Protection Unit investigated. Hamilton was reported to the Procurator Fiscal at Stirling for consideration of 10 charges, ranging from assault, contravention of the Children and Young Persons (Scotland) Act 1937 and ultimately obstructing the Police. It was also noted by the Police that the supervision levels were inadequate and this was reported. Hamilton had advertised that there would be between 4 to 6 adult leaders supervising 15 to 20 children. The Procurator Fiscal at Stirling decided to take no proceedings.

"Janet, Sam and myself all shared the view that he hated kids, especially little girls" (Doreen Hagger, Daily Record 15 March 1996)

"I formed the view that his interest in health and fitness and outdoor pursuits was ideologically tinged with authoritarianism redolent of national socialist propaganda" ie. Nazism (Iain Macfarlane, The Herald 16 March 1996)

George Robertson MP also described Hamilton's clubs as "looking like the Hitler youth". He and another parent – Stewart Hart – had visited the club and been dismayed to see "a large number of small boys in shorts stripped to the waist being bossed around by two or three middle-aged men, swaggering around in a very military-type way".

CHAPTER 4 :

PAEDOPHILIA AND HOMOSEXUAL
ACTS IN PUBLIC PLACES

In the book and BBC TV series, "The Hunt for Britain's Paedophiles", the question is posed, "what makes a photo or a film of a child indecent?" The authors, Bob Long and DCI Bob McLachlan respond, "pretty obvious you might think, but this is not so as the law currently stands". There are four pieces of legislation in place to prevent children being sexually exploited through photography, but none of these Acts of Parliament provides a legal definition of what is or is not 'indecent', leaving the decision to.... the jury. It was therefore relatively simple for Lord Cullen to conclude – from what was made available to him – that Thomas Hamilton's photographs and videos did not constitute indecency, or what we commonly refer to as 'child pornography'. Yet Hamilton regularly destroyed the images he created. Other photographs that children said had been taken have never been retrieved.

In the course of investigations after the events at Dunblane Primary School on 13 March 1996, the police found 445 photographic slides, 548 photographs and 4,260 photographic negatives at Hamilton's home at 7 Kent Road, Stirling. Thirty seven video tapes were recovered which appeared to have been made by Hamilton on a camcorder and depicted scenes recorded at his various boys clubs. Sixty three pairs of swimming trunks were recovered from his house. A colour break down revealed: black - 54 pairs; blue - 7 pairs; red - 2 pairs.

During the 1991 investigation of Hamilton's Summer Camp, one child, SR, received special treatment by Hamilton. He was the only child to be issued with small ill-fitted red coloured swimming trunks for wearing during "private" photographic sessions. None of the photographs were recovered. In 1988, the boy in red swimming trunks was L, a young blonde lad. Hamilton followed him everywhere.

In evidence at the Inquiry, forensic scientist Michael Baxter stated that 11 pairs of swimming trunks found in a Littlewoods bag were generally stained with a white substance. Part of this white substance was analysed and found to be a paint-like substance. All sixty three pairs of swimming trunks were further examined and nothing further of significance was found. The Lord Advocate then asked Mr Baxter to explain to Lord Cullen and those present what sort of substances he was looking for. Mr Baxter replied, "any obvious bloodstains or signs of the presence of semen; all presumptive tests for the presence of semen gave negative results." So that's all right then? **No it is not all right**.

For some reason Thomas Hamilton wanted there to be the *appearance* of semen on certain of the swimming trunks, as if the boys had been excited and ejaculated. It doesn't take much imagination to think of the intimate type of photographs Hamilton was able to take of boys hanging upside down in skimpy swimming trunks over a bar in a gymnasium or elsewhere. In June 1993 a report was forwarded to the procurator fiscal at Stirling after complaints were received from parents whose children had attended evening classes with Hamilton at High Schools in Dunblane and Stirling. On one occasion a parent found Hamilton locked inside the gym at Stirling High School with just one boy, dressed only in "very scant trunks", who was being made to do press-ups while Hamilton took photographs. On another occasion a child was made to sit "crouched on his knees, between the legs of another boy. He had to hold this boy's neck whilst the boy carried out sit-up type exercises. This caused (the boy) to go across the body of the other child, almost in a lying position, and Mr Hamilton photographed this". The procurator fiscal refused a request by Detective Constable Taylor for a warrant to search Hamilton's house.

The fact that a variety of photographs were taken is beyond dispute. Many of these photographs and negatives were burnt in his back garden, presumably when he was tipped off about a raid. On another occasion, Alexander Robb tried to retrieve photographs and negatives of his partner's son. A few days later a small selection of photographs arrived at the address of Mr Robb's partner. The pictures had been destroyed but left enough to identify them as being pictures of G. From G's report of the photography sessions, these were not all the photos that had been taken. Included with the photographs was a receipt attached for bleach. Mr Robb assumed this was used to sabotage the photos. Mr Robb was later required to attend Dunblane Police Office where he was told to leave things in the hands of the Police. The police, as we know, did nothing.

Perhaps Lord Cullen knows nothing of this as he didn't read any of the preparatory material for the Inquiry. Can we therefore trust Lord Cullen's opinion that Hamilton did not take indecent images of children? We most certainly cannot. Furthermore, the question of whether Hamilton was a 'supplier' was never addressed by Lord Cullen, yet witnesses gave evidence to the fact that Hamilton had regular male visitors, many of them smartly dressed men, arriving in large expensive cars. Some stayed only a few minutes.

Just because Thomas Hamilton is dead doesn't mean these other men won't still be involved in the business of making, distributing and using indecent images of children. The hunt for Britain's paedophiles must take another look at the background to the Dunblane massacre. Britain's children are still not safe whilst such men remain at large.

By making contact with other paedophiles, the least that would happen, even for those who could not bring themselves to feel fully comfortable with what they did, was that they would no longer feel alone with their guilty secret. If they understood that what they had was a problem, at least other people had it too… because of technological infancy, pre-Internet days held a demand for pornography that outstripped the supply available (Long & McLachlan).

Obviously, not all the squad's officers were crooked, but those who were operated a 'licensing system' to allow the pornography dealers to continue trading (Long & McLachlan referring to the Metropolitan Police). Did a similar system operate in Central Scotland?

More than anything, this contact with other paedophiles reinforced their moral position. Most paedophiles are very keen to share their collection and do their bit for their community.

At the Inquiry, a portrait emerged of Thomas Hamilton as a sadistic paedophile who took pleasure in the suffering and discomfort of young boys. Photographs of the boys, which could have been innocuous, could have served the same purpose as pornography. Dr John Baird said, "I wonder how a man such as Hamilton who, over 20 years, had attracted such attention as being unfit for the Scout movement and a persistent litigant, could have been a suitable person for holding firearms and allowed to retain them". When preparing his first report into the behaviour and personality of Thomas Hamilton for the Inquiry, Dr Baird held the view that neither psychological nor psychiatric examination would have alerted anyone to Hamilton. But later evidence presented to him indicated items of behaviour in relation to firearms and Hamilton's paedophilia that, had they been taken seriously and set alongside the disquiet of parents, could have indicated deep-rooted problems. But he added: "It was, if anything, his tireless campaigning – characteristic of paedophilia – that prevented decisive action being taken against him." (see Notes 4).

In Scotland, during Hamilton's heyday, there was no national registration of people working with youngsters over the age of 8 and no requirement for any formal qualifications or references. This was not the case in England and Wales. Hamilton was able to drift from area to area unhindered running clubs and camps for boys aged eight to 14.

In 1994, police raided Hamilton's home after a tip-off that **he was dealing in paedophile photographs**, but no charges were brought. Just eight months after Thomas Hamilton carried out the atrocity at Dunblane Primary School, a clampdown on paedophile activity in Stirling was initiated by Central Scotland Police. Note, that although the boy who these men were having sex with was only 13 years of age, these men are referred to as "gay", not as paedophiles. Further note, that the men are referred to as being the boys' "clients", not that he is the victim of their abuse.

GAYS FACE COURT OVER BOY; SPY CAMERA USED
(The Herald 20 Nov 1996)

Up To A Dozen Gay Men have been interviewed by police in Stirling who are investigating allegations that they shared a teenage male prostitute. Most of them are expected to appear in court in three weeks' time, charged with indecency towards the 13-year-old.

Two homosexuals have committed suicide within the last four weeks after being confronted by police, who had installed a spy camera at public toilets allegedly used by homosexuals as a meeting place in Beechwood Park, Stirling, near Stirling High School.

One of the men accused of indecency towards the boy was a Stirling Council Youth & Community Worker, Mr Cameron Daisley, 48, who hanged himself at the weekend following the police undercover operation at the toilets, which were allegedly being used by the boy and his "clients". A month ago, Mr Michael Cummings, 60, allegedly caught committing a homosexual act in the same toilets with another man, jumped to his death from the Forth Road bridge.

The secret camera installed at the toilets revealed that they were a regular haunt for homosexual men. Four men appeared in court last week and pled guilty to committing homosexual acts other than in private. A fifth asked for his case to be continued without plea.

The council is insistent its rigorous vetting procedures introduced following Dunblane will not be affected by the incident. A spokesman for Central Scotland said they could not comment on the death of Mr Daisley or matters surrounding it. A report on the incident will go to the procurator fiscal. However, the force's action came under fire last night from homosexual rights groups for installing the camera in the toilets. Mr Ian Dunn of homosexual pressure group, Outright Scotland, said the actions of Central Scotland police fell below the professional standard he expected. Mr Dunn condemned the police actions and claimed that it had led to the suicides of both Mr Daisley and Mr Cummings.

"If reports that a young man was prostituting himself in the toilet are correct, Outright Scotland wants to know how and why this was allowed to go on," said Mr Dunn. Despite a number of attempts for an official statement on Mr Dunn's comments, Central Scotland police said no-one was available for comment. But Stirling Council's convener of community services, Councillor Gillie Thomson retorted: "The gay lobby is doing itself no favours by making this sort of attack. If there was a paedophile ring operating around these toilets, the police have to gather evidence".

A Dunblane parent, who did not want to be named, said: "The awful lesson of Thomas Hamilton is that paedophiles will go to any lengths to get close to children. The school authorities say they knew this man was a homosexual. Never mind equal opportunities: knowing that, they should have known better than to give him an office in a school with lots of young boys to ogle at."

On 17 September 1986, the Stirling Observer reported that Cameron Daisley was setting up a boys' club in St Modan's High School for boys in the St Ninians area of Stirling. A cutting of this article was supplied to·me by Stirling Council following a Freedom of Information request relating to Thomas Hamilton. Hamilton had circled the article and sent it to the former Central Regional Council (now Stirling Council). On it he wrote, "after our termination at St Modans by Mr Daisley due to no accommodation being available". Signed: Thomas W Hamilton. So, one paedophile was vying with another for access to boys…

Below, from Scotland on Sunday (24 Nov 1996)

Daisley had been one of around **60 men from throughout Scotland's central belt** caught in a major police operation centred on a dingy toilet in Stirling. Astonishing details of a covert exercise involving secret cameras and surveillance teams began to surface. And far from being an isolated case, Daisley was the second man ensnared in the police web to have taken his life. Central Police said the undercover investigation was set up to substantiate claims that adult men were using the toilets to pick up the teenage boy for sex. One thing is certain: it is a case that will not go away quietly. Six men have already appeared in court and been fined between 250 and 400 pounds each for committing homosexual acts. At least three others are due in court next month in connection with more serious allegations about the teenage boy. SoS understands a prominent businessman from East Lothian is among those expected to face charges.

The surveillance operation, using a hidden video camera, began in early September and continued for six weeks. A police team armed with more cameras also kept watch from a nearby building. Suspects' cars were tailed and, as evidence was gathered, the arrests began.

And below is media coverage surrounding another scandal involving homosexual sex in a public place in Central Scotland.

SEX SHAME DOC CAUGHT BY COP VIDEO:
UNI BOSSES ACCUSED OF COVER-UP
(Sunday Mail 16 Sept 2001)

A University GP jailed for molesting male students was secretly filmed during a police probe into an earlier campus sex scandal. Bosses yesterday were accused of a cover-up. For Allan Buchan was allowed to keep his job despite being caught on camera during the 1994 gay sex inquiry. Buchan, of Dunblane, Perthshire, was jailed for two-and-a-half years on Wednesday for a campaign of sexual assaults on young male patients dating back six years.

He assaulted them by taking down their trousers and fondling them after they consulted him for problems as varied as flu and dermatitis. The scandal came to light in 1998 when a German student complained to Buchan's partners at the NHS-run Airthrey Park medical centre on the campus. **But the**

Sunday Mail can reveal that Stirling University bosses were warned that he and other men were involved in a gay sex ring.

He was identified after the university's security team called in police to probe complaints that homosexuals were using toilets in the MacRobert Centre for gay sex. **Five men working at the university, including Buchan and a senior member of the university staff, were reported to the management.**

An insider said: "The university were terrified this would come out at his trial. It suggests they had evidence he was a possible risk to young people but did nothing about it". Central Scotland Police confirmed the inquiry took place.

This story was not followed up by any other newspaper. Isn't that strange? Who were the other four men caught on camera in this gay sex scandal? I made a Freedom of Information request to Central Scotland Police asking for a copy of the incident report. They claimed they had no record of this and told me not to believe everything I read in the press. So I made a Freedom of Information request to Stirling University to ask for copies of all documentation relating to their investigations into this matter, but they refused, claiming it wasn't in the public interest to release such material. Both applications have been referred by me to the Scottish Information Commissioner. Whilst homosexuality is not illegal, homosexual sex in public places is, especially at an educational institution housing thousands of young males.

DOCTOR MAY FACE JAIL OVER SEX ASSAULTS
(PA News, 15 August 2001)

A doctor was tonight facing the prospect of a jail sentence after he was convicted of molesting three male patients. Dr Allan Buchan, 40, from Dunblane, was found guilty of carrying out five sex assaults on the patients, all students, while working as a GP at Stirling University.

Buchan had been charged with committing eight sexual assaults on six men at the Airthrey Park Medical Centre and the Occupational Health Unit in the grounds of Stirling University between January 1994 and September 1999. He was convicted of five of the charges, found not guilty of one, with the two other charges found not proven.

All three students, who cannot be named for legal reasons, were in their late teens or early twenties when they were molested by Buchan during appointments with the GP at Airthrey Park Medical Centre. During the nine-day trial, one of the victims told how he had gone to see the doctor after injuring his ankle playing sport in March, 1998. The man, an exchange student at Stirling who is now studying in Germany, said after examining the joint, Buchan began massaging the muscles at the top of his legs and then touching his genitals. He told the court he was left "surprised and stunned" by what happened.

Another student told how he was molested by Buchan on two separate occasions. He first went to the surgery in November 1998, two days after he had been involved in a car crash, suffering from whiplash injuries and a sore knee. He also had a chest infection. The student said Buchan pulled his trousers down, stood near him in "a sexual way" then pulled down his underpants. The doctor then began lightly brushing his genitals.

In September the following year, the student went back to the surgery for treatment for a bowel complaint. He was given an appointment with Buchan and although he insisted he only wanted a chat, the doctor began examining him again. While examining his abdomen, the doctor undid his belt and lowered his trousers before starting to touch his genitals. The man was so concerned by what had happened he reported Buchan to the centre. He said: "I felt that I had to do something about it because I didn't think Dr Buchan should be in a position where he could do that to his patients."

Buchan was also found guilty of assaulting another student during two appointments. The victim told the trial that in March 1995, he went to the surgery complaining of flu, but during his examination the doctor began stroking and massaging his penis. Then in December the same year, the man went back to Airthrey Park complaining of dermatitis on his foot and Buchan touched his penis and testicles while examining him.

A spokeswoman for Stirling University said: "The university treats the welfare of its students as a matter of the highest priority. It is deeply concerned at the evidence of abuse that emerged during Dr Buchan's trial. It has fully cooperated with the appropriate authorities during their investigations of the allegations and will offer counselling support to any of its students or former students who were victims of Dr Buchan".

UNIVERSITY GP FACES JAIL AFTER MOLESTING PATIENTS
(Daily Express 16 Aug 2001)

Dr Allan Buchan, 40, faces up to three years in prison for sexually assaulting Stirling University students at his surgery during check-ups for conditions including flu, dermatitis and whiplash injuries. Stirling Sheriff Court heard Buchan turned into a "gay predator" because of his "desire to satisfy his sexual urges".

The GP, who has more than 14 years experience and was at one time the club doctor for Third Division club East Stirlingshire FC, undressed the patients and forced them to take down their underwear before fondling their private parts. Buchan, from Dunblane, was convicted of five charges dating back to 1995 following an eight day trial. On two others he was found not proven and not guilty on an eighth. The married GP had already been banned from practising without a chaperone by the General Medical Council when the allegations first came to light. He now faces being struck off the medical register.

Politicians and student groups said they were "shocked and horrified" by the catalogue of abuse. In 1997, the student newspaper BRIG met with university officials and threatened to print an expose story unless action was taken. Former students believe "dozens more" may have been assaulted and one added: "There were so many people talking about it who were just embarrassed to tell officials."

Buchan claimed he had uncovered a plot to kill his wife and said he believed a nurse at the surgery had worked with Thomas Hamilton to plan the Dunblane massacre *(writer's note: I wrote to Allan Buchan to ask for further details about this, but he never responded to any of my letters).*

Depute fiscal Amanda McGowan said: "Dr Buchan used his position as a doctor to abuse the opportunity his job gave him to get access to the bodies of young men and satisfy his own sexual urges. Doctors are not above the law. It is a long way for him to fall but doctors have to be held up to account for their actions."

PERV Y DOC WAS A 'GAY PREDATOR'
(Daily Star 16 August 2001)

A twisted GP was yesterday convicted of sexually molesting three male students during routine medical examinations. Dr Allan Buchan, 40, faces up to three years in prison after assaulting the men at his surgery during check-ups for conditions like 'flu, dermatitis and whiplash. Stirling Sheriff Court heard the doctor turned into a 'gay predator' who preyed on the students to satisfy his sexual urges.

After the court case yesterday, politicians and student groups said they were 'shocked and horrified' by the catalogue of abuse. Former students said they believed 'dozens more' may have been subjected to assaults and have been afraid to come forward. One said: "There were so many people talking about it but many were just too embarrassed. There will be dozens more in the closet."

Dr Buchan, also a registered children's GP, was convicted of five different offences against the men at Airthrey Park Medical Centre, in Stirling University. The court heard the abuse began in 1995 during an examination on a student who complained of minor 'flu symptoms. Depute fiscal Amanda McGowan siad Dr Buchan molested the students as part of a 'seduction scene' to fulfil his sexual needs.

German student teacher Markus Pissarek has been left with a deep mistrust of the medical profession after being abused by disgraced GP Dr Allan Buchan. The keen sportsman was just 25 when he visited Airthrey Park Medical Centre after spraining his ankle. Now 28, Markus, said: "This has been a very bad experience for me. He has not harmed physically but I feel badly misused and let down. I was brought up believing I could put my trust in a doctor but that perception has now gone. I know all doctors are not like that but it makes me wonder every time I go into the surgery now".

Allan Buchan has never shown any interest in appealing against his conviction. Since his release from prison, Linda and Allan have separated. Buchan was involved in a gay sex scandal at Stirling University that was busted in 1994. His access to easy (gay) sex was therefore removed. His only other options were the public toilets in Stirling, but he was a married man with children. The facility for gay sex during his working day clearly fulfilled a certain need. When it was withdrawn, his assaults on young male patients began... the very next year...in 1995.

It is hard to avoid the conclusion that Central Scotland was a magnet for paedophiles and homosexual predators. Why were they drawn to the area? Before Hamilton committed the atrocity at Dunblane, most of us were oblivious to this dark underbelly of life involving clandestine paedophilia and homosexual sex in public places. Just how long had it been going on?

CHAPTER 5 -

THE COVER-UP

A lot of people ask how a conspiracy on the scale I allege could have been covered up, when so many people had to have been involved. Let me explain. Immediately after the massacre happened, there was inevitably a lot of media coverage and a lot of probing questions were asked. Then a curb was put on media reporting by the Crown Office and Lord Cullen. It was said this would prejudice the evidence of witnesses called to the Dunblane Inquiry. In an article in the Scotsman (5 April 1996) Ian Bell explained: "Scotland's most senior law officer threatened editors with proceedings for contempt if they continued to investigate the circumstances of the Dunblane massacre. As though to sharpen the point, the Crown Office said the remarks of Lord Mackay of Drumadoon, the Lord Advocate, were themselves "not for publication or broadcast". The curb on reporting is not to be reported". So all went quiet for a few months until the Inquiry began.

At the Inquiry, there was the Crown representing the Crown: that is the Lord Advocate, The Lord Mackay of Drumadoon; Advocate Depute Mr Ian Bonomy and Advocate Mr Lake.

Mr Campbell and Ms Dunlop represented the families of the deceased children, the families of the injured children, the children absent from class, Mrs Harrild and Mrs Blake.

Mr Gibb represented Mrs Mayor (deceased) and the Educational Institute of Scotland.

Mr Stephen represented the Association of Head Teachers in Scotland and Mr Ronald Taylor.

Mr Jones represented Stirling Council and "others".

Mr Taylor represented Central Scotland Police.

The Dean of Faculty and Mr Kavanagh represented individual officers of the Scottish Police Federation and Lothian and Borders Police.

Mr McEachran represented the Scottish Target Shooting Federation and Mr Scoggins the British Shooting Sports Council.

Who represented the public? Well, the Crown of course. Who organised the cover-up of the truth? The Crown.

Central Scotland Police carried out the investigation for the Inquiry and thus, even if the Crown Office was not involved in the cover-up, Central Scotland Police was given carte blanche to withhold any witness statements they didn't wish to be seen, for whatever reason.

This material was passed to the Crown who then summarised it (see Notes 5) and passed it on to the above named representatives, who in turn passed it on to their clients (or at least they passed on *some of it)*. These documents were not released to the press, nor did Lord Cullen read any of this preparatory material. There were a total of 1,655 witness statements taken, from a total of 1,240 witnesses. Only 171 witnesses gave evidence at the Inquiry, thus the evidence of 1,069 witnesses was never heard.

Lord Cullen wrote his report on the basis of the oral testimony of just 171 witnesses. The fact that some of these witnesses, police witnesses included, lied on oath, was therefore not known to him (or was it?) All the evidence prepared for the Inquiry was then locked away for an astonishing 100 years, until the Crown Office released *some* of the documents in October 2005. It was almost impossible to ascertain WHAT had been released, and what withheld. It was only through making a total of 60 requests for information to Central Scotland Police under the Freedom of Information (Scotland) Act 2002, that I started to discover just how much material had still been held back by the Crown. So, on 19 December 2005, I made a Freedom of Information request to the First Minister (who, I discovered, is not exempt from the FOISA). I asked for details of the number of statements that are available at the National Archives of Scotland and the number that have been held back. Mr McConnell passed my request on to the Crown Office. Over two months later, on 22 February 2006, the Crown Office replied as follows: "I can confirm that your request is receiving attention and we will respond to you further as soon as possible". Why is it such a difficult question to answer?

So how did they cover-up the truth on the day? Remember that in the gym nearly all the children were dead or critically injured. Their teacher was dead. One child who did not sustain any injury obviously told her parents something of what she saw in the gym, and this was then relayed by her parents to their solicitor. I repeat, they state that they saw two bullet holes in the south wall of the gym, about 2 inches apart and just 6 inches from the ground. Their statement continues, "There were no other bullet holes in that wall and I noticed that there were quite a few bullet holes in the other walls which would confirm my (words are blanked out here.............) that he fired into the walls at the bottom end of the gym where Hamilton had entered the gym". So, WHO fired into the walls at the bottom end of the gym when Hamilton (re-entered) the gym through the fire exit door at the south end?

The injured teachers and some of the less critically injured children were hiding in a storeroom off the gym. They weren't fully aware of what was happening outside that room. However, Eileen Harrild testified that someone entered the gym BEFORE Hamilton stopped shooting, and Mary Blake thought Hamilton might have surrendered. Basically – and understandably so – they had no idea what was going on.

The people that we know for certain entered the gym immediately after Hamilton's death were the headteacher, the student teacher, the janitor and the off-duty police officer. Of these four people only the headteacher gave evidence at the Inquiry. We know the names of the student teacher (David Scott) and the janitor (John Currie). Through my own private investigations I ascertained the name of the off-duty police officer (Grant McCutcheon) and obtained a copy of his statement from Central Scotland Police under the FOISA. It is astonishing that this statement was withheld from the Inquiry. Mr McCutcheon should have been called as a witness at the Dunblane Inquiry because his evidence contradicts that of the janitor John Currie and the Scene of Crime Officer Malcolm Chisholm. ALL the evidence should have been examined. The Inquiry was set up under the 1921 Tribunals of Inquiry (Evidence) Act to find out the full truth about an event that had caused serious public concern and enormous distress.

On the day itself, the bereaved parents were locked away in a staff-room for up to five hours before being told their children were dead. Central Scotland Police claimed this was to ensure the identity of all the children before telling the parents. However, all of the children bar one had been identified by midday. It is much more likely that the scene of crime was being tampered with during those five hours, in order that the police and the Crown got their story straight, ie. that Hamilton had turned the gun on himself after a three minute shooting spree. If the truth is – as I believe – that Hamilton was shot and killed on scene, far too many uncomfortable questions would have been asked about how the person who killed him got there so fast. The only feasible explanation is that Hamilton was under surveillance that morning. Perhaps the intention was to try and apprehend Hamilton BEFORE he shot anyone. Central Scotland Police – and others – had had enough of Hamilton but seemed to have little evidence against him to get a prosecution, never mind a conviction. If he was found in or near a school with guns and ammunition, they had him. He would have had his firearms certificate removed, he would have faced jail, and his unsavoury activities with boys would have been finished. It was a plan that went tragically and horrifically wrong.

At the Inquiry, a picture emerged of wholesale incompetence by Central Scotland Police in their handling of Thomas Hamilton and his firearms applications. DCC McMurdo took the flak. All the representatives damned the maladministration of firearms procedures at Central Scotland Police. Who would dare to make further criticism when certain officers had already been excoriated?

Well, further criticism is necessary, because it is possible that illegal activity was going on in Central Scotland Police – and Central Regional Council for that matter – during Hamilton's long years of gun ownership and access to boys. In her summing up on Day 25 of the Inquiry, Ms Dunlop said, "He described himself to particular individuals, for example Mr Moffat, as a gym teacher. He referred to himself as having qualifications in gymnastics when the evidence discloses in fact the only qualification he'd had was that of an assistant coach and........."

Lord Cullen tried to stop her there, with "Under supervision", to which Ms Dunlop replied, "Under supervision of adult females". This had been carefully concealed throughout the previous 24 days of the Inquiry, but Ms Dunlop at least saw to it that it was mentioned in her summing up. However, Lord Cullen chose to ignore this in his final report. The fact is, that in the original inquiry papers, the truth about Hamilton's gymnastic qualifications was detailed for all to see, and the truth is that Central Regional Council had known he wasn't qualified to teach boys or to teach them unsupervised. How much influence Hamilton's local councillor Robert Ball – a lecturer at Stirling University – brought to bear on this can only be guessed at. Given how strong an advocate he was for his constituent though, Mr Ball could be said to have assisted Thomas Hamilton in getting lets of school premises for his clubs, when Hamilton was in no way qualified to train boys in gymnastics.

But I digress. In her summing up, Ms Dunlop refers to the extent to which the events of 13 March 1996 were planned. Although there was evidence of Hamilton having quizzed a small boy about arrangements at Dunblane Primary School and had stockpiled ammunition, she continued, "it may be thought that there was a degree of compulsiveness about the location". Indeed. The CCTV sightings of Hamilton's van on the morning of 13 March 1996 show him exiting the Burghmuir Roundabout on to the Kerse Road. Kerse Road is NOT the exit that leads "on to the road to Dunblane". It leads to Braehead Primary School in Bannockburn. Did Hamilton set off for this school initially? I don't know, because the Crown Office refuse to answer my question about why DC Capes was allowed to give wrong CCTV evidence. As Ms Dunlop concludes, "The evidence in this area is perhaps in some respects contradictory". But bear in mind that Hamilton had quizzed a former police officer about whether all stations kept firearms and was informed that only those that were manned 24 hours a day did. This is perhaps why he chose Dunblane in the end. The Primary School at Bannockburn was too close to Stirling Police HQ – which kept firearms.

Did Hamilton stockpile ammunition because he planned to flee and go on the run? Hamilton attempted to pay for the hire van in advance. He also bought some new shirts. Does this indicate an intention to commit suicide, or something else? As Ms Dunlop concludes, "It is difficult in fact to make much of the evidence about the shirts given that there was in fact the purchase of new shirts at all". And what did he do with all these new shirts? In the Property Register of the search done on Hamilton's house on 13 March 1996, the only item of clothing found was a jacket. She continues, "There is also evidence of his having booked the school for the Easter camp…(and) there is evidence of his attempt to book the minibus for the 14 and 19 March".

Mr Campbell, in his summing up, states "What appears to have happened is that isolated incidents were considered on their own and then forgotten or at least ignored when further incidents occurred. In this regard, sir, I note, and indeed Mr McMurdo agreed with this, that the bulk of what is now known about Hamilton after this whole Inquiry was known to the police before the 13 March".

The bulk of what we discovered about Hamilton **after** 13 March WAS ALREADY KNOWN by Central Scotland Police **before** 13 March 1996. This is a very important point. Was a friend – or friends? – of Hamilton's diligently removing items of criminal intelligence on him all that time? Keeping his firearms file clean? It is certainly a possibility. Hamilton had friends within Central Scotland Police, as Clive Wood testified to in his evidence on Day 4 of the Inquiry.

Mr Wood himself was not asked any particularly probing questions. As an STV cameraman, he regularly visited Hamilton in his STV logoed car. Outside of Hamilton's friends within Central Scotland Police, Clive Wood was Hamilton's longest standing associate. They had known each other since about 1981. Mr Taylor, representing Central Scotland Police, obviously wished he had asked further questions of Clive Wood, given that Wood in his evidence made reference to Hamilton's "police friends".

On Day 25, in his summing up, Mr Taylor states, "Clive Wood, for example, was never asked to comment on the quality of his relationship. He might well have given valuable evidence in this regard. When Mr Wood was in the witness box it was not known to the parties that there was an intent to use the information on character as a basis for analysis by a psychologist and psychiatrist. Generally when witnesses applied labels they were not asked to explain what they meant". The man representing Central Scotland Police was obviously a little piqued that he hadn't had the chance to question Clive Wood more about his friendship with Thomas Hamilton, when Wood himself had referred to Hamilton's friends within the police.

It is hard to avoid the conclusion that the public inquiry headed by Lord Cullen in the summer of 1996 was conducted improperly. Many guilty people walked free. It was always the case that they would. The Inquiry was not a criminal prosecution – it was a show trial. An *attempt* at justice being "seen to be done". On the whole, it was cleverly conducted, including a weeping Deputy Chief Constable (Douglas McMurdo), an unflappable witness who refused to have words put into her mouth (Doreen Hagger), a varied selection of Thomas Hamilton's friends who were desperate to tell us what a boring man he was (which obviously explains why they spent so much time with him), some extremely insignificant witnesses who testified to train tickets being bought, and some vital witnesses such as the staff of Dunblane Primary School who were caught up in this horrific tragic incident. There were certain witnesses who were notable by their absence, for example, the student teacher David Scott, whose statement was read out at the Inquiry by DCS Ogg. And the off-duty police officer who was first on the scene...

So, what was happening in Thomas Hamilton's life that caused him to enter that school that day and shoot those children? The truth was swept away under Lord Cullen's carpet, and there it was meant to rest in peace. But you can't do that to the truth. It forces its' way out, any way it can. It battles on looking for those who will believe it and then quietly nestles itself inside those who do. But let's get something straight here: most of us knew that the Cullen Inquiry into the Shootings at Dunblane Primary School in 1996 was a cover-up job. Our indignant but ultimately weak voices continued protesting for several years after the show trial. Then all was quiet for a while, until the beginning of 2003, when the cover-up started to show its' gaping holes, and the frayed edges started to unravel...

If it hadn't been for the persistent and valiant efforts of a retired businessman from North Berwick, the truth about the background to the Dunblane Massacre would probably still be buried. William Scott took it upon himself to challenge the Scottish legal establishment about their 'right' to hide information for 100 years. Although I had been incensed to discover about this 100 year rule – which only came to the attention of the general public in 1999 – it simply never occurred to me that it could be challenged. William Scott's remarkable campaign to get answers from the Crown Office about the legality of this rule eventually paid off, and the greatest lie in Scottish history was about to unfold.

The words of William W Scott

My interest in the Cullen Inquiry into the Dunblane Tragedy began in November 1999 when I read that Lord Burton had requested that a report to the Inquiry by a Sergeant Hughes be placed in the House of Lords library. He was informed by Lord Sewell that this was not possible due to it being subject to a 100 year closure order. This exchange is recorded in Hansard. The Lord Advocate at the time warned Lord Burton not to make any further enquiries.

I thought that 100 years was rather a long time since Cabinet papers are only sealed for 30 so I wrote to my MP who at that time was Mr John Home Robertson. After devolution and the creation of the Scottish Parliament he became MSP for the constituency of East Lothian. He wrote to the Lord Advocate on my behalf. After five months and repeated reminders the Lord Advocate informed Mr Robertson that the closure was imposed to protect the identity of children. He accepted this explanation but I could not see why a felt tipped pen could not have been used to blank out the names of children mentioned in the report as was the case with the Lawrence Inquiry and the Waterhouse Inquiry "Lost in Care". The Lord Advocate in the same letter categorically stated that the closure was proposed by the Scottish Record Office and that other documents were also subject to the 100 year closure.

I asked my MP who was responsible for the closure since Lord Sewell claimed it was Lord Cullen and the Lord Advocate said it was the Scottish Record Office. I further asked since the plural was used how many other papers were included in the closure and why was it not possible to use a felt tipped pen to blank out the names of children. The fact that Thomas Hamilton legally held a firearm certificate also troubled me so I wrote the following to Mr Robertson : "Mr Thomas Hamilton held a firearm certificate at the time of the Tragedy although from press reports after the shooting it would appear many people considered him to be an unstable character unsuitable to hold such a certificate. There was also believed to be a police report confirming that he was indeed unsuitable. Is it public knowledge who signed the documents to allow Thomas Hamilton to legally own handguns or is that information covered by the 100 year closure? Surely the matter of how an application for a firearm certificate from such a person as Thomas Hamilton was successful must have been put before Lord Cullen and considering the magnitude of the misjudgement it seems only right and proper that the public should know the facts." I concluded by asking if he would prefer that I wrote to the Crown Office direct.

Mr Robertson ignored all my questions and replied that he understood the fundamental reason for the 100 year restriction was to protect the identity of children. He added that I should feel free to write to the Crown Office. I wrote to the Lord Advocate putting the same questions as I had to my MP. He replied with legal jargon to confuse the matter of Sergeant Hughes' report, but was emphatic that it was the Scottish Record Office that proposed the 100 year closure.

Further correspondence produced the address of the National Archives of Scotland (formerly the Scottish Record Office) and continued insistence that the closure was to protect the identity of children.

My next move was to communicate with the Keeper of Records at the National Archives of Scotland regarding his imposing of the 100 year closure. His reply left no room for misunderstanding. He informed me that he had no responsibility whatsoever for the imposition of closure periods and that it was entirely a matter for the body responsible for the creation of the records. He further went on to explain that there is no statutory basis for the closure of records created by Scottish public bodies. The Public Records Act 1958 specifically excludes any body which is wholly or mainly concerned with Scottish affairs, or which carries on its activities wholly or mainly in Scotland.

I of course made Mr John Home Robertson aware of this information provided by the Keeper of the Records of Scotland and requested that he assist me in obtaining access to Sergeant Hughes' report. He wrote in reply that he noted that there may be different accounts of how the closure was initiated but the key point seemed to be the fact that the decision was specifically confirmed by Lord Cullen. He went on to say that he thought it was entirely appropriate to protect children and that he could see no good reason to support my request for disclosure.

My next letter to Mr Robertson pointed out that I was surprised that he was not concerned that the Crown Office provided him with false information. I put it to him that the next time he made an enquiry on behalf of a constituent how could he be sure of the accuracy of the reply. I went on to suggest that the "good reason" might be found in the report, might well be in the public interest and only by the reading of it could it be judged whether the closure was justified or not. I also thought he would want to know why the Crown Office and others had given the impression that the closure order is backed by law when this is not the case. I asked him to reconsider his position. Mr Robertson replied that if Lord Cullen was satisfied there were good grounds for the closure order he would be reluctant to question his judgement. It did not seem to occur to Mr Robertson that "good grounds" to Lord Cullen might be something quite different from the protection of the identity of children which he seemed so passionately to believe in.

At last, 16 months after I first wrote to my MP, the Crown Office admitted that "the Public Records Acts are not applicable to Scotland." The letter stated that officials recommended to Lord Cullen that a 100 year disclosure be put on the papers but it did not state what department these officials belonged to. The letter closed with the following: "If you are able to set out reasons why you consider it necessary to have access to the report, I will, however, consider the matter further." I never was of course permitted access. To quieten public fears of a cover-up to protect the identity of important persons was not considered a 'necessary' reason. **However, this proved beyond doubt that there was no legal closure. If there had been I could not have been offered access under any circumstances.**

The Crown Office sent me off on a wild goose chase by suggesting that much of the information I sought could be found on the internet. Fortunately I did not waste much time on this as it was obvious that information they wished to hide would not be freely available on the web. **Since it had been established that there was no statutory authority for the closure, I wondered from where the Lord Advocate derived the right to deny access.**

Mr Robertson wrote to the Lord Advocate on my behalf. The reply was a typical lawyer's letter with much that was irrelevant. However, he wrote the following after referring to the England and Wales Public Records Act 1958: "Although there is no similar statutory obligation on Government departments in Scotland, the same practice is followed administratively." *Followed administratively* hardly explains the authority to either allow or deny access to the documents.

My question about the authority to deny access has never been answered, but I was sent a paper entitled 'Guidelines on Extended Closure' which I suppose they hoped would satisfy me. After studying the criteria detailed I could not find one that covered the plans of Dunblane Primary School nor Thomas Hamilton's autopsy report. I pointed out to my MP and the Lord Advocate that since the Guidelines had been sent to assist me I should be grateful if they would inform me which criterion covered the two examples mentioned. I have not had a reply and in fact, the Lord Advocate has stated that he will not respond to any further letters from me. But for reasons unknown, correspondence has recommenced. Possibly the questions I ask are covered by the Freedom of Information Act and the Crown Office has no choice.

After further correspondence Mr Robertson closed a letter with the following: "My understanding is that Lord Cullen imposed the closure and that the Crown Office is implementing that decision." Apart from Lord Sewell, nobody at any time has suggested that the idea for closure came from Lord Cullen. The general consensus was that the proposal for a 100 year closure was put to him by officials unknown and he agreed.

In fact the decision to impose the 100 year closure was taken at a meeting held on 13 January 1997. At that meeting were the Clerk to the Inquiry and representatives of the police, the Scottish Records Office and of the Crown Office. Lord Cullen in a letter to me stated unequivocally that those present at that meeting did not have the authority, *individually or collectively*, to do so. The Keeper of the Records of Scotland and the Lord Advocate agreed that the imposition of a closure order is entirely a matter for the body responsible for the creation of the records. However, in a later letter the Lord Advocate wrote, "Records are usually deposited in a records office by a department and that department is thereafter responsible for deciding on the closure period....... In this case since the public inquiry office was ceasing to function the Crown agreed to assume the role of depositing department with the responsibilities to which I have referred".

Assuming the role of the depositing department and being the creator of the records is hardly the same thing and it must not be forgotten that Lord Cullen said that none of those attending the meeting on 13 January 1997 had the authority to impose a closure order.

It is accepted that the Records Act 1958 does not apply to Scotland but the terms of that Act are applied 'administratively'. When I questioned why legislation was required in England and Wales but not in Scotland I was informed that the Lord Advocate and the Scottish Executive were within their rights to apply the 1958 Act to Scotland. If this is indeed the case we now have a form of dictatorship in Scotland where the Lord Advocate and the Scottish Executive can do as they please without consulting the Holyrood or Westminster Parliaments.

In October 2002 my MP wrote: "If you can let me have one good reason why the identity of children who are referred to in the Dunblane Inquiry should be disclosed to you, I might be prepared to take this matter further." I have never at any time made a request to know the identity of children and indeed on numerous occasions suggested the use of a felt tipped pen to blank out their names. I was not at all pleased at such an accusation being made and asked for an apology which I have never received.

It must be tedious reading what has been written and the replies received, but I felt that it was necessary to provide the background to my struggle to uncover the truth and to show how it became much more difficult when my elected representative refused to help. He may not see it that way as he dutifully forwarded my letters to the Lord Advocate and passed on his replies but the fact of the matter is that he acted as post box and nothing else.

It turned out that the other documents mentioned earlier were 105 productions apart from Sergeant Hughes' report amounting to tens of thousands of pages and taking up 20 feet of shelf space. That there were 106 productions on the closed list was known quite early on but the quantity held only came to light when the Lord Advocate gave it as an excuse for the delay in cataloguing all the material. As with most of the information released by the Lord Advocate or the Crown Office it just raised more questions. How was such a vast amount selected for closure? How can they justify claiming for so long that the closure was intended only to protect the identity of children when it is ridiculous to suggest that each and every one of these pages contains the name of a child?

Lord Cullen stated that there was no evidence of criminal behaviour on the part of Thomas Hamilton prior to the shooting, but of course he may not consider the abuse of children a criminal offence. So who are the children named in the productions? If they were not abused by Hamilton, who was guilty of interfering with these children? I bet they are now wishing that they had only imposed a 30 year closure as, if that had been done, it is unlikely anybody would have shown interest.

Even now the Lord Advocate is only agreeing to release some of the papers since there are some, he says, that are too sensitive to be made public. He claims that police reports are routinely closed, the identity of witnesses as well as children must be protected, the Data Protection Act must be considered and distress must not be caused, but none of these conditions surfaced until after it was discovered that there was no statutory basis for the closure order.

I asked how many of the productions were police reports, but of course, as usual, never received the information requested. What can be so sensitive that it cannot be made public for 100 years? I realise that in some cases witnesses have to be protected for their own safety, but it is difficult to see how this is relevant in this instance.

The authorities obviously realised that even those three conditions could not possibly cover the tens of thousands of pages they were trying to keep hidden which is probably why they were now attempting to use the 1958 Act.

Witnesses were not called who could have provided crucial evidence. A police officer was in the school at the time of or shortly after the shooting. He advised the first ambulance crew to arrive that it was safe to enter the gym as Hamilton was dead. On a matter as serious as this a police officer would have confirmed the facts himself before advising the ambulance crew, so he had definitely been in the gym. Here is an officer present at the scene, trained to observe and give evidence, so why was he not called to give evidence to the Inquiry? When I raised this point the Lord Advocate in an attempt to minimise the importance of the police officer's non-attendance informed me that a trainee teacher had seen Hamilton shoot himself. This only made me more suspicious as the trainee teacher was not called to give evidence either and his statement read to the Inquiry by a police officer did not exactly say what the Lord Advocate claimed. An injured schoolboy is alleged to have said that he saw the "bad man" (Thomas Hamilton) being shot, so a lot of questions remain unanswered. Thus, there is doubt as to how Thomas Hamilton died. The gun that it is claimed he used would it is alleged have just about have blown his head right off, yet the headteacher Ron Taylor thought he saw Hamilton's body move. The senior ambulance officer, John McEwan, remarked on seeing Hamilton's body that he wanted to kick it, even though its head was blown off.... !

Hamilton's body was quickly cremated which of course makes it now very difficult to discover exactly what happened in the last minutes of his life. The autopsy report cannot now be questioned by other experts and the authorities have complicated matters further by attempting to have part of Thomas Hamilton's autopsy report hidden for 100 years. What on earth can be in an autopsy report that requires it be kept secret for 100 years unless there is proof that he did not commit suicide? Is it normal for autopsy reports to have closure orders placed on them and to arrange cremation so quickly?

When reading the transcript of the Inquiry I noticed that a Dr Beattie when questioned about the bodies in the gym confirmed that there were a number of dead children and one dead adult. He agreed when questioned further that the body of the dead adult was that of the teacher Mrs Mayor. On the evening of the shootings Dr Beattie, with events still clear in his mind, told reporters at a press conference that he did **not** see Hamilton's body in the gym. He had ample time to consider that response before giving evidence to the Inquiry but chose not to alter what he had told the representatives of the press. There are many theories concerning Hamilton's death and the moving of his body, but I have restricted myself to the almost certain fact that at 10.15am on 13 March 1996 the body of Thomas Hamilton was not in the gymnasium and have endeavoured to find conclusive proof. Dr Beattie seemed to be the obvious person to settle the matter so I wrote to him at Yorkhill Hospital although I was not certain that he still held a post there. I sent copies of the original as I had not received a reply. My letters were not returned so I had no way of knowing if Dr Beattie had received them. I decided to send an e-mail to the hospital with a request to let me know if Dr Beattie had left. This prompted a reply from Dr Beattie by e-mail which I now reproduce below.

I only reply lest your conspiracy theory is reinforced.

I simply suggest you read all the evidence.

For my part, please note that I will regard any future contact from you or your group as harassment and will take the necessary action.

Please do not contact me in any way again.

I considered that to be a very strange response to such a simple request. All I had asked was whether the body of Thomas Hamilton was in the gym at

10.15am or not. There was no mention on my part of any of the doubts many have over the death of Hamilton so why did he mention a conspiracy theory? What he did succeed in doing is to convince me that somebody advised him to answer as he did. Now who would do that? He suggests I read the evidence. It was because I read the evidence that I decided to write to him. He mentions my group but there is nothing in my letter to suggest I am working with others so what put that into his head? He almost threatens me with harassing him but I sent one letter and an e-mail which can hardly be described as harassment. Admittedly I sent copies when I did not know if he had received the original but they would never have been sent if he had shown a little courtesy and answered my letter. It is true that I often send copies of correspondence to other people who I believe have an interest in the Cullen Inquiry but in no way can they be described as a group taking concerted action. Most would not welcome the information I send them if they thought they were being so labelled. The body was either there or it was not. A simple yes or no would have sufficed. Why did Dr Beattie choose to stay silent? It could have been because it would have been a lie to say the body was there and to admit that it wasn't would have raised many very awkward questions, or was he warned as Lord Burton was in 1999?

When writing to Dr Beattie failed to produce the information I wanted I decided to attempt to communicate with a member of the first ambulance crew to arrive at the scene. He phoned me and we had a lengthy conversation although he informed me at the start that he had been advised by his supervisor that he could not discuss the matter I had written to him about due to the Data Protection Act. He gave me the name and address of his superior in Stirling who he thought might be able to help me. Before I had time to write to Stirling, a letter arrived from Mr Gordon, the General Manager of the Scottish Ambulance Service based in Dundee claiming that the gentleman who phoned me had passed the letter to him as he was uncertain how to respond. I did not like the tone of this letter so informed him that he employed his staff but did not own them. My letter was obviously shown to the person in charge at Callander but I am sure the member of the ambulance crew did not request that it be sent to Dundee. He had no reason to as he had advised me to approach his superior in Stirling. So how did my letter with a simple request about Hamilton's body finish up in Dundee? As with all aspects of the Cullen Inquiry there are no answers, just more questions. I have heard that the Data Protection Act does not apply to dead bodies, so I made Mr Gordon aware of this but never received a reply.

I thought that with so many questions arising from the presence or otherwise of Hamilton's body it might throw some light on the subject if I could obtain details of the quantity, type and position of the bullets and shell cases recovered from the gymnasium and area surrounding Dunblane Primary School after the shooting of sixteen children and a school teacher. I applied to Central Scotland Police for the information but was notified that under

Section 37 of the Freedom of Information Act the knowledge I sought was an absolute exemption. That seemed definite enough but an expert on the subject advised me that section 37 could not possibly apply so I wrote again to Central Scotland Police. Forty working days had passed since I was refused so an appeal against their judgement could not be considered. The Scottish Information Commissioner confirmed that this was indeed the case but helpfully pointed out that if I wished I could start the process again from the beginning. This I did. As the information collected by the scene of crime officers was gathered as routine police work and not at the time for the Cullen Inquiry, section 37 should have no influence on its release.

Central Scotland Police, although stating that they could not divulge the information I wanted, suggested that I approach the Crown Office. It seemed strange, as does everything surrounding the Cullen Inquiry, that it could be possible for a department to release information that another department had said it was impossible to do. Anyway, I wrote to the Crown Office. I received dozens of pages which at first sight did not appear to contain the details I requested. On pointing this out I was sent, by a different person, another batch of the same pages. Closer inspection of the material revealed that a report and photographs were mentioned which were likely to contain the details I wanted. I requested copies. It was then that I was told that the report and photographs were among the tens of thousands of pages that it was intended should be hidden for 100 years.

Many might say it is of little consequence how Hamilton died and that it is good riddance. However if he was murdered it has to be asked why and by whom and for what reason? Did somebody already try to do away with him? It is alleged that a senior police officer provided him with an expensive launch that he certainly could not have afforded to buy himself. Why would he be given such a generous gift? Was it for services rendered? He was on board that boat when it blew up and sank. He survived. Why was there no investigation? The police, I believe, salvaged the boat at taxpayer's expense and claimed it was a training exercise.

The more I have delved into this matter the more frustrated I have become and due to the evasive answers I have received I am now totally convinced that there has been a cover-up. It could have started with something as simple as a small lie to protect the identity of someone in the public eye who at one time had known Thomas Hamilton but now did not wish that innocent acquaintanceship to become public knowledge. Of course more lies have to be told to cover the original and the whole process snowballs. On the other hand there could be a paedophile ring operating and that is much more serious as they are still free to continue their sordid practices.

The Cullen Inquiry seemed to raise more questions than give answers and the obstructive attitudes of the authorities over the years has convinced me that they are certainly trying to hide something. Surely an inquiry is set up to make clear exactly what happened, who was involved and why it happened.

The only certain fact is that sixteen children and a teacher died on that dreadful morning in March 1996.

After Dunblane, there were demands for a ban on handguns. There is no doubt that many people genuinely felt that ownership of guns should be banned. However, the outlawing of these guns did not reduce crime. The number of crimes involving the use of guns has risen every year since 1996 and only 2004 showed a slight decrease. It was almost unknown for legally held weapons to be used to commit a crime, but unfortunately, due to the almost hysterical campaign, the spotlight fell on law-abiding sportsmen and women. The incompetence of the licensing authority, Central Scotland Police, or more seriously, on the favours given to Thomas Hamilton by the police, were ignored. The anti-gun campaign did of course divert attention from the question as to why a serious investigation was not carried out into all aspects of Thomas Hamilton's life including his associates.

Central Scotland Police carried out the investigation into the tragedy that occurred in Dunblane, whereas the force should have been under investigation for possibly being responsible, although not actually pulling the trigger, for the deaths on 13 March 1996. It was reported at the time that all the opposition parties were against Central Scotland Police being given the task.

How different from the inquiry into the killing of two little girls in Soham which even forced the resignation of a Chief Constable. No serious attempt was made to discover what drove Hamilton to commit such a crime, if his friends had an influence on him or to find out where he was and who he met on the morning before he arrived at the school.

A housemaster at Queen Victoria School alleged that Thomas Hamilton had access to the facilities at the school and that there were other unauthorised visitors. He reported his suspicions to his superiors, but instead of being praised, his flat was raided by the police, his computer confiscated and he was forced to resign. A very strange string of events which it would appear require to be investigated. This creates a difficulty as it would seem that the action taken by the police would have to be part of any investigation. However, I believe Strathcylde Police have been given this task. Will they do their job or become part of the cover-up?

William concludes, "Given that it took several years to prepare the papers for release and that some will remain closed, I do not believe anything of importance will be found in the pages the public are now allowed access to. **Only a fresh inquiry will be able to establish who is being protected and why**".

****

We thought it was all "wrapped up", the atrocity known as **Dunblane**. The pain and shock have subsided over the years, although immense damage was done. It wasn't a subject I particularly wanted to revisit. I had written many words condemning Central Scotland Police, perhaps even more than I condemned the actual perpetrator, Thomas Hamilton. He was dead afterall. They are still here, alive and kicking, pensioned off, resigned from their posts, moved on, gagged, silenced, or busy gagging and silencing others. Nobody would want a revisitation to Dunblane. What would be the point? All it would do is bring back the sense of shock, disbelief, horror and incredulity we suffered for so long after 13 March 1996. Alas, we must revisit Dunblane. We must take a closer look at Thomas Hamilton's *friends* and ask how much they knew, how much they were involved in his paedophilic activities, how much they aided and abetted him, and how he managed to plot and plan for 13/3 without any of them *apparently* knowing a thing. They are still in our midst and I think we should know more about them.

Dunblane has been a much neglected subject (after the initial aftermath). As I fully supported the handgun ban, my motivation in uncovering the truth was vastly different from that of the gun lobby. However, one of the arguments in support of the ban was that the children and their teacher had been murdered by a *legally* held weapon. It is my contention that Hamilton held his guns *illegally* – that he supplied paedophilic material in return for access to guns...

The greatest irony of all of course, is that Hamilton's death was caused by one of those weapons he so loved. His guns were his "babies" – his friends. Hamilton loved the power and control his guns gave him. Six-year-old Matthew Birnie who was injured in the incident, said from his hospital bed a few days later, "I know the bad man is dead because the policeman shot him". Eleven-year-old Laura Bryce, listening to what was happening that morning from Hut 7, said she heard a man scream and guessed that was when Hamilton shot himself.

So, Hamilton faced the same terror just before **his** death as the children had before **theirs**. Quite literally, hoist by his own petard – destroyed by a gun, one of his "babies". And ruined by his own devices against others. Like Michael Ryan, did Hamilton find himself wishing he hadn't got out of bed that morning? The Hungerford massacre unfolded as a result of a plan that went wrong – Ryan's intention to rape a woman. Her resistance to his attempted rape resulted in him killing her – and then there was no going back. It is likely that Hamilton set out to kill Ron Taylor, the headteacher of Dunblane Primary School. He planned to do this in front of Assembly, in particular, in front of the Primary 7 boys. It was an eye-for-an-eye. In Hamilton's eyes, Taylor had humiliated him by warning the boys in Assembly to have nothing to do with him. He was out for revenge. But his plan was foiled. As a consequence, "the massacre" happened.

What we must all remember when we think about Thomas Hamilton – as hard as it is to care – is that, prior to 13 March 1996, he genuinely believed he was not guilty of any crime. Not the sexual or physical abuse of children, nor anything else. He was surrounded by people who not only failed to take him to task about his "behaviour", but positively encouraged him in his activities. He also had a coterie of like-minded paedophile friends. It is unlikely that he ever had reason to believe his behaviour was in any way 'abnormal'.

Unlike other big murder trials, the general public stayed well away from Lord Cullen's Inquiry into the shootings at Dunblane Primary School in the summer of 1996. It felt like the only respectful thing to do. And it was clear by then that the bereaved parents had formed a close-knit group and were receiving messages of support from all over the world. Everything seemed to be taken care of and besides, what could any of us really do?

It seems obvious, looking back, that the Inquiry was far too hastily convened. Central Scotland Police would *appear* to have conducted a fairly thorough investigation, even though then, as now, I find it incredible that they were assigned to this task, given their relationship with the murderer Thomas Hamilton. The senior investigating officer, DCS John Ogg, now retired from the force, said as recently as June 2003, "I can reassure you that the investigation into the Dunblane incident was absolutely thorough, and we covered every angle". If the Inquiry was conducted improperly, as I believe, then whoever had overall responsibility for searching for the truth is guilty of perverting the course of justice – a crime which as we have seen in the Soham murder case, carries a sentence of imprisonment. Many witnesses gave statements who were not called to the Inquiry to give evidence, so if they had something vital to say, how will we ever know? And through my own enquiries over the last three years, I know for certain that the Crown Office did not release ALL the witness statements when the documents were opened to the public in October 2005. It is a damning indictment of the Scottish legal system that this has happened.

A Report was cobbled together by Lord Cullen, published in October 1996 to angry noises from the Snowdrop Campaign – the campaign fighting for a total ban on handguns – only to find that Lord Cullen did not make such a recommendation. In the media frenzy that followed, firearms were in the firing line. Not "the truth" and whether "justice had been seen to be done" – but whether Lord Cullen had the guts to anger the gun lobby. And as we know, he didn't. Or perhaps, given that he knew the truth and that there was so much more behind what caused the 13 March 1996 to happen, he knew that whilst banning handguns might appease the bereaved parents, it was actually beside the point. Thomas Hamilton had been a 'protected' man. The law had been sufficient to stop him, and many police officers and others had tried. But Hamilton had friends in high places. That was the truth of the matter, and that was the truth that was so conveniently lost in 1996.

So let's call the Dunblane Closure Order by its' true name – the One Hundred Year **Gagging** Order. Let's talk Plain English here. Does the Scottish legal system understand that? Lord Cullen shot himself in the foot – that's where firearms are really useful – when he told us in 1996 that there was no evidence to suggest that Thomas Hamilton abused boys. Then, when a few agitators started asking questions about the legality of hiding information away for **One Hundred Years**, Lord Cullen told us that it was to protect the child victims of Hamilton's abuse. It is only natural and right that we should be confused.

They can't have it both ways. Did Hamilton abuse boys or not? I think from all the evidence – both that in the public domain and that that is hidden away – we can fairly safely and horrifyingly conclude that he did. So where are these 'boys' now? Were they asked for witness statements at the time of The Cullen Inquiry in 1996? Of course not. The One Hundred Year Gagging Order was imposed for quite a few reasons, and sadly, the least of these was to protect the abused children, or for that matter, the feelings of the bereaved parents. "Sorry, but your child wasn't killed by a lone madman whose actions could never have been predicted, but by a frustrated paedophile who had long been considered a danger to children and sought revenge when he could no longer get easy access to boys".

The boys Hamilton abused – and Lord Cullen has now admitted that there were such boys – are now young men. Even at the time of The Cullen Inquiry in 1996, many of them would have been in their late teens. It should have been their choice whether they gave evidence or not. The boys at the 1988 camp on Inchmoan Island in particular must surely be traumatised by their ordeal. Doreen Hagger had to leave the island in the middle of the night for her own personal safety and to get help for these boys. The distress and guilt she felt at having to leave the boys behind when they pleaded to be taken with her, lives with her today.

In his final write up into the shootings at the primary school in Dunblane, Lord Cullen stated: "The only evidence which the Inquiry heard as to any acts of indecency on the part of Thomas Hamilton comprised two incidents" (page 25, para 4.15) And of these two incidents he only believed one of them. And that incident *only* consisted of thigh rubbing – about the most innocuous thing that Hamilton ever did to one of "his boys".

In February 2003, I petitioned the First Minister of Scotland with a demand for a new inquiry. Here is the case I made:

*The Cullen Inquiry into the Shootings at Dunblane Primary School in 1996 was carried out under the terms of the Tribunals of Inquiry (Evidence) Act 1921. In his opening statement, Lord Cullen commented, "I would emphasise that this is to be an Inquiry held in public. As matters stand I do not foresee that I would require to exercise my power to direct that any part of it should be held in private." Obviously, at some point during the gathering of evidence, Lord Cullen decided that aspects of the inquiry could **not** be heard in public. And hence the 100 year closure order.*

*However, **accountability** lies at the heart of the role of a tribunal appointed under the 1921 Act. On the rare occasion when a matter of grave public concern needs to be investigated thoroughly and to the full satisfaction of the public, a tribunal is appointed under the terms of the above Act. There* can be no doubt that the events of 13 March 1996 constituted one of these very rare occasions. Yet Cullen's Inquiry failed to generate public confidence and actually served to reinforce the suspicions of the general public that there was something to hide.

For example, Central Scotland Police was given the crucial role of investigating the background to the massacre, in which they themselves were heavily implicated.

Furthermore, Lord Cullen could obviously pick and choose which witnesses were called to the inquiry. In his opening statement he admitted that: "Since this is an investigation I will have the ultimate say as to whether or not a person should be called to give evidence".

Of these witnesses, there was an arbitrary system of cross-examination, some witnesses being exposed to rigorous questioning, whilst others waltzed in and out of the witness box, with very few questions asked. Lord Cullen himself stated that he would decide the extent to which witnesses should be questioned. This resulted in such anomalies that Doreen Hagger's evidence for example, runs to **40** A4 pages, whilst two of Hamilton's friends – Geoffrey Clive Wood and James Gillespie – ran to a mere **8** and **6** pages respectively. This begs the question, why were Hamilton's friends given such an easy time?

In his final write up, Lord Cullen then filtered the evidence heard or presented to the inquiry and left out whatever did not fit with the picture he wanted to portray, that of the "lone madman" seeking revenge on Dunblane. In his opening statement he admitted as much: "The criterion which I will apply is whether what is proposed is likely to be of assistance in achieving the objects of this Inquiry."

Thomas Hamilton's "friends" have been protected for the past 7 (now 10) years and it is time they faced full scrutiny. As for the boys whom Hamilton and his friends abused – well, where should they start with their claims for criminal damage? At the bottom: with Hamilton's friends? Or at the (so-called) top: with Cullen? Is this the real reason why they were silenced? The criminal injuries bill for these boys would run into millions. The financial cost of a public inquiry that never even set out to find out the truth is a scandal of enormous proportions. It is time we fought for justice for all Hamilton's silenced victims.

Make no mistake, this – the long years of Thomas Hamilton's reign, the Dunblane tragedy, the aftermath, the Cullen Inquiry, the hidden documents – this, is Scotland's Shame. At every stage, those involved have sought to conceal the truth. 'They' would have got away with the Dunblane cover-up if Lord Burton had not asked Lord Sewell a question about DS Paul Hughes police report on Thomas Hamilton. It was only by accident that we – the public – discovered that documents from Lord Cullen's Dunblane Inquiry had been locked away for 100 years. Even when Lord Burton asked the question of Lord Sewell, the latter chose to hide the truth from his fellow peer. And even before the Inquiry began, the bereaved and injured children's parents were not advised about having legal representation. One parent said, "It wasn't made clear to us until some time after the events had taken place that the parents would require legal representation. I feel that this should have been brought to the attention of the parents immediately they were informed of the tragic circumstances. It was mainly by accident that my husband and I became aware that we did require, like other parents, to be legally represented". Another said, "The Procurator Fiscal did not tell us about the importance of the role of the parents at the Public Enquiry and specifically he did not advise us that we should appoint a lawyer for that purpose".

The Government-ordered cover-up was put into operation immediately. According to Frank Cook MP, there was a meeting at the House of Commons the day after the shootings to discuss how the situation was going to be handled. A carefully staged question was asked in the House by one interested Member of Parliament to another, George Robertson to Michael Forsyth. An Inquiry was going to be held under the 1921 Tribunals of Inquiry Act and the truth about the incident would be uncovered. So that was alright then.

Scotland's Shame continues. Lord Cullen, the Lord Advocate and the First Minister's refusal to answer questions put to them about the Incident and the Inquiry perpetuates the scandal. We can only assume that the reason for locking documents away for 100 years was very grave indeed, and whatever the truth is, we are not to know it – not ever. Dr Peter Anderson, a deputy keeper at the former Scottish Records Office, has confirmed that while most 100-year cases were reduced to 75-year closure in the late 1980s, documents still under a 100-year ban include anything involving children; plus rape victims (for instance, the identity of Carol X); sectarian politics in Northern Ireland; and the royal family. The purported reason for the Dunblane Closure Order was to protect children. This is simply not true.

When Lord Cullen was chosen to head the Dunblane Inquiry, there was a good reason for doing so. He was known for toeing the establishment line. When Lord Hutton was chosen to chair the Inquiry into David Kelly's death in 2003, the former Labour MP and Guardian columnist Roy Hattersley mused on how judges are chosen for these tasks. If one judge is deemed more appropriate than another, doesn't this call into question the notion that they all perform their tasks with equal and absolute objectivity, as they should? He concludes his surmising with the observation, "So, if he remains true to form, we can expect his inquiry to end as so many inquiries have ended. The report will be balanced and judicious, as is always the case. No one will be unfairly blamed, as they never are".

DCC McMurdo took the brunt of it after Dunblane. How does he feel about that now? At the time of his resignation he said that he had no regrets and would take the same course of action again. He – presumably – believed he had done nothing wrong. And maybe he hadn't. When the furore about the 100 year rule hit the press early in 2003, McMurdo was contacted by a journalist at the Scottish Mail on Sunday. McMurdo stated that he had never spoken to anyone from the press about his situation or about the incident. If he is 'innocent', how can he live with having had to carry the can for Britain's worst massacre? Did Michael Forsyth do a deal with McMurdo to keep himself out of the frame? When Forsyth lost his seat at the general election in 1997, his relief was almost palpable. He was going to "get a life" he said. Forsyth knew he had only just scraped through the whole Dunblane/Hamilton situation unscathed. The Snowdrop Campaign had distracted everyone from the truth and attention was focussed solely on the gun issue. Judicial inquiries rarely end with an explicit criticism of a minister's integrity or the honesty of a senior civil servant. The hapless, arrogant McMurdo would do instead.

Well damn you then – damn the lot of you. Your apathy and indifference to the truth speaks volumes. What kind of a nation are we? Sixteen five-year-old children went off to school one morning and were shot dead in their gym class. Do you think we know the truth about that? About why it happened? I can assure you we don't.

In Lord Cullen's final write-up of all the evidence heard at the Inquiry in 1996, there are many untruths. To give just one example – on page 40, Cullen writes "His qualifications were checked and found to meet the requirements of the Regional Council". This check on Hamilton's gymnastic qualifications was made in February 1993.

However, in the Crown Office Summary of Evidence (a document that was initially locked away for 100 years), it states that Hamilton lied to the Regional Council about his qualifications. Having done a check with the British Amateur Gymnastics Association, the Council discovered Hamilton's lies.

This check produced the following information: *Hamilton was the holder of a Women's Assistant Coach Award, Class 5, which would qualify him to assist in the teaching of women's artistic gymnastics while under the supervision of a Class 4 Coach or above. Qualified Assistant Coaches may work under the direction of a qualified coach but must not work unsupervised.* Thus, Hamilton was not qualified to teach boys gymnastics, nor to do so alone.

In his article, Ian Bell continues, "Be aware, further, that much of the investigative work into possible official failures attempted by the press in the aftermath of the massacre have proved fruitless, simply because the very sorts of people Lord Mackay now seeks to protect – police officers, councillors, and local authority officials – have taken cover behind Cullen. It seems the public interest, and the public's right to know, are to be allowed only one representative. Such are the number of potential witnesses to the long, squalid career of Thomas Hamilton, indeed, that the media need hardly now dare speak to anyone. Meanwhile, the police, the subject of most lay criticism, are given the job of investigating themselves. The suspicion grows, therefore, of an attempt simply to prevent the press from investigating what happened at Dunblane".

Bell adds, "What scrutiny is there when the press is forbidden to look, far less to speak? What happens when a press that calls itself free is drawn into direct conflict with a legal system that calls itself just? The answer is that one or the other has ceased to live up to its name.

"Tribunals of inquiry," says one standard work, "are appointed to investigate serious allegations of corruption or improper conduct in the public service, or to investigate a matter of public concern which requires thorough and impartial investigation to allay public anxiety and may not be dealt with by ordinary civil or criminal processes."

Is it seriously proposed that the press could hinder the utterly impartial Lord Cullen? Conversely, are we expected to believe that public anxiety is allayed when the media is fettered? The only possible interpretation of the Lord Advocate's note is that policemen and officials have come complaining because the press is asking questions. How would the public feel if the press, after Dunblane, did not?"

Bell concludes as follows, "The massacre was unprecedented, as was the public's heartfelt response. Now the Lord Advocate steps forward to create a precedent of his own with a patchwork of law, administrative procedures, and jurists' reports. It is bad, it is dangerous, and it does not reflect well on a Scottish legal system whose pride and glory is the claim to proceed, always, from principle".

In the first six months after the massacre, there was a lot of media concern about the conduct of the Inquiry. A spokesman for the Lord Advocate said that *Lord Cullen's powers outweigh those of the police and the procurator fiscal.* "If he is unhappy with any aspect of the investigations he can order further investigations as he chooses, and into whom he chooses," he added. However, as we know, Lord Cullen did not read any of the preparatory material for the Inquiry. He simply sat and listened to the oral testimony of selected witnesses – witnesses selected by the Crown.

On 9 June 1996, Graeme Smith, writing in Scotland on Sunday, observed: "The order is not strict – one minute the inquiry is hearing about concerns over a Hamilton club at Linlithgow Academy in 1988, the next it is back to a social worker to hear how relatives were comforted on March 13 – and daily witness lists issued to lawyers and journalists are becoming increasingly redundant with other names suddenly being dropped in and others never appearing. On Wednesday for example, only 3 witnesses from a list of 25 were heard and DS Gordon Taylor, one of the last officers to investigate Hamilton, has been on the list twice but has not yet given evidence. There is disquiet among other parties at the inquiry that they are not having enough time to prepare for late changes, or cope with the deluge of paperwork from thousands of files standing floor to ceiling in a corridor outside the main hall".

On 11 June 1996, less than two weeks after the Dunblane Inquiry opened, the media reported that, "A row has broken out over the refusal by the Scottish Office to provide MPs with a transcript of the inquiry. The Scottish

Office minister, Lord James Douglas-Hamilton, stated it would be "inappropriate" because the purpose of the transcripts was to help the chairman of the inquiry and interested parties. Willie Ross, Ulster Unionist Party MP for East Londonderry said, "When you think about the importance of this and the grave public disquiet caused by Dunblane, not least by the evidence given by the police officer the other day, then the transcript should be given to members". It is astonishing that the Scottish Office even considered NOT giving a copy of the transcript to MPs.

On 24 June 1996, it was reported that Colin Campbell, QC, asked Detective Sergeant Gordon Taylor if he was satisfied with the explanation given by the Stirling Procurator Fiscal's office for refusing him a warrant to search Hamilton's home. He had been told there was no evidence of acts of criminality to justify the warrant. However, before Det Sgt Taylor could answer, Ian Bonomy QC for the Crown, intervened to argue that in law such decisions were not for scrutiny for a court or tribunal. ... the Scottish Liberal Democrat's legal spokesman, Menzies Campbell, QC, who formerly served in the Crown Office as an advocate depute, led a call from politicians for the officials to be questioned. He said, "I shall be extremely disappointed if the Lord Advocate insists throughout the Dunblane inquiry on the policy of confidentiality in relation to the actions of the Procurator Fiscal. It is quite true that he has the right to do so, but it is a matter of legal convention and not statutory requirement. Mr Campbell pointed out that on at least one other occasion, a Glasgow rape case, the Lord Advocate of the time departed from the policy, though he had acknowledged the policy's validity in almost every other case. Mr Campbell continued: "Dunblane is unique, and it must surely be in the public interest to know what detailed consideration, if any, was given by the PF to the possibility of prosecuting Mr Hamilton. The Lord Advocate should not prevent scrutiny of the authorities in this wholly exceptional case". Mr Campbell was backed by the SNP's home affairs spokeswoman, Roseanna Cunningham QC who said a clear explanation should be given by procurators fiscal.

In a statement read to the inquiry by Mr Bonomy, the Lord Advocate said that Alfred Vannet, regional procurator-fiscal for Grampian, had compiled an 18-page history of Hamilton's encounters with the procurator fiscal service. This report would give the "stated reasons" for the decisions which were taken and the Lord Advocate said that if the inquiry wished, present or former fiscals who had dealings with Hamilton could be called as "witnesses to the facts".

Mr Bonomy said: "It would however be incompatible with principle and practice... for the tribunal to subject the soundness of the decisions made in relation to Hamilton to detailed examination at the inquiry". The statement continued that it was a "fundamental principle" that prosecution decisions in Scotland were taken independently and free from outside pressure, by prosecutors accountable only to the Lord Advocate.

John McFall, Labour's Scottish home affairs spokesman, said: "Given the gravity of these matters, I would like to see the fullest discretion allowed to Lord Cullen who is, after all, an eminent judge appointed by the Government to carry out this inquiry as he sees fit."

Menzies Campbell, QC, home affairs spokesman for the Scottish Liberal Democrats, said: "The Lord Advocate has gone some way towards meeting the legitimate concern of the public that the Cullen Inquiry should have all the relevant information available to it."

Mr Campbell said the Lord Advocate should not take "an unduly restrictive view about what will be asked in questions. The rule is a convention, not a statute, and though the public interest lies in the confidentiality of prosecutions, **that can be overridden in these unique circumstances where the public interest lies in knowing exactly what happened in the run-up to the events at Dunblane**."

Lord Cullen ruled that the procurators fiscal who decided not to prosecute the killer Thomas Hamilton four times in five years should not be forced to justify their decisions. He substantially upheld the view of Scotland's senior law officer, the Lord Advocate, Lord Mackay of Drumadoon, that while the fiscals could appear before the inquiry, they could not be questioned on the correctness of their decisions. But he allowed leeway for submissions to be made on the decisions taken by the fiscals, including opinion on the correctness of those decisions.

Colin Campbell, QC, for the families of the 16 children who died at Dunblane Primary, argued against limited questioning, saying that the Lord Advocate had no "absolute veto" preventing scrutiny of decisions by public prosecutors. Mr Campbell argued that it was difficult to understand the purpose of providing a full explanation of what happened – a reference to an 18-page report on the fiscals' dealings with Hamilton prepared by an independent procurator fiscal – and then to deny the inquiry and Parliament the opportunity to consider the merits of what had been done.

Lord Cullen said he was satisfied on the one hand it would "not be proper" for the inquiry to require the prosecutors to justify their decisions or to entertain submissions as to the sufficiency of what was put forward in justification of these decisions. But he added that he saw no good reason why the inquiry should not entertain submissions based on the available evidence, saying: "I am not going to draw any hard and fast line to what can or cannot be submitted. It would certainly include the possibility of submissions as to whether a relevant charge could have been granted or whether in some circumstances some other decision could have been taken.".

Lord Cullen said he did not wish to inhibit submissions but it had to be clearly understood that they were to be based on available evidence "and do not enter into a review, in one form or another, of the decisions reached". He added. "I am content this inquiry should not require the soundness of the decisions be subjected to detailed examination of submissions, but I do wish to hear submissions based on the available evidence". Earlier, Mr Campbell noted there was potential conflict between the public prosecutor's independent, impartial role and the accountability of the law officer to Parliament. This conflict still exists.

He said: "However, it is one thing to leave it to the Lord Advocate or the fiscal to decide whether or not a prosecution should take place but another matter altogether whether, in appropriate circumstances, and in the public interest, it is appropriate to examine decisions already taken." It did not follow, he said, that the Lord Advocate had an absolute veto on all scrutiny on all acts and omissions of public prosecutors in Scotland.

The tribunal's purpose, he said, was not to influence decisions but to assist Parliament in considering the full circumstances of what happened and "more important than that, to assist Parliament in learning any necessary lessons and making necessary reforms in the public interest." The Crown counsel, Ian Bonomy, on behalf of the Lord Advocate, said either the principle existed or it did not. The result of infringing the principle would be that every decision made would be made under the threat of being called to account later. "It would be wrong for the inquiry to review the decisions made in the sense of reviewing the exercise of discretion undertaken by the fiscal, or for the inquiry to endeavour to do the job of the fiscal and decide what course of action would have been appropriate," he said.

So much for the public interest and knowing what happened in the run-up to Dunblane....

Gordon Crawford, the secretary of Stirling Rifle and Pistol Club where Hamilton occasionally shot, said that it was a pity that his club and Callander club were not legally represented at the Cullen Inquiry. "Blame has not been laid at the police's door where it should be," said Alex Boyd, the chairman of Callander Rifle and Pistol Club, which refused Hamilton membership just before the massacre. "Lord Cullen's report does not explore how Hamilton's lies went unexposed, nor the police's lack of understanding."

Good reasons for revocation or refusal of his licence abounded. However, Chief Constable William Wilson said that based on evidence heard by Lord Cullen, "there was enough" to contest any legal action by the parents (the parents never took any legal action against Central Scotland Police).

If, during the immediate aftermath, the media played their part in shutting down any real attempts to understand why 'Dunblane' happened, they appear to have no intention of re-examining all the evidence even now, ten years on.

On Sunday 2 October 2005, freelance journalist Marcello Mega had stories in several Scottish newspapers about the Dunblane parent Mick North claiming that "Top secret documents dispel the rumours of a cover-up". Those of us who have been campaigning for a New Inquiry into the Dunblane massacre for the last few years were not consulted and Mick North's views were reported as the truth. This is deeply irresponsible and dangerous journalism. Many of the points made by Mick North could easily be challenged, but those of us who have done the most work were not even contacted and have been given no right of reply. Thus, William Scott wrote directly to the journalist himself:

Dear Marcello, I was amazed to see that you used the headline, 'Top secret documents dispel the rumours of a cover-up', for your article in the Sunday Express. The documents released will certainly not dispel the belief that there has been a cover-up.

They are copies, not the originals, so there is no way of knowing if they have been tampered with or if in fact they have all been released. Since there is nothing of any consequence in the released papers why was it thought necessary to have them hidden for 100 years? They were only released yesterday and Dr North only recently took an interest in them so how could tens of thousands of pages be studied in such a short time to enable you to state so emphatically that there was no evidence of a cover-up?

Of course I never thought for one minute that the released documents would assist in the search for the truth. The Crown Office have known for quite some time that some of the papers would have to be released and have produced what they hope will be enough to stop any further questions being asked. It appears that in your case their efforts have been successful.

Some details of Hamilton's post mortem have been released. It was known that there was damage to his digestive system which suggested that he might have received a wound to a part of his body other than his head. The Lord Advocate explained that the damage was to the palate which is considered part of the digestive system. What has never been explained is why part of the autopsy is to remain hidden for 100 years. Questions about Hamilton's death remain unanswered.

As far as a paedophile ring is concerned you surely did not expect, if one exists, that proof would be found in the released papers? He had many visitors in expensive cars, some chauffeur driven, who were never identified. Why not?

It is ridiculous not to consider it a serious omission that a policeman, trained to observe and give evidence, was not called to appear before the Inquiry. It makes matters worse now that we know that there were two officers in the school and one at least was there at the time of the shootings. The Lord Advocate in an attempt to minimise the importance of that omission stated that David Scott, a student teacher, saw Hamilton shoot himself. However Mr Scott was not called to give evidence either and it is clear from the portions of his statement read to the Inquiry by a police inspector that he definitely did not see Hamilton shoot himself. Although the Lord Advocate named the teacher he refused to divulge the identity of the policeman.

Dr. North says "The QVS is barely mentioned." That in a nutshell sums up what was wrong with the Inquiry. It is what was not said and who was not called to give evidence that is behind all the suspicions.

For nearly six years I have been trying without success to establish where the authority came from to allow the imposition of a closure order. I suspect this is because there is no such authority as the Keeper of the Records of Scotland advised me some years ago. However if there is authority for the closure how can it be waived by the Lord Advocate to permit release of some of the documents? If the authorities are so evasive about the existence of a closure order why can they expect to be trusted over any other information regarding Dunblane?

You wrote "One neighbour said she had seen him getting out of a grey car at his home before walking to the van he had hired for his last journey. The grey car and its driver were never traced." That simply is just not true. The lady you refer to said that she saw a man in a grey car. The Lord Advocate informed me that the man in the grey car was another neighbour. If this was the case surely the lady would have named him and not referred to a neighbour as "a man in a grey car." This matter could not be resolved as neither was called to give evidence to the Inquiry.

I still feel there is doubt about the time Hamilton took to drive to the school. For many years I drove daily to and from Edinburgh and the time taken, irrespective of driving conditions, varied little. More recently I visited Grantshouse regularly which entailed a 30 minute drive. Again no matter whether I was in a hurry or the road congested the time taken varied little. On a fifteen minute journey the possibility of increasing or decreasing the time taken becomes even less. Of course if there had been an accident or road works causing a lengthy detour to be made then an increase in journey time could be expected but that explanation has never at any time been suggested.

You quote Dr North as saying that there was no evidence that friends in the Police Force had given any significant support to him. That may be so far as the released documents are concerned but a very valuable boat seized by Strathclyde Police was sold to Thomas Hamilton for the paltry, considering the quality of the vessel, sum of £5,000. There was no public auction. While he was on board there was an explosion or fire and the craft sank. It was recovered by police divers as a training exercise. From February 1977 to January 1996 Hamilton purchased an assortment of pistols, revolvers and rifles amounting to twelve guns in all. From January 1983 to October 1984 he had in his possession six hand guns and rifles. If nothing else these facts must arouse some doubt.

Lord Tebbit once wrote to me that what was needed was a good investigative journalist. Unfortunately that need is still there.

On 14 October 2005, William emailed me to say that Marcello had phoned him. He wrote:

He supported Dr North and suggested that I did not understand journalism but this was no more than I had expected. He tried to make out that the articles criticised the police but that was just waffle as the main thread through all the papers was that we should now accept that this was the end of the matter and that all the guilty parties remain untarnished. He tried to make out that he was only reporting Dr North's views but that was not made clear in the many publications under his name. I am no wiser as to why he wrote as he did. I know that it seems a ridiculous accusation against a journalist but could he somehow have become enthralled by Mick North?

CHAPTER 6 –

IN THE BEGINNING

7 December 2002 - And this is how it began. I was browsing around women's websites and I discovered 'Quines Online'. Saw a Research Request as follows:

Hi! I'm looking for an old newspaper, a copy of The Scotsman from 1996. It has to be the edition sent out on subscription, the First or Highlands & Islands Edition (it says that somewhere on the front, I'm told), and for Saturday 29 June 1996. No, it's not available at the British Library, they archive only the final, Edinburgh edition. No, the company deny having a copy of the article I remember reading in a paper sent to the NGO I was a volunteer for in 1996 which had the paper on subscription. I'm specifically interested in a report from the final day of the 1996 Cullen Inquiry into the Dunblane Massacre saying that McMurdo's police chauffeur had given evidence he'd been driving McMurdo to Thomas Hamilton's flat to visit him as a friend for years.

I'd greatly appreciate people living in The Scotsman's Highlands & Islands edition area taking a look in drawers and cupboards for the copy of the paper with this report in it. If you have any other information on the Dunblane Massacre, or any other relevant cuttings/papers – particularly from local papers, I'd be interested to hear from you. Regards, Norman Bassett.

I was curious and emailed a brief note to Mr Bassett.

Have you been successful in your research request, for a copy of The Scotsman from 1996? I have a friend who attended the Cullen Inquiry and might be able to cast some light on the evidence given by McMurdo's police chauffeur on the final day. What is your angle on this? What aspect of the Dunblane Massacre are you researching? Do you remember what you read exactly?

7 December 2002 Sandra, Hi, I'm very pleased to hear from you. Would you tell me who put you on to me? I was working as a volunteer for the Charter 88 pressure group in London in 1996 when the Dunblane Massacre took place. The organisation received all the major daily newspapers to keep an eye on the Press output. Among the papers was a SUBSCRIPTION COPY of both the Socialist Worker and The Scotsman newspapers.

Being interested in shooting I was reading The Scotsman's account of the 1996 Cullen Inquiry and read an article covering DCC McMurdo's final testimony on the last day of the eyewitness part of the Inquiry. The article said that DCC McMurdo's retired police chauffeur had given evidence that he'd driven McMurdo as a personal visitor to Thomas Hamilton's flat for three years about fortnightly. McMurdo then went on the witness stand again and confirmed this and said he'd previously been a friend of Thomas Hamilton's father.

I looked in the other newspapers and the Socialist Worker had a very simple report covering the same facts. No other newspaper had anything on the matter. The date on the two newspapers was Saturday 29 June 1996 and I read them approximately the following Thursday, that being the delay caused by the second class postal rate.

Tragically, I expected fireworks and allowed the copies of the newspapers to be discarded. No fireworks came along and I've not been able to obtain copies of these newspapers subsequently. It's a coverup.

The Scotsman comes out in FIVE DAILY EDITIONS and the First or Highlands & Islands Edition is the one sent out on subscription, the Final or Edinburgh edition is the one held on archive in Edinburgh, London etc. The Scotsman's archivist tells me they have no record of this article. The Socialist Worker's editor has sent me a personal letter saying he can find no trace in the SW archives of the article in question and I've looked at the archived edition in the London Newspaper Library and it's not in that. He says there was only one edition.

I've been up to Glasgow three times and to Edinburgh twice (from Manchester) looking for more information. I was given the name and phone number of one of the 10-14 journalists present at the 1996 Cullen Inquiry and he agreed completely with what I'd read in The Scotsman. I have to tell you that the Clerk to the Inquiry has flatly denied that this evidence was ever given. The journalist when I asked him to sign a witness statement to cover what he'd told me refused to do so. I have to conclude that he has been subject to some pressure.

If the shooting fraternity could obtain a copy of either of these newspaper reports or a witness statement from someone who'd been at the 1996 Cullen Inquiry and was willing to sign a witness statement to that effect and stick to their story, the entire 1996 Cullen Inquiry would be exposed as a sham, a coverup.

I've also been told that Scots BBC and ITV evening news reports from the Inquiry on that Friday evening covered McMurdo's testimony and said from outside Stirling Police HQ that they'd been told there was nobody available to comment on McMurdo's testimony. Both Scots BBC and ITV say to me they are unable to find any videotape or record of such a news item for Friday 28 June 1996.

In short, Sandra, your friend would be walking on hot bricks if he/she came out and confirmed that McMurdo had given testimony that he'd been a personal friend of Thomas Hamilton. They would be under pressure to shut up, but a signed witness statement or videotape of an interview with them would be very hard to dismiss. As would any newspaper article or copy thereof which covered this matter.

This remains a major political hot potato with all the considerations that derive from that. In short, it's a matter of courage and justice, but your friend can expect to be under pressure if they give personal testimony. If on the other hand I was supplied with a copy of The Scotsman or the Socialist Worker's article, I'd do the business and support what I've been telling the shooting fraternity publicly for the past six years with some evidence.

It's in short a paedophile coverup and reputedly Thomas Hamilton was the boy-supplier to Conservative Party Central Office. Getting the 1996 Cullen Inquiry exposed as a coverup even very partially (as above) would help unravel the coverup but wouldn't do the whole job, obviously. Let me know a bit more, please.

8 December 2002 Hi Norman, to put you in the picture, I came across your request for information on the Quines Online website last night (presumably you put it there because of its connections with the north east of Scotland). I was intrigued that someone was still searching for this kind of information after all this time.

There is no doubt in my mind that the Cullen Inquiry into the Shootings at Dunblane Primary School was a whitewash. It is extremely frustrating (understatement) that certain information has been "hidden away" under the 100-year-rule. I suspect that the material you are looking for will be contained within that. My friend says he doesn't recall hearing such evidence at the inquiry, but has heard this rumour – about McMurdo – before. Do you consider it to be a Freemason link? I have a press cutting from 22 March 1996 ("Masonic link may explain Hamilton's 'charmed life'") and could forward a copy if that would be of any interest to you. I would be interested to know how you get on with your search for the truth, but it doesn't look like I can help.

Hi Sandra, It would be MOST beneficial to me to obtain a copy of either The Scotsman's or the Socialist Worker's news reports I mentioned. A personal witness, curiously, might be of less use, although welcome. I've left my mark in the north of Scotland because that's where the Highlands & Islands edition of The Scotsman I'm interested in was distributed. DCC McMurdo had throughout the 1996 Cullen Inquiry up to his testimony on the final day said he'd only ONCE met Hamilton in the flesh, so he was "outed" by his police chauffeur on the final day of testimony as a perjurer. That's the real significance of his testimony and that's why the existence of his testimony is being denied.

54,000 pistol shooters had their pistols bought off them by force and then private pistol possession in England, Wales and Scotland was banned, so the passing of the years has made no difference at all to how they feel. The Inquiry buried two lots of information – a list of the boys the police had interviewed about sexual activity with Hamilton and the autopsy results on the victims. Either would be most interesting. If you come across anything more, do let me know, I'm permanently interested.

9 December 2002 Norman, How do you know the Cullen Inquiry buried these 2 lots of information (the list of boys interviewed about sexual activity with Hamilton, and the autopsy results on the victims?) I was aware that the post-mortem results were not to be disclosed, but are they actually held under the 100-year time-seal? I thought we (the public) were not informed what information was being witheld under the 100 year rule....

9 December 2002 Hi Sandra, You can write and ask the Scottish Office. The information was given on TV and in the papers at the time. The boys information has a 100-year seal on it, the post-mortem results are just being held as too personal to be available to the public/media. Post-mortem results are not too personal from other Public Enquiries, though. A strong smell of dead rat emanates from that, too. Here's the Official Transcript of the 1996 Cullen Inquiry on the web:

http://www.scotland.gov.uk/library3/justice/dunblane/dunblane-00.asp

And the 1996 Cullen Inquiry Report:

http://www.official-documents.co.uk/document/scottish/dunblane/dunblane.htm

You can search them both with a little more difficulty in the latter one. You can get a printed copy of the 1996 Cullen Inquiry Report for about £20 from the Stationery Office, the Transcript is not available in hard copy but can be inspected in Edinburgh, Stirling Council's archives and by MPs only in the House of Commons Library. The Transcript in hard copy is about 14" high and having visited it in Edinburgh once I got it put on the web with the help of a shooting association I'm a member of, the BASC.

Getting confirmation that McMurdo and his chauffeur gave that testimony that he'd been a personal visitor to Thomas Hamilton's flat for years would bust the whole coverup open and I think in time it would be WIDE open. If it could be shown that Cullen deliberately falsified his Inquiry Transcript and Report the government would not be able to resist calls to open the whole can of worms up.

One of the witnesses at the Inquiry said that a policeman was one of the three most regular visitors to Hamilton's flat – Mrs Grace Ogilvie on Day Three of the Transcript – but her testimony as printed in the Transcript is very mildly ambiguous and the questioner didn't ask any more questions about it. That's like the end of a ball of string sticking out, it just needs pulling on, but apparently Mrs Ogilvie was being less that clear on the subject when interviewed recently.

The whole business stinks, Sandra. I can trust hardly anyone I know in the shooting line to be honest about this. It's a really HOT hot potato politically. Paedophile policemen and politicians. But such have been mentioned before when various boys' homes scandals have been opened up. Keep asking questions!

9 December 2002 Hi Norman, Already have a printed copy of the 1996 Cullen Inquiry Report. Haven't ever read the Official Transcript though, but have started to do that now. The link you gave me for the Official Transcript, is that the one you organised to be put on the web (with the help of BASC)? Have now read Mrs Grace Ogilvie's testimony and it didn't seem at all ambiguous to me. Given the degree of questioning of witnesses in the previous 2 days, I am astounded that no further questions were asked when she referred to Hamilton's regular visits by the police.... . Who was it who interviewed her recently? And what exactly did she say? Was it a face-to-face interview, or over the phone? Was she interviewed by a man or a woman?

Why can't you "trust hardly anyone you know in the shooting line to be honest about this?" Honest about which bit? That the Cullen Inquiry was a police/paedophile cover-up? I wasn't sure from what you wrote....surely your fellow shooters have the same goal in mind as you? How does your view differ?

I have a friend who is going to the Outer Hebrides for Xmas/New Year, and have spoken to him about looking for the issue of The Scotsman you are seeking (perhaps you have already looked in Stornoway Library?) It is very much a needle-in-a-haystack though, isn't it?

It will take me a while to get through the transcript, but I was also surprised to read that the Headteacher, Mr Taylor, did not make a 999 call (just an "ordinary" call) when phoning for help, and no questions were asked about that either (like who did he call? Dunblane Police Station?) He has subsequently been "removed" from his job by the way.... Keep supplying answers!

10 December 2002 Hi Sandra, There are two principal documents involved: (1) The 1996 Cullen Inquiry Transcript, and (2) The 1996 Cullen Report. Note that Lord Cullen did a public inquiry into the Piper Alpha Disaster previous to the 1996 Dunblane Massacre Inquiry and has co-hosted a twin rail disaster inquiry in England since then. THREE public inquiries have his name on them.

The 1996 Cullen Inquiry Transcript is the one I got the British Association for Shooting and Conservation (BASC) of which I am a member to push the Scottish Office to encode for the internet. I had previously asked them in my own name to do that, but they had refused on the basis of lack of public interest. I got Bill Harriman the "Head of Firearms" at the BASC to propose it additionally to my request – they have 110,000 members – and the Scottish Office put it into Adobe Acrobat format for the web and it's been up since about January 2001.

Mrs Grace Ogilvie's testimony CAN be misunderstood. I think you've just done that. If you read the start of her examination she was specifically asked about regular visitors to Thomas Hamilton's flat, as I recollect over the five year period previous to the Massacre. She mentions THREE REGULAR VISITORS by their vehicles. The STV (Scottish TeleVision) liveried vehicle whose runner's testimony is given in the Transcript and "The Police". In the context in which the questions were posed "who were his regular visitors" you have a choice of seeing that as "who were his regular PERSONAL visitors" or not. In fact both the STV and gardener confirmed that though theirs were business vehicles they were visiting Hamilton as personal friends. "The Police" refers to the vehicle Mrs Ogilvie saw and it's ambiguous as to whether that was one individual – ie McMurdo in a chauffeured police vehicle – or various policemen in various police vehicles visiting Hamilton on official police business. Nobody at the Inquiry suggested that for five years fortnightly/monthly Hamilton had a policeman in a police vehicle visit his flat. The implication is that though there's a little ambiguity which isn't cleared up by further questions, the visitor was a personal one and the same person. McMurdo's testimony on the final day of the witness part of the Inquiry confirmed what his police chauffeur said – ie he was a regular personal visitor about fortnightly for over three years to the knowledge of his police chauffeur.

A lady researcher under contract to the BBC, whose name and local contact I can give you if you wish, interviewed Mrs Ogilvie on camera and in the presence of her husband and the interviewer's local contact to the best of my knowledge. The local contact says she said when asked that it was a traffic police sergeant who she saw. That's where ambiguity creeps in, since I imagine that would describe the police chauffeur to McMurdo. The BBC's lawyers, so the researcher told me, said that either she had sufficient evidence to accuse McMurdo of paedophilia and they'd broadcast it, or she didn't and they should not broadcast it. In their opinion she didn't have that evidence and the program was therefore canned. She's now in the USA and though I can give you her local contact's details and her last email address she has not responded to my emails recently.

Read Mrs Ogilvie's testimony PREAMBLE again, she's asked for regular visitors and the implication is they're regular PERSONAL visitors. The point about Mrs Ogilvie is her address is in the Transcript and you can work out her age – go around and visit her in person, I'd suggest to you. She failed to respond to my letter to her asking for further details and is obviously ageing, but my letter was mentioned by her to the BBC researcher.

The reporter – stringer – who was one of 10-14 such at the Inquiry and who confirmed what it said in the two news reports I saw – says there were a great deal of witnesses and they all got into the box and out again promptly so they could all be interviewed. Obviously they could be questioned either more or less according to choice or instruction.

Trust – if I had a copy of those two reports in my hand today I'd spread copies of them around far and wide and put photos of them on the internet. I suspect that copies have been sent to some of the shooting organisations and they've said nothing.

This is a CONSERVATIVE PARTY coverup – they were in power at the time. The Usual Suspects in paedophile scandals are "policemen, politicians and local businessmen". There are paedophiles in all four Scottish parties and presumably that's why it's such a good cover-up. Anyone who's a homosexual, a homosexual paedophile or a heterosexual paedophile is liable to be blackmailed or in covert associations. They conspire together, they can be blackmailed, they have criminal records they'd like to remain publicly unstressed. Whether this is their own scandal or they wouldn't like it to come out if they were involved in something similar, there's a lot of people in the UK – 270,000 according to one police estimate given on Radio 4's Today program – who are active paedophiles.

The reporter who confirmed the newspaper articles I read lives on Orkney, incidentally. I've written and emailed around the public libraries in Scotland – they keep back issues for only six months before discarding them. Yes, it's a needle in a haystack, but what a needle... Keep asking.

10 December 2002 Hi Sandra, I was looking you up on the google.com and found the below letter referred to (bottom). So you actually live in Dunblane? Could I suggest a couple of lines of inquiry – did Thomas Hamilton know Gwen Mayor personally? did Thomas Hamilton know the children he murdered from somewhere? It seems curious to me that Hamilton would murder only ONE of the three teachers present and not murder ALL the children. He killed himself in possession of 4 working pistols and hundreds of rounds of working ammunition.

Mrs Ogilvie's evidence in the Transcript includes her home address. I'd get round and speak to her pronto. I've considered visiting her but it's expensive from Manchester and I don't really want to knock on her door without a female companion and a videocamera, so I've held off doing that. I'd also suggest you speak to some of Hamilton's personal enemies – I'd miss Comrie Deuchars off that list, were I you. Speak to the ladies who threw muck at him in Stirling – Mrs Hagger, was it, and her daughter?

Incidentally, one of the computer options when looking at the 1996 Cullen Inquiry Transcript is to load the whole file into your RAM and Search it (binoculars symbol) end to end. I'm using an internet café's equipment and it has endless RAM, but if your PC can manage it it's a lot easier searching the whole Transcript for STV, Gillespie (the contract gardener), McMurdo etc than Searching day by day.

I think you could ask around Dunblane about wife-swapping clubs, too. I suspect Hamilton was bisexually paedophilic and you should be listening out for family-sex swapping clubs, a simple extension on wife-swapping clubs. Be appropriately careful and make sure someone reliable knows what you're doing and where you're going and who you're going to see.

Oh, Gwen Mayor's injuries appear to be from a press report one shot through her forearm and upper arm, a shot in the groin and once across the chest and one to finish her off in her eye. If she was shot through both breasts and in the genitals that would be relevant, but I can't tell that from the press description.

"DUNBLANE MASONIC PAEDOPHILES"

The following letter is copied from Scotland on Sunday, page 16, 30 August 1998, Sandra Uttley of Dunblane.

"It was good of C Martin McGibbon (grand secretary of the grand lodge of Scotland) to write in your paper confirming that Dunblane killer Thomas Hamilton was never a member of his organisation (Letter 23 August). However, William Burns (16 August) is correct in stating that many people are flabbergasted that the Cullen Enquiry seemed to ignore Hamilton's Masonic affiliation. It is a question that has never been addressed, which is why the issue of Freemasonry cannot be disregarded...

According to the Scotsman (22 March 1996), a senior Scottish freemason told the paper that Hamilton had been a Mason for a number of years and had visited functions at different lodges. Given the evidence we now have about the number of senior police officers who are themselves Freemasons, the link between Masons and Hamilton's actions, both prior to March 1996, and on the day, must be examined if we are ever to find a "satisfactory answer to the question why" that William Paul (Spectrum 9 August) believes we will never know. Whether Hamilton was a mason or ex-Freemason (thus presumably anti-mason), the lack of exploration of this issue and the total unaccountability of Central Scotland Police (bar one resignation) leaves a festering wound over the already massive scar of Dunblane. To simply describe Hamilton as a "warped human being" doesn't do justice to the complexity of an individual's relationship with certain organisations, be it police, local government or a Masonic lodge. The pernicious influence of freemasonry on all our public bodies – and potentially on the new Scottish parliament – is ignored at our peril."

On 10 December 2002 I discovered a website named <u>Cullen Uncovered</u> set up by Greg Lance Watkins. Quote from Hansard 12 May 1998: Lord Burton asked Her Majesty's Government:

Whether they will place in the Library of the House a copy of the Report by Sergeant, now Inspector, Hughes, of Central Police, into Thomas Hamilton; to list all the charges to which he recommended consideration for prosecution; and whether they will state why the Report is not listed in the index or appendix to Lord Cullen's Report into the Dunblane tragedy.

Lord Sewel: This report was made to the Procurator Fiscal while Thomas Hamilton was alive. It was therefore not a submission to Lord Cullen's Inquiry, but the Inquiry took account of it as a production. Lord Cullen did not list productions in the report or in the appendix. Mr Hughes' report is, however, referred to at pages 34-36 of the Cullen Report.

Lance Watkins also includes the following letter on his website: this letter was first sent in November 1996 to The Press & Journal of Aberdeen, HRH the Duke of Edinburgh and The Gun Club of Great Britain. No response was received. The substance was as a result sent to The House of Commons subsequently no response thereto was received.

"With regard to recent publicity correlating secret organisations with paedophilia, particularly the Free Masons, I would like to bring to your attention the link between the abuse of boys at the Queen Victoria School (QVS), Dunblane, the large presence of Freemasons in that establishment and the slaughter of 16 children and a teacher at Dunblane by Thomas Hamilton on 13 March 1996. As far as I know no such link was revealed in the Cullen Report. In June 1994 I released a report about my own experience as a housemaster at QVS. A copy of my report was sent to almost every Scottish education authority in July 1994. I believe that, had my allegations in 1991 been properly investigated, there is a strong possibility that Hamilton would have been discovered. His signatures in the visitors log have been removed. The awful slaughter in March 1996 could have been prevented by an impartial police investigation..

In my report of June 1994 I accused the Ministry of Defence (MOD), the Scottish Office and the Procurator Fiscal of a deliberate cover up and of maladministration at the QVS. The Masonic presence in the local police and the QVS was strong. It is a fact that Hamilton was enrolled in Lodge Number 1417 (Garrow Hill) in 1977. He was granted a firearms certificate in 1977. It was no idle boast when Hamilton claimed he was "a friend of the police" (Masons). In March 1996, just after the slaughter, Hamilton's file went missing. Hamilton was a regular visitor to the primary department of QVS. I saw him on several occasions as a friend of a housemaster. He was one of many visitors. I presume the school security had cleared him. Nothing of this was in the Cullen report. Lord Cullen is a Mason with a duty to protect brother Masons. There is evidence to show corruption and maladministration by the police".

Greg Lance Watkins' meeting for the Cambridge University DM, by Idris Francis: A small but respectably sized audience seemed spellbound as Greg spoke eloquently on the subject of "The Abuse of Power" and the remarkable defects of the Cullen report into the Dunblane shootings. The defects in the Cullen report into the Dunblane affair were covered in considerable detail with documentary provenance – the extraordinary suppression of a Police report on the murderer Hamilton prior to the shootings and other documents, embargoed for the extraordinary period of 100 years, the refusal of the Government to answer Lords questions on the documents or their suppression, the trainee teacher "witness", neither named nor listed in the report, who claimed to have seen Hamilton shoot himself TWICE in the mouth (remarkable enough in itself) in glaring contradiction to the sworn evidence of the headmaster that he had seen Hamilton breathing and moving when lying on the gymnasium floor afterwards, the suppression of the autopsy on Hamilton, the absence of any evidence relating to bullet matching or injuries, and of the solicitor who had been found drowned in his car in a lake with 2 bullet wounds in the head (verdict suicide).

Nothing was documented by Cullen about Hamilton's known activities as a supplier of pornography and worse to local deviants, and associated blackmail, nor about the boat, seized by police from an unconnected person and given or "sold" to Hamilton, without record of payment. Greg systematically painted a picture which could not make sense unless very senior people were involved in the affair and the cover-up. George Robertson, now NATO chief, was the local MP at the time (*writer's note – this is incorrect – it was Michael Forsyth*), and some believe he might have signed Hamilton's firearm application. Masonic links are believed to exist between some of the players, and other links are believed to exist to rumoured activities and proclivities of Cabinet Ministers. It is suspected that Conservative co-operation in the suppression of part of the Cullen report may have been agreed with the then Opposition on a quid-pro-quo basis.

William Palfreman: After Greg's excellent talk, I have come to the considered conclusion that the events surrounding the Dunblane massacre, and the subsequent submissions to the Cullen enquiry that have been put under to 100 years of secrecy, far outweigh in political significance issues such as our opposition to the EU and what it entails. It is inconceivable that T Blair, Jack Straw and Gordon Brown can survive in office as this matter becomes known. It totally undermines the Labour government, and could easily be a case of the Queen feeling she has to use reserve powers to call an emergency general election, such would be the loss of confidence. This scandal is far more important than anything that has happened here in living memory, in fact I can think of no parallel for it. It certainly pisses all over anything that happened to Kennedy or was done by Nixon. I am surprised, given the gravity of this matter, that attempt has yet to be made on his life, for surely we are dealing with desperate people here. It also explains a few strange things, such as just why T Blair and co were so keen to ban all handguns, and why such obviously talentless nobodies like George Robertson have risen from being backbench nobodies a couple of years ago to Defence Secretary, and now Secretary-General of NATO.

Put it together yourself. Ostensibly, Thomas Hamilton, a man who has moved from town to town in Scotland setting up 'Boys clubs', suspected of paedophilia for years, took his guns into the Dunblane school gym and brutally murdered a large number of five year old children inside, before turning the gun on himself (ALLEGEDLY). Nowhere in this is there a national security risk so great, that documents – part of the public enquiry – are now state secrets to be held for 100 years? Funny kind of public enquiry. Why, when Thomas Hamilton's application for a gun licence was turned down, due to him being regarded as a man of unsound character and him being the object of several paedophilia investigations, did his MP, our friend George Robertson (*again, Hamilton's MP was Michael Forsyth*), write him a glowing character reference, and personally see to it that his application was successful, when he knew the grounds for the original refusal were because he was suspected of procuring boys for sexual services?

Or take a boat seized on Loch Lomond by the Strathclyde Police. It is a very rare thing for assets to be seized in the UK, as there are no asset-forfeiture laws. When it does happen, there is normally a trial at least, with things only being seized if they are proven to be bought with money proven to be the consequence of a proven crime. Even then, they are sold by public auction. How come, then, was this very valuable boat sold for the tiny sum of £5000, without an auction, to none other than our friend Thomas Hamilton, a man of no financial means whatsoever, nor a sailor, nor lived anywhere near any open water. Why did not the boats owner complain about having their property stolen from them in this manner? I can only conclude because it was being used for some very serious criminal activity, and those on board were merely glad to escape prosecution. Also, it seems rather odd in such circumstances that not only were the owners happy to avoid prosecution enough to lose a valuable boat, but that the Strathclyde Police were not willing to prosecute. And yet, after these improbable events, it wound up in none other than our friend Hamilton's hands. Could he have been a blackmailer as well as a paedophile?

But the main thing is what might explain sections of the public enquiry that are now under the hundred year rule. There are only three levels of secrecy in the UK for state secrets, the 30 year rule, the 80 year rule and the 100 year rule. Normal secrets, like Cabinet discussions, government papers, espionage, all that, are under the 30 year rule. Only a very small number of things ever reached the 80 year rule, particularly events in the Sudan with Kitchener in 1902, where it seems that an act of genocide was committed, and some things that happened 1914-18, as well as things like potential peace negotiations in 1941, and just about everything to do with the IRA (after all, people are still alive after 30 years) come under the 80 year rule. Of them, the darkest of state secrets, when the events of '02 were getting a bit close to their limit for comfort, a further class of secrets was created to last a hundred years, and a tiny number of things were put in it – eg. Kitchener in '02, some World War 1 things.

But none of these things can be said to apply to Dunblane. That was ordinary murders, of a kind that happen from time to time. Even if a backbench Labour MP was implicated, or may have been involved in a large paedophile ring in Scotland, that is not a matter of vital national importance. You have a prosecution, there is a bit of a scandal, everyone is disgusted and one MP goes to prison. Big deal, such things happen. You certainly would not make such information a state secret just to save one unnamed backbench nobody's miserable neck. Governments simply don't go to such extreme lengths to save nobodies – power broking just doesn't work like that. There must be issues of profound national importance working here, and I put it to you that anything that involves certain events in Scotland is more likely to be someone of cabinet level than anything else. If Thomas Hamilton was the centre of a paedophile ring in Scotland that procured boys to people of the highest rank…. the government would fall.

What the hell had I got myself into?!?!!!!!!!

11 December 2002 – My next email to Norman: First of all, I would be very interested in having the journalist's name, address and phone no (perhaps he would tell me who the other journalists present were? Or have you already asked?) Also, who is the "local contact" you refer to? I'm not rushing into anything. I really do want to read the whole transcript first. As you say, my angle is completely different from yours, and my interpretation of certain aspects of the inquiry will also differ (for example, I have always been dubious about the headteacher – from the moment he made his little speech about "evil visited our school today" – to the situation surrounding his leaving Dunblane Primary School a year or so after the massacre. Reading the transcript about his not making a 999 call has made me even more suspicious).

I have often wanted to go and interview certain people, like Doreen Hagger (her daughter died from a drugs overdose a few years ago by the way, and the implication was that she couldn't handle not being believed about Hamilton, and wished she could have done more….) I would also like to talk to Anne Anderson, the last police officer to deal with Hamilton's firearms certificates and who was extremely uncomfortable when she was with him in his house (she has since resigned from the service). But I don't have any "authority" to do so, although I am now inclined to just give myself that "authority".

In the first few years following the atrocity here, I waited for the bereaved parents to take legal action against the police. They had up to 3 years to do this, and in the end, they didn't. As far as I'm concerned, Central Scotland Police has got away with murder. And as far as Dunblane, the town/community is concerned, they like to pretend the massacre didn't happen, particularly our local Tory councillors (one of whom is involved with a mason – Dunblane is riddled with freemasonry).

When the legal action against the police didn't happen, I decided I had no choice but to get on with my own life, which I did. My particular interest is "women's issues, aka feminism" which is how I came across your research request – looking at Scottish women's websites. So it's a bit of a fluke that we have ended up communicating, because we are poles apart. You, a shooter! Me, a feminist! You are my supposed 'enemy', and I would like to bet that you have no time for 'feminists'…. My particular angle, you see, is "male violence", and I am very angry indeed that one of the worst examples of that has been swept under (what I call) a Cullen-made-carpet.

I really don't want to get into any discussion with you about either your interest in shooting* , or my interest in feminism. We will never see eye-to-eye, of that I am sure. But as you say, you are not me (and I am not you!) but you are being helpful... and I believe I could be too. Your information about these newspaper reports is the first concrete evidence I have had about the 'cover-up' about Dunblane, and I admire your tenacity in trying to track down copies of these. When you actually live in a place where something like this has happened, it is hard to separate rumour from fact, and as a consequence, everything gets put down to rumour. There are enormous pressures here to let this whole matter go. I am so disgusted by that, I continually think about leaving.

It was never my intention to 'revisit' the Cullen cover-up, but as I say, I accidently came across your research request. A lot of what you have to say strikes a chord with me, and maybe I should just try and find the confidence to go out there and ask a few questions, instead of retreating from the whole thing once again. I don't know what will happen.

Thomas Hamilton brought the spectre of paedophilia out into the public domain, but only in a very limited way (because of the cover-up). Bizzarely, it was the death of just one child (Sarah Payne) that brought it right out into the open. I think the deaths of 16 children was just too much for people to cope with and that's one of the reasons why the lid has been clamped down on this. But it is my belief that most cover-ups start to unravel about 10 years after the event, so only 3 years to go... Time to read some more of the transcript.

* presumably you want the handgun ban lifted, but uncovering the truth about the Cullen Inquiry doesn't automatically mean that will happen – Cullen himself did not advocate a handgun ban – it was a political decision – and I believe it will always remain so...

12 December 2002 Hi Sandra, Here's the details on the journalist: BV, Orkney, Tel ******* His wife usually answers the phone and he's out and she doesn't know when he'll be back. I leave it up to you if/how you introduce my name into it, but bear in mind that he has threatened to get the police onto me if I "harass" him further by phoning him or writing to him again. I leave that to you. The most he can do is to confirm, if he's willing to do so, that he was one of 10-14 journalists present at the 1996 Cullen Inquiry into the Dunblane Massacre and to tell you what he recalls of the Inquiry. I asked him about the other journalists present but he said he was unable to identify them in detail.

If I were you I would tape-record all your phone calls to him. You can get a pocket cassette-recorder for about £25 from Argos and a microphone with a cup to attach it to the side of your phone to pick up the phone call probably from Sinclair Electronics or Tandy shops for about £5. (I could send you one or both items if you wish, but I'd expect you to refund the money). I really would advise recording the phone conversations – had I done that before phoning him I'd have had at least that confirmation to support my recollection of the newspaper articles. If you send someone round to his house, they can turn on such a tape recorder in their pocket to record the conversation on the doorstep, turn the tape over in the toilet etc. If you were talking to Mrs Ogilvie I'd ask her permission first.

My local contact is a shooter: J, Tel: ******* Email: ******** The BBC contract researcher is now a friend of J above but he tells me she's working in America – MIGHT be back for Christmas, note – ASK ABOUT THAT. I've had no response to my latest emails to her, it's possible she has another email address – ask J for it. J is the one who I believe was with S when she interviewed Mrs Ogilvie and he tells me she said that the policeman was a sergeant in traffic division – that's a man in uniform with sergeant's stripes on his sleeve. That MAY be DCC McMurdo's chauffeur she's talking about, J and S don't seem to have pinned her down about that. I'd ask around your feminist circle if anyone recalls the Friday evening TV news report (28 June 1996) from outside Stirling Police HQ. That could be very useful confirmation and you could make a friend that way.

You'll find that in the US a lot of women carry pistols for self-defence and that's a major part of shooting in the USA. You'll find a lot of US feminist websites advocating women carrying pistols to defend themselves on the internet. US feminists are NOT opposed to shooting – it's empowering. Get in contact with them by email – they're all opposed to violence against women and they could be very encouraging under the circumstances and very helpful to you.

I really would advise you to make contacts locally as indicated – with Mrs Hagger, with Mrs Ogilvie, with the policewoman you mention, with the two teachers Hamilton didn't seem to want to kill. I think the distribution of £6 million from the Snowdrop Fund probably took the impetus out of the families' desire to sue the local police. Keep communicating.

12 December 2002 Norman, Must stress, I do not believe Hamilton's victims were targeted personally. Given that you are aware of the paedophile/police/possible conservative party (maybe freemason) cover-up, I'm surprised you think he had it in for the teacher Gwen Mayor (in particular) and the individual children who died. I am 100% certain that is not the case. The 2 teachers who survived crawled away into another room, and in his shooting spree he obviously forgot about them (and the 4 or 5 boys who hid in the store room with them). If they had still been 'visible' to him, I'm sure he would have "finished them off" (to use your expression).

One of the teachers has said she thinks he lost track of time and that sounds perfectly feasible to me. He had previously made enquiries about how long it would take for a police hit-squad to arrive on scene in the event of a mass shooting, which is why he didn't ultimately use all his ammunition. It would appear that he intended to kill everyone in the school, but got his timing for school assembly wrong – and only came across the gym class. As far as we are all aware, he hadn't killed anybody before that day, and he wouldn't have known how he would react once he had. Basically, he killed himself before the police got the chance to kill him. You are reading too much into the fact that 2 teachers survived (you should read more into the fact that so many girls died, and not boys...)

13 December 2002 Hi Sandra, Hamilton according to the Transcript was instructing boys on how to use airguns and crossbows when he was a teenager. As a man he was instructing boys in his clubs in gymnastics and running them through PT like a PT teacher. That's a personality characteristic. I suspect he was trained as a gym instructor somewhere – maybe for just a few months – and that may be the tie in to Gwen Mayor. Anyhow, with no further investigation to bring out more facts, it's just theorising.

Have you spoken to J? It's possible S is going to be visiting him over Christmas and you could get the chance to talk to them both. With reference to the small Sony cassette-recorders, I discover mine in fact has NOT got a phone-bug input socket, this one is different from other models which still have those, but I'm pretty sure just holding it beside the earpiece would pick up conversations. I do urge you to speak to J and get over and see him, he's in your neighbourhood. Soon, I think, would be a lot better than after Christmas.

14 December 2002 Norman, Why isn't the police chauffeur's evidence on the internet version of The Transcript? (silly question) Do you think it's likely to be in certain hard copies of the transcript? I am going to look at my friend's hard copy of the transcript this weekend (I doubt that the chauffeur's evidence is in any of the archived copies – it has obviously been spirited away).

Have emailed S with a view to meeting up. Will let you know if/when I hear from her. I'll contact J if I don't hear anything by early next week. I can assure you that I am doing lots of work in terms of contacting people locally, but don't want to say anything more at this point.

14 December 2002 Hi Sandra, I've been to Edinburgh like I said previously to look at the hard copy of the 1996 Cullen Inquiry Transcript and there's nothing in it at all on that final day of eyewitness testimony about any police chauffeur's evidence or DCC McMurdo concurring in it. The Clerk to the Inquiry in Stirling and three solicitors for parties at the Inquiry deny any recollection of it. There are only TWO hard copies of the Transcript available to the public – the one in Stirling Council's archives and the one in Edinburgh National Library. There's another the public can't get to inspect in the House of Commons Library. I doubt that the testimony is in any of those copies but I can only vouch for the Edinburgh copy and the online Transcript. I know that hard copies of the daily Transcript were initially being sold at the Inquiry and after a few days and a Parliamentary protest given out free to interested persons.

That's what I've been saying, Sandra, I've seen two news reports about McMurdo's final day's testimony in confirmation of what his police chauffeur said, the one in The Scotsman and the one in the Socialist Worker, which the papers concerned deny the existence of.

That's an email address for S I've not had any luck in getting a response from for over a year. I would consider it a dead duck and move directly on to contacting J – preferably today. S may well be visiting him over Christmas.

14 December 2002 Hi Norman, A neighbour of mine works at The Scotsman and has agreed to look for the copy you are searching for. Obviously, as the archivist has told you they have no record of this article, The Scotsman is going to great lengths to keep it hidden. Do I tell my neighbour this? If I don't, he might just think he can be upfront about what he's looking for. Then again, if I do tell him, he might not want to do it (putting his job in jeopardy). So, I'm not sure how to handle this. I also asked him about a list of organisations/individuals who received it on subscription, but he hasn't commented on that (obviously assuming he'll find the copy himself). One of his sons went to Hamilton's club at Dunblane High, but only 3 times because they weren't happy with the way the club was run, specifically that the boys had to strip to their shorts, but also that the gym doors were locked (which I hadn't heard before). So he probably is keen to help, but I'm not sure how much to tell him. I was sounding him out first about whether he would help me find the relevant paper and he seems willing to do that. Please advise. Sandra

Fumbling around – still trying to understand all this – I wrote to my friend for advice, who wrote to a friend of hers. Her reply:

15 December 2002 Yes, he said that the media contact the relevant government departments (where he is concerned, MOD) usually to get clarification or a statement. If the subject is seen to be of a nature threatening to national security, the Govt dept will put a "D" notice on the subject, asking the media not to broadcast part or all of the subject matter. The media does not HAVE to take notice, but I suspect it usually does. He said the D Notices are usually issued before anything has gone to press, but it is possible that they can be activated after the first broadcast. He also said that the "library" will hold copies of all the editions of the newspaper. What he didn't clarify was whether he meant the Scotsman's own library or the National Library. But a phone call to the Scotsman would quickly clarify this. Hope the above helps!

15 December 2002 Norman, Have you heard of "D" Notices? This is what might have been slapped on the newspaper report after the first edition went out. A government department can ask the media not to broadcast all or part of the subject matter. The media does not HAVE to take notice, but I suspect it usually does. D Notices are usually issued before anything has gone to press, but is it possible that they can be activated after the first broadcast. All copies of each edition are apparently on microfiche, but don't know whether the person I was speaking to meant the newspaper's library or the main library in Edinburgh. Perhaps my neighbour will find out for me. I intend to speak to him tomorrow about his search on Tuesday. Hope you can get back to me before then. Sandra

Oh boy, how naïve I was back then...

16 December 2002 Hi Sandra, First, all emails are read by the US National Security Agency and our equivalent (GCHQ) for military intelligence reasons. So, you can expect The Scotsman to be forewarned about your neighbour's neighbour's (your) intentions. If you intend to do anything remotely potentially offensive to the UK government, then don't tell me about it on the internet via email, or by mail, or on the phone. In my opinion The Scotsman's files have been sanitized and there's nothing left in the offices or archives or computers to find. On the other hand, asking people in the printing department about what they recall being pulled off the First Edition may just hit gold.

You don't need a D (Defence) Notice to get things out of the newspaper, you just get a solicitor to phone up the newspaper's solicitor and say unless this unwarranted allegation is removed from your newspaper we will commence a libel action against you. That's usually enough to get anything but the Editor's particular interest out of the paper and the newspapers having the attention-span of a housefly anyway it's not likely to get put back in Monday's newspaper if it was taken out of Saturday's. There's also the usual Old Pals Network where someone influential – like the Lord Lieutenant of the County or someone from the Scottish Office or Conservative Central Office in Edinburgh – phones up the newspaper proprietor and asks him for a small favour.

I don't think your pal would be in any danger of losing his job unless he pushed hard in areas where his curiousity was unwanted. It's really a matter of intelligence-gathering – it's not impossible at all but you have to expect them to expect you and to be appropriately cautious. So, if you're making confidential enquiries, Sandra, don't tell me about it in emails, letters or on the phone if you want to keep it confidential and to get somewhere.

A question for YOU: What is the current status of the Snowdrop Campaign Money? Was it all given out? That's an estimated £6 million donated during 1996 on the basis that it was to help prevent the suffering of siblings of the murdered children. That means in practice to fund repeated visits to Disney World in California, to buy their parents houses etc.

16 December 2002 Norman, Why do you want to know about the money? What does that have to do with uncovering the Cullen Inquiry?

16 December 2002 Hi Sandra, The money was not collected nor distributed by a registered Charity, so it has not received the usual legal regulation – which £6m in donations obviously deserves. Nor is it an easy matter to either enquire about it or find out how it was disbursed. Apparently some retired Colonel did the disbursing. There has been some press interest – the press helped publicise the Snowdrop Appeal, so that's not unreasonable.

I'm interested in uncovering where the money went and to whom for what – a dependent coverup, you might say. If there were any funds left over and the money could be converted for the uses of a legally-constituted Charity with appropriate objects then it could possibly be used against paedophiles and to help in uncovering Thomas Hamilton's paedophile activities. I think you're pretty soon going to be told by J and S that with some money for expenses a lot more could be done to open up the Hamilton affair.

17 December 2002 Norman, Just to clarify one point: the Snowdrop Campaign to ban handguns (now defunct) was completely distinct from the Dunblane Fund. The former had no money, but was supported by the Sunday Mail. It was set up and run by volunteers, some of whom were bereaved parents. The Dunblane Fund on the other hand (run by the local authority), was established as a result of people sending in donations. Its primary purpose was to "use the funds and any income accruing to make provision for the relief of loss suffered by those affected by the tragedy". And payments were not confined to the bereaved and injured children's families. Subsidiary purposes included provision of a suitable memorial, and provision for the benefit of the community. The Fund closed in 1999 and the residual balance was passed on to the Dunblane Community Trust, the primary purpose of which is to fund and support a Youth Centre in the town (now underway). Tell J and your fellow shooters that.

As I previously said to you, there is great pressure here to forget about what happened. "The money" was itself a great source of contention amongst different groups (I have heard worse insults here about how the money was used). The families themselves never requested money, and there was no attempt to have fund-raising schemes. The general public simply wanted to "do something".

You are way off the mark with so many aspects of this tragedy (the word "atrocity" seems more appropriate to me). You are only involved in this because you want the gun legislation over-turned. I am involved because I want genuine justice for those who died, their bereaved families, and let's not forget, all those injured children. Unfortunately I don't belong to a particular "interest group" like you, and I have felt very isolated in my belief that a gross injustice has been done here. That isolation will obviously have to continue.

17 December 2002 Hi Sandra, It's a great pity the public who wanted to do something didn't contribute to an investigatory fund or one which combated paedophiles, isn't it? My interest in un-gunbanning is to do with enabling people to better defend themselves against criminals and criminals in government, Sandra, it's perfectly moral and very important to everyone, not just me. I've never thought depriving children of a school gymnasium and substituting a garden of remembrance was very constructive. I wonder exactly how the rest of the money was spent.

DO get in touch with J, Sandra. If you delay you might just miss the chance to talk to the BBC investigator when she was visiting him and that would be a very great pity. Just make that phone call. If you're a feminist, that's an interest group with 51% of the population in it, Sandra. Sounds like you could be very influential to me and that means you could change things from the present coverup. Contact J Contact J Contact J.

113

18 December 2002 Norman, I had already contacted J (on Sat). Thought you knew that. Had email back yesterday. Hope to meet up with him some time in the next week. Sorry for my fit of temper! Was reading McMurdo's evidence last night. Wish I had his email address. I'd have strong words for him. Sandra

19 December 2002 Hi Sandra, The problem with my knowing from the reports in The Scotsman and the Socialist Worker that McMurdo had perjured himself is that he was in charge of the investigation of the Massacre. Just as a single question more to Mrs Ogilvie might have opened a can of worms up at that stage of the eyewitness testimony, I'm aware that there is NO material evidence, eyewitness or report that McMurdo could not have fiddled or modified. I have to wonder what part if any of the case presented at the 1996 Cullen Inquiry is true. Good luck with J.

Could I say to you that dissemination of a copy of just that single sheet of newsprint from The Scotsman with that report on McMurdo's testimony would in itself break this case. It would mean he could be shown to have perjured himself and it would be the end of Cullen's credibility in the Dunblane and two other Inquiries he's taken part in to date. It would tear the Scottish Office apart. It would ruin John Major and Tony Blair's reputations. All from one piece of paper. I know it may not be your specific interest, Sandra, but you can't say that about many pieces of paper, can you? Only a sworn witness statement or a videotaped interview from McMurdo's police chauffeur repeating his evidence at the Inquiry would be as useful. It's just possible that the ex-policewoman you mentioned might be able to assist here. Somewhere in Scotland, at the back of a cupboard, lining a drawer perhaps, maybe between the leaves of a book as a cutting, that piece of paper sits today. If every woman in Scotland could be put on the alert for that news report, or could be got to search her memory for the BBC/ITV early-evening TV news report from outside Stirling Police HQ for Friday 28 June 1996, the whole case could be broken open. Let me know how you get on with J.

19 December 2002 Norman, As this is the first bit of evidence – albeit on your word only – on how the Cullen Inquiry ended up corrupted, I can assure you I will do everything I can to unearth that piece of paper (likewise about memories of the TV news report). It is all slowly starting to make sense to me and I am going through all the material I have on the massacre to help get a bigger picture.

19 December 2002 Hi Sandra, You'll have to come to your own conclusions about how reliable my recollection of reading the two press articles is. At some stage you're going to have to speak to the journalist or his wife on the subject, or to try to get someone else to do that on your behalf. He was completely PLAIN to me initially about witnessing the testimony of McMurdo's chauffeur and of McMurdo's corroboration of it. He has only refused to give me a signed witness statement confirming that "for very personal reasons". According to him there were between 10 and 14 reporters at the 1996 Cullen Inquiry who all heard what was said in court. Presumably any of them will corroborate what he said which was in The Scotsman's report.

The woman who told me about seeing on TV a reporter outside Stirling Police HQ saying on that evening that Central Scotland Police had nobody available to comment on McMurdo's testimony of that afternoon said it to me without my asking for it. I'd never heard of that previously. The recollection of that news report is probably the most common piece of evidence you are likely to come across – in Scotland. Thinking about it, there must be court ushers and presumably other policemen who were there, too.

27 December 2002 Norman, J doesn't know when S will be over next, so we delayed our meeting till the new year. I wanted to continue reading the transcript and getting my head around all this stuff. Hope to meet up with him next week. Have you been in contact with Greg Lance Watkins at all?

27 December 2002 Hi Sandra, Did you get S's email address from J? Please do ask him for it. Look up Greg Lance Watkins on the google.com – he's idiosyncratic but that's about all. I don't think he's got any new information but he's obviously against the pistols ban and presumably could be relied on to relay anything new on his websites and email lists. Yes, to answer the question, I've emailed him and told him the tale I've told you. We haven't made any other progress together.

For other local (Edinburgh) pro-shooting activists you could try Johnny Pate – http://www.dvc.org.uk/-johnny/ whose "arms" visual pun might be wearing a little thin by now but I see he's still fond of it. He's keen and annoyed about the pistols ban but hasn't made any steps forward. There are a number of "resources" – relevant reports etc some to do with shooting, some to do with Dunblane – and he lists them. You'll no doubt benefit by scanning through them lightly.

In my opinion you need to talk to someone who's local and who's interested in the child abuse side of it – Mrs Hagger seems an obvious choice. From the pro-shooting side of it, we need to roll a six to get the wagon rolling again, things are in the doldrums on this investigation. There's obviously a very great irritation over the handgun ban and at least most of the shooters would be delighted to get any new information about Thomas Hamilton – and his friends – into the public spotlight.

To put it shortly, the paedophiles of Dunblane/Stirling have a lot of enemies in the shooting fraternity but those enemies need some fresh shit to throw. I've publicised the two newspaper articles and the TV evening news report, but failed to substantiate them publicly. That's to say, I've asked the journalist to publicly corroborate what he said to me and he won't, but I've not asked the two ladies to do the same for the evening TV report snippet because pressure appears to have been put on the journalist to shut up.

J for S's email address and Mrs Hagger, I think. Is there a local feminist network you can associate with?

6 January 2003 (letter by post) Dear Norman, You said you didn't know who to trust anymore. Please explain to me why you trusted J. Go back and read his evidence on Day *-*. For someone who didn't think Hamilton was a paedophile, it is rather strange that he is now – allegedly – involved in a "project" looking to expose paedophiles.

Of course "the project" doesn't exist. I even wonder if S does. Or if she does exist, he has put the frighteners on her and that's why she's disappeared to America. He has really pulled the wool over your eyes Norman. Fortunately I twigged just in time. I was just about to go and meet him this week. He is busy covering his tracks because he knows how damning his evidence in the transcript is. I am now busy covering my tracks because he is looking for me (he knows where I walk my dogs, and it won't be long before he has my address). I am pleading innocence, as if I think you're a nutter, okay? You must continue your communication with him exactly as before. I am going to pretend I have no interest in going any further with this.

I can see now that he persuaded you to think you'd misinterpreted Mrs Ogilvie's evidence. He claims he lived in Dunblane till the end of 1997. In one of his emails to me he said my "lack of haste was commendable". He doesn't want to be found out, so it is in his interest to discourage people looking for the truth about 'Dunblane'. He really succeeded in throwing you off the scent.

I am putting my trust in you Norman. Please do all you can to cover my back. Tell him I'm ill (I'm not by the way). I am going to try and arrange for someone to go and "interview" him before he disappears from T, assuming that is a genuine address.

6 January 2003 To: J As I haven't heard from you, I guess this week isn't convenient. I'm writing to say I'm pulling out of this search for the newspaper reports that Norman told me about. I reckon he's got it very wrong. He said there were many witnesses that day, but quite clearly there weren't, so either he's got the date wrong or remembered what he read wrong. That was all that got me interested and I haven't got anywhere with it. It was his suggestion that I meet up with you, but there seems little point. I haven't got any further information that would be of any help. No doubt I'll hear about the project you and S have been involved in when it comes to a conclusion. I'm writing to Norman this morning to tell him the same, but I'll be diplomatic because he quite clearly believes what he's told me and I wouldn't want to offend him. You obviously know the guy and would understand better than me what has set him off in this quest, which I believe is a hopeless one by the way. But spare his feelings!

6 January 2003 From: J

My Dear Sandra, The reason you hadn't heard from me is that I haven't checked my email for a few days. I will in fact try to make Friday, at least for an hour, but it still depends on the work I am currently drowning in. When we meet – eventually – I will try and give you a short account of how things stand. I will also explain how I think that Norman's deductions make too much of what may be a correct original sighting. He is indeed a bit one track on this, and difficult to shake. I no longer try. J

9 January 2003 From: Norman Bassett (by post)

Hi Sandra, Though what you're suspecting that G = J is possible, I've had nothing to support that except a lot less pro-shooting effort than I'd have undertaken in his location. J has been contributing to Cybershooters BB for the past 6 years. If you want to check J and G out the easiest means I can suggest is the local Electoral Registers. You make a phone call to your local Council and say you want to do some Family Research – looking up long-lost relatives – and ask where are the Electoral Registers kept for Doune, Dunblane etc. Don't supply them with the name, make up a name and write it down on a scrap of paper. I'd be a lot happier were I in touch by email with S because J has told me very little about what they talked to Mrs Ogilvie about. I'm not sure how intimidatable the Ogilvies are – she has a husband, I believe. It's not impossible that you're right about J. I've said absolutely NOTHING about you at all to him. The only reason I put you onto him was that he's a pro-shooter who contributes to Cybershooters BB and I've communicated by email and snailmail with him. I've never met him and I've never spoken to him on the phone. I've not been persuaded to doubt the evidence of my senses as regards the two articles I saw in The Scotsman and the Socialist Worker, I'm just puzzled that what J says Mrs Ogilvie said doesn't match up with those two articles, the journalist I spoke to and the woman who told me about the TV news snippet she saw in 1996. Why don't I trust some shooting people? I've come across too many who are pulling their punches and I'm puzzled why. Don't be scared, be careful. DO get onto the Electoral Registers and see what you can find out. Stay cheerful.

12 January 2003 (by post) Dear Norman, Thanks for your letter. J's name was spelt one way during the inquiry (G), and another way in the list of witnesses at the end of the report (J). He is listed in my telephone directory as G (not J) and still residing at _____ (as of Nov 2001) – although I realise that doesn't mean very much. There isn't a J or G listed for T. He seems to have another email address too (see attached).

Although it only states " _____ " in the transcript, I have seen a copy of his original statement, and that quite clearly states his occupation. The spelling of his name there is G. You were very patient with me when I had to get up to speed in terms of fully understanding what you were saying about those newspaper reports, and I will be patient with you whilst you take on board what I am saying about this man. I freaked out the other day when I realised this, and I found myself not trusting you either. That's why my first letter was so harsh in tone. I have calmed down now and can assure you that I am being **very** careful. However, if you don't take this on board fast, you will potentially endanger me!

If you could explain more to me about how and when you got in contact with J, and whether he put you in touch with S (or the other way round), I will be able to start piecing things together. I will do an electoral register check, but I have no doubt in my mind that they are one and the same person. It starts to make sense of a lot of what we know. J is also referred to as * and ** throughout the inquiry. There are many misspellings in the transcript, but again I have no doubt that C is J as well. Did you pass on the journalists name to J? If so, guess who got him to shut up.

I have been in touch with Greg Lance Watkins – by email and phone – and although he is as you say, "idiosyncratic", he is well connected and is as determined as you to get to the truth of all this. If we can put something together about J (comparing what he's told me with what he's told you), I'm sure Greg could organise for someone to interview him. The initial enquiry could simply be about the "project" to expose paedophiles.

I am informing a third party of all that I am doing just now (including names and addresses), and that includes my communication with you. I am still endeavouring to get J off my case, although I suspect it is too late. I think he knows that I know. He seems more keen to meet me now that I've backed off. He knows that I've been reading the transcript, and he must have known that some day somebody was going to twig.

You are going to have to believe for the time being that I am telling you the truth (that J is G) and then think about all the ramifications of that. Then you will realise what a dangerous situation I am in. I've considered the possibility that you are in cahoots with him, but if that is the case, I've already had it. If it isn't the case, then lets start working as a team and get the show on the road!

17 January 2003 To: William Scott

Hello, Just had phone call from Greg Lance Watkins and he gave me your email address. I would be interested to know more about the present situation re DS Hughes report. In my own small way, I am looking to uncover the truth about 'Dunblane'. Don't know if he's mentioned me to you. I live in Dunblane and am incensed at the cover-up in the Cullen Report. Hope this reaches you.

18 January 2003 From: William Scott

Delighted to hear from you. If we can co-operate on this I should be overjoyed as it has been an uphill struggle. At the start I encouraged about a dozen others to write but all but one gave up when they received a reply which was of course worthless.

You may wonder how Mr Robertson was involved as recently as June and August of last year. I asked him about access to closure orders that were not legally valid and he wrote to the Lord Advocate on my behalf but quickly withdrew when he realised it was Sergeant Hughes' Report I was interested in. Hope we can find ways to take this forward together. Here's to success. William W Scott

18 January 2003 (by post)

Dear Norman, How much more proof do you want about this man? I am sending this lot to GLW as well, but I am beginning to think he can't be relied on. He eventually phoned on Friday evening, but doesn't appear to be interested in the cover-up at this low level. He's more involved in getting the 100 year time-seal over-ruled. Fair enough, and I hope it happens. He admitted that Dunblane only occupies about 5% of his time – most of his energy goes into campaigning against "Europe". I need to be in touch with someone who is prepared to specifically focus on this. It is a major issue in its own right after all.

Do you have a postal address for S? If she only left for the States recently – and we only have J's (worthless) word for that – it's possible she'll have a mail redirection set up. Do you have a copy of the newspaper snippet about Mrs Ogilvie that you mentioned to S in one of your emails? There appears to be a suggestion that D is a paedophile too????? How come you haven't mentioned that before? Your email correspondence with S has opened up even more questions for me. .

Anyway, I will soon drop this whole matter if those I am in contact with aren't more focussed. It's not supposed to be a half hearted venture, something just for fun. I am only too aware that those who say they will support you invariably don't. I will not allow myself to be shafted on this one.

You were not at all vague about those newspaper reports Norman, but please try and address issues as they come up, without me having to prompt you! I shouldn't have to keep asking questions like "did you put J on to BV?" Can't you see how important this is? It is very worrying to me that you didn't see through J. Is there a reason for that? The fact that you are prepared to spend money to go all the way to France so that you can still "shoot" emphasises yet again that your primary motivation in all this is simply to overturn the handgun ban. For me, it is very different. For S it was probably different too – she was wanting to make a documentary that would presumably establish her name... Yes, we all have very different motivations, but as I've said before, if we don't work together, the truth will forever remain hidden. That's not what you, GLW, S, myself and many others want (even if that is J's goal).

20 January 2003 Hi Sandra, Try focussing on Mrs Doreen Hagger.

Meanwhile, J wrote to Norman, who sent a copy of the letter to me. It was headed J*, Accountancy, Crunluath Ltd. No accountancy qualifications. No VAT registration number. I did a company check to see what kind of business it actually was, and this said "none registered". J was listed for about 6 other companies (I have all this documentation), and I decided to check out one called PPP.

Here is J's letter to Norman in full:

10 January 2003

Dear Norman

Nice to hear from you. S returned from the US to get divorced and sell her house here, and has now left again for the States, probably permanently if she can get work out there. If I can raise the standard of evidence we have to that demanded by the BBC (much higher than their normal requirement) she will return to co-produce with me any programme commissioned.

I am not working on the project at the moment, because the run-up to the tax return deadline is my very busy time. However, I will be starting again in February, this time with some hopes. In the first place, I hope to have some funding, and in the second I have a new source of information which promises to take me straight into the local police.

This may give us a chance to clarify the information provided by the Ogilvies. As I understand it, they were aware of a police sergeant regularly visiting Hamilton. This fellow was in Traffic, and was recognised by Mr Ogilvy, a former fireman who often needed the cops to keep traffic diverted when he was on a job, but John Ogilvy could not place the name. You recalled a report in the News of the World referring to Douglas McMurdo's driver, which I think we will have to consult the News of the World's physical archive to track down. Or have I got the reference wrong?

I have a difficulty with the second point. The chief constable would probably rate a full-time driver, given the public relations and political aspects of his job which would keep him much on the move. The Deputy would tend to be more stationary, as would the Assistants; the Deputy would be standing in for the Chief, and the Assistants would have their divisions to run. They would probably be able to call on a pool of drivers, probably from Traffic, as they needed transport but none would be likely to have a dedicated driver. Recall that CSP is a very small force.

Suppose we have a sighting of a policeman connected in some way with McMurdo. He could easily have been there on his own account, or on behalf of another senior officer. <u>According to the parents of a witness who committed perjury at the Inquiry, their son was blackmailed and threatened into doing so by a police sergeant.</u> I think this is probably the man, but the only police source willing to point the finger so far associates him with the target we have had in mind from earliest days.

My new source seems to know everybody, and I am hoping to put him to good use next month. I am praying too for the funds, for bribes and to be able to hire private detectives.

Sandra did indeed get in touch with me, but then as you say withdrew, just a couple of days ago before we had a chance to meet. It is quite likely that she would be nervous, especially living in Dunblane, so don't be hard on her. She didn't tell me whether she was any sort of professional, so I don't know how much help she could be. If she wants another chance, she knows where to find me.

The Dunblane funds, both of them, were extremely secretive and I don't know if they have to publish any sort of Accounts. At the moment, I don't have any contacts within them, but I do remember that one of the bereaved mothers told me she didn't think much of them at all. Perhaps later there might be time to do some looking, because after chatting with that mother it wasn't at all clear to me where all the money had gone. The whole subject was surrounded in bitterness, with a three-sided fight among the bereaved families, those whose children were shot but survived, and indeed the rest of the community, who saw the chance to get some public facilities built. A bit of a viper's nest, and I would be more nervous of getting involved there than I am of the present investigation. It is conceivable that some at least of the "missing" money was invested for the surviving children, some of whom have lingering injuries.

If you do get to a Paris Club, please let me know how you get on. There are cheap flights from Edinburgh and Glasgow, and if I got the chance and the money to combine a dirty weekend with some range time, I would jump at it.

Yours

(illegible initials)

In an email to me (12 January 03), J wrote, "Norman is not a friend, and in fact I have never met him. We do correspond occasionally about the project, but while I am probably as obsessed as he is, I am not monomaniac about the point he raises, and in fact if I come to accept the story he has somehow heard, I won't necessarily put on it the same interpretation he did. I should certainly stay away from Doreen Hagger. Perhaps eventually I will go and see her myself, but with sceptical misgivings. As I said in my last message, you are owed an explanation, and I will do my best to make a chance to give you it if you wish."

20 January 2003

Hi Norman, Interested in the following?

Crunloath (the name of J's company) doesn't make much sense. "Crun" means a crown and "luath" means fast. However, a "crunn-luth" is a musical term meaning a quick measure in pipe music. Make any sense? What's the context? (from my Gaelic speaking friend at the BBC)

20 January 2003 Hi Sandra, J is welcome to call his company what he likes, of course. Most company names are meaningless. Why not do something constructive and contact Mrs Doreen Hagger, or get someone in the web Electoral Roll business to look up G for you for a few quid? Or Mrs Hagger AND G for a few more quid, since you're interested in G?

21 January 2003 Dear Norman, You will have received my letter by the time you get this email. To quote your own words to me, "the whole business stinks". I am going to return to my other interests. There is nothing in this for me. I am not the slightest bit interested in overturning the handgun ban, and it seems to me that the only people who are interested in uncovering the truth about Dunblane are aggrieved ex-shooters (as if I didn't know that before). As I've said before, I waited for the bereaved parents to take action against CSP, and they didn't. The only other "concerned" group appears to be your lot. So it is your battle. Not mine. Don't forget to carry on with your war crimes work mind. That is very important indeed.

I think when the 100 year time-seal is over-ruled (as being illegal), the truth will spill out. Why not write to William Scott offering your support in that regard?

Look out for my feminist website! As I said, I stumbled accidently on your research request whilst doing research of my own (ie. what websites already existed for feminist minded women). When my website is up-and-running, I feel sure I will write about "Dunblane". If you wish to contribute, I will consider your submission! However, I imagine you will be too busy with other matters... If you can be bothered, I would appreciate an update every now and then. If you can't, I will understand.

21 January 2003 Hi Sandra, Thanks for your three emails and your letter. J's company was registered in March 1999. Doesn't seem connected with anything but an interest in making small videos – like S was later commissioned to research for the BBC. You could check out the accounts figures to see how much trading it's doing.

No, I don't have S's address of any kind. Try a Search of the Divorce Registry – presumably there's one in Scotland? She's obviously a distant relative of yours, so you should tell the registrar, so could you have a copy of her divorce registration for Family Research purposes? That should have an address on it. Otherwise you can try to get to her through her email provider? Or there appear to be a number of US companies offering search facilities through the official databases for not much cash.

I presume you're saying G and J are currently at their Electoral Register addresses. You can check that each is paying FULL Council Tax minus any annotations, which would mean they were different people. I think I'll back the "two people, similar names" hypothesis.

Let me know your feminist website address – if you'd put up a permanent request for any further info on Dunblane you could put up the details of those newspaper cuttings I'm after. The real problem is there's no single major feminist website in Scotland, so good luck with that.

22 January 2003 Norman, It is precisely that view – "two people, similar names" – that puts me in a very difficult position. I trust you will continue to keep quiet about my hypothesis – one person, different spelling? Just for your interest, S is the Director of PPP Ltd.... Does that at least make you suspicious? Why have you got such a problem with this? In your earlier emails you seemed to want to hunt down the paedophiles of Central Scotland. Either you are one yourself and you feel you now want to protect J, or you are embarrassed at having been hoodwinked by J and S. So, which is it? You just think it's coincidence that J and G both work in **? Finally, T is a business address. D is the home address. I hope you are bringing more rigour to your other investigations. The truth is staring you in the face, and you can't face it. That makes me very suspicious about you.

You can check that each is paying FULL Council Tax minus any annotations, which would mean they were different people. You're the one with the problem here. Criminals – be it war criminals, paedophiles, rapists or murderers – as you well know, go to great lengths to disguise themselves. J hasn't even changed his name. Just the spelling!

I guess you did put either J or S on to BV, and that is why he went from being frank and honest about what he heard at the inquiry, to angry and hostile about you "bothering" him. You undid all your own work Norman. If you continue with J as a contact, you will get nowhere. Remember that all our correspondence has been passed to a third party and I have now forwarded all my info to an investigative reporter. And that's why it's time for me to resume my work on my feminist website. Stinks? A bit of an understatement I'd say.

22 January 2002 Sandra, If I personally wanted an alias, I would change both parts of my name. I can't accept your hypothesis as reasonable. What I told S was exactly what I've publicised on Cybershooters for the past 6 years. Apart from the journalist's contact details which I sent to a number of persons in the shooting world as well as to her. The reason he's not willing to give me a witness statement is he's gutless, Sandra, or being blackmailed into keeping quiet. I have no idea what his "very personal reasons" are and he's refusing to tell me. If S is a Director of PPP then you should be able to force her address from the company (ie J) through Companies House and contact her directly.

Porn is a very complex and international business, Sandra. I'm not saying that some innocuous stuff would not help provide cover but frankly the electronic side of things comes into the amateur range of equipment nowadays and you basically don't need cover. On the other hand a production company of your own would be an enormous help when selling documentaries.

I think you're being paranoid. Do stop being paranoid and do some more investigating. Check out the Council Tax records. Have you been around in person to the T address? Have you been around in person to the D address? Do you have no personal contacts in either place who could check things out directly for you? Get your web search company to locate Doreen Hagger for you – or go talk to her neighbours and leave a message.

22 January 2003 Norman, I must clarify one point. What I am alleging is that Hamilton used equipment provided by J. It is hard for us all to remember how things were before the mid 1990s when the internet really took off. Paedophiles had limited access to child porn. Most of it was dated to the period 1969-74 when Denmark legalised all forms of pornography, including child porn. The service Hamilton offered in Scotland was fairly unique. He didn't just take photos. He made videos. I believe his reputation went far and wide, making Central Scotland a magnet for paedophiles. His curtains were always drawn at his house and he had 3 regular visitors who one can only assume visited him to view his material. I believe there are many others who didn't visit his house – he visited theirs.

Yes, I have been out to D and what I gleaned from that visit still backs up my theory. I am often called paranoid, and I read a quote once about how "paranoia is rarely right, but usually sensible" (or something to that effect). So I operate on that basis. I am very sorry for my fits of temper. As my 'friend' J says, don't be hard on me. I am bound to be nervous, living in Dunblane! However, because I totally believe my hypothesis, it is inconceivable that I write to S (whose address I now have). I hope I will get DH's address soon. Thank you for bearing with me.

22 January 2003 Hi, Sandra, 1996 is some time after the introduction of videorecorders – about 1965? What G could have been helping TH with prior to 1996 would be the use of video-editing equipment, which was and still is a bit pricey. TH was in the retail camera business after he closed his Woodfit concern down, so it says in the Transcript. That's not just still-film cameras but videocameras too. I don't think he needed any help from anyone in supplying cameras or producing films, but maybe he did in producing a more professional product. There's no overt evidence that I'm aware of that he produced any child porn at all. But the photos and videos of boys at his camps and in his clubs clearly are only a step away.

You're short of evidence on which to hypothesise, Sandra. You need to get some more. Get around and talk to your contacts about these things and about how wife-swapping leads on to other things. See what they know. Putting a big map on your wall would probably help.

10 February 2003 Dear Mrs Hagger, I do hope you are the same Doreen Hagger who gave evidence at the Cullen Inquiry in 1996, as I urgently need to find out more about Sam Davie and James Williams, who I believe attended as helpers at Thomas Hamilton's summer camps.

Just to put you in the picture, as you see, I live in Dunblane... I am aware that you had to endure a very "hostile examination" at the inquiry. I have subsequently read your evidence and believe you were treated very badly indeed. If you would like the opportunity to speak out again about what you knew about Hamilton's camps, I would love to hear from you. I have also attached a news report from yesterday's *Sunday Herald* just to show you that there might be an opening for the real truth about Dunblane to come out in the not so distant future.

It is my understanding that allegations of indecency were made against 2 youth leaders who helped Hamilton, and I wonder if you have any information relating to that. Did you have any suspicions about Sam Davie and James Williams? You also referred to "strangers" visiting the camp, and I would like to know more about that.

Please do get in touch with me. You must be very angry indeed about how you were treated at The Cullen Inquiry. Thomas Hamilton's "friends" on the other hand were asked just a few questions and were not subjected to any cross-examination... I look forward to hearing from you.

Doreen phoned me at 7.30 the very next morning, as soon as she received my letter. We began working together immediately.

23 March 2003

Given that I knew before meeting with J that he was looking for the funds to hire private detectives – and offer bribes – it seems quite strange that I did not consider before or during our meeting that the man I was talking to WAS NOT J, or even G or C. It was only *after* our meeting that I realised he was in fact a private detective. If J is as guilty as I believe him to be, he was never going to show his face to me. Well, at least I figured it out shortly after. Others might not have worked it out at all.

We met at 11.30am in front of Dunblane Cathedral, by the noticeboard. It was my intention that we conduct our entire meeting there, but he nervously stated that there were two men in a white van over the road who had been watching him. I simply said "hello" as I walked round the back of him. He was reading the noticeboard and turned round and said "Sandra?" and shook my hand. If I could re-enact this scenario, I would say, "And you are J? Could you provide me with some I.D?" But I didn't. In a quiet voice, he just said his name as he shook my hand. My first mistake.

He insisted we go for a walk, and I insisted it had to be in a public place. So we walked down the High Street, which was very noisy and busy. We sat on the bench at the bottom of the High Street. He wanted me to do the talking. I said no, we were here for him to tell me what he knows; that he already knew how much I know, from the press release I sent him. And then it went instantly wrong. I hadn't taken to him from the moment I met him, but when he said "look Sandra, YOU came to ME", I bristled and retorted, "NO J, this time YOU came to ME". He threw the line back at me that I had written in my last email; "J, tell me what you know". And for some reason I was momentarily thrown by that. I think I then said something about he wouldn't tell me anything by email, or over the phone, and it didn't look like he was going to tell me anything face-to-face either, so if that was going to be the case, I might as well go straight home. He remarked that we didn't seem to have hit it off, and I agreed. He wondered if it was "the chemistry". I told him that quite simply I didn't trust him; that I knew nothing about him or why he was involved (apart from the fact that he had lived in Dunblane back in 1996, which he seemed to think was sufficient reason to be involved, but I commented that the majority of people in Dunblane didn't give a damn about what happened, so that just didn't wash with me). He repeated what J had said to me on the phone, that I hadn't told him why I was involved, and I repeated that he had never asked me, and that I would have been willing to tell him. He wanted me to explain, but I repeated that I was only there to find out what he knows. So then he started off on one of his laborious unconvincing "speeches" : I must remember the shock we all felt – that a police officer he knew couldn't even describe what he saw in the gym that day. I remarked that as I had been in the ambulance service back then, I knew what an awful scene it had been, even though I wasn't there.

He told me he was a shooter, but didn't do much shooting these days. I said, "does anybody?" He said they were small in number anyway, and made some comment about them being exonerated. I asked if that was why he was involved then, to be exonerated? And he said yes, the shooters should be exonerated. I told him I agreed that the shooters were right to feel aggrieved that they lost their "hobby" as a result of Thomas Hamilton's actions, but that was not why I was involved in the search for the truth. I told him I wanted the handgun ban to remain in force, and that was not my motivation at all.

He remarked that the difference between us was that I was a "campaigner", and he was an "investigator". I said that for an investigator, he was very vague on "facts" (dates, names, etc). We had a difference of opinion (fact) about when S went to visit Mr and Mrs Ogilvie (he thought Mr O was called John, but I told him it was Jim). I told him Mrs O said it was about 4 years ago, as did Frank Cook MP. He said it was about 2 years ago, and that nothing much had happened in the last couple of years. I said that Norman had seemed to think it would be useful for me to meet S. He said she had already gone back to the States by the time I got in contact. I said that seemed odd, given that S had sent a package to Mrs Ogilvie within Britain at the end of Dec '02 and I had first contacted J about mid Dec.

Interestingly, he did not remember warning me off meeting Doreen Hagger. He asked me to tell him what he had said in his email!; he reminded me that as I live in Dunblane I should consider whether I want to have enemies, as he has; he remarked that I was not paranoid enough, but I stressed that I was more than paranoid enough; he wouldn't give any names of the very vague people he referred to; he asked if I had a copy of the transcript and had I read it; he referred to me being in contact with a journalist and said "he/she?" I simply confirmed that I was in contact with a journalist; I told him that those of us who were prepared to stand up and be counted were sharing information, but that he didn't seem to be prepared to do that; I told him that we had some of the hidden documents; he went on and on about the BBC wanting 110% proof, and I told him not to bother with the BBC – produce your programme independently; I asked what the angle of his programme was and he said something vague about "you have to ask the right questions"; I repeated that I was interested to know what the angle of his programme was, and he said it started off being about gun ownership, but then moved into the possible abuse of boys; he talked about the visitors to Hamilton's flat, who obviously called by to collect dirty videos, usually only staying a minute or two. I replied that some of his visitors stayed for a long period of time, up to an hour; he commented on Mrs Ogilvie's evidence, and how after she said "the police", there was no further questioning on that (re Hamilton's visitors); he talked about Hamilton's photographs and was a bit coy here – I said I knew he took photos of naked boys, and he agreed – but he went on to say that Hamilton's videos were mostly just of his boys clubs and that there was nothing overtly pornographic in them; he referred to a police friend of Hamilton's as "Willie Mac"...

This is William MacDonald's sworn evidence from the Inquiry:

WILLIAM MacDONALD (56), Sworn:

EXAMINED BY MR BONOMY: I live in Invernessshire. I am a retired police officer.

You I think knew Thomas Hamilton for a number of years? – Yes, approximately 15 – round about 1981.

How did you first get to know him? – When he opened his Woodcraft shop in Stirling, and it was about the only one in Stirling at that time. There was no B&Q at that time and suchlike. It was well-known.

Did you have an interest in do-it-yourself? – Yes.

And were you a customer of the shop? – I was indeed.

Over what period did Mr Hamilton have that shop? – On recollection I think he had it for about six years or so. I think it closed down in 1986 if I remember.

Do you know anything of the circumstances which brought it to an end? – Not really, no.

He never said anything to you about that? – No.

While you were dealling with the shop was it, as far as you were concerned, a reasonably good shop? – Yes, it was a very well equipped shop.

Did it appear as though it was a popular place? – Yes, it was popular.

So it would be for at least a period a successful business? – Yes, I would say so.

Did Hamilton know what he was about in the business of selling that type of material? – Yes, I would say that he was very well up on it, yes.

Now, you I think developed an acquaintanceship as it were beyond simply being a customer with Hamilton. Is that a fair way of putting it? – An acquaintanceship, yes.

Did he contact you for example outwith the shop? – Not much, no.

Occasionally? – Occasionally I would say, yes.

Was there anything in particular that would cause him for example to phone you or visit you? – No, the only times he visited in that time would be possibly transporting materials and suchlike. I am talking about wooden panelling and suchlike that I had ordered.

That is a delivery? – A delivery, yes.

So did your contact initially not really go beyond the relationship between customer and shop? – Yes, that is correct.

Now, he had a boat I think? – Yes, he had a boat on Loch Lomond.

Were you ever on it? – Once, yes.

Could that be described as going beyond the sort of customer/shopkeeper relationship? – Possibly, yes. I think I recollect in this instance he had delivered material one evening and he mentioned the boat to us.

And did you and your wife go on the boat? – Yes, and there was also a couple of friends I believe at that time.

Where was it kept? – It was kept at Balmaha at Loch Lomond.

What kind of boat was it? – It was a cabin cruiser. I think it was round about 27 feet in length and an onboard engine.

What became of it? – I think he sold it. He obviously sold it. I think, yes.

You didn't know anything about it being destroyed at all? – He had one after that that went on fire.

This one was sold and he got another one? – Yes.

And then the later one went on fire? – Yes.

Is that something you just heard about from him? – I just heard about that, yes.

Now, can I take it that the end of the shop meant that you didn't see Mr Hamilton for a while? – I didn't see him possibly until maybe....or remain in contact with him until maybe 1990 or so.

And who contacted whom on that occasion? – It was him that happened to meet my mother who was down here on holiday at the time and he gave her a lift home.

And did your mother live near to him? – No, my mother was down on holiday with me at that time and he obviously recognised her in the town and gave her a lift down the road.

And did you speak to him on that occasion? – Yes, I did.

Was there something concerning him? – No.

Nothing that he told you that was a cause of concern at that time? – Not that particular day but I did meet him one day in the town afterwards.

And was that when he told you about something that was concerning him? – He did mention he was getting a bit of harassment with the Region about school letting and suchlike for his boys' clubs and I did mention to him at that particular time that he would be better forgetting his boys' clubs and doing something worthwhile as he was quite a talented person.

In what respect was he talented? – Well, he had a lot of knowledge in relation to building and he had his cameras etc and he seemed to have quite a lot of knowledge and I thought it was wasted with what he was doing.

When you first met him did he already have an interest in photography? Back in 1980? – No, I can't recollect at that stage.

When were you first aware of the interest in photography? – It would be in 1990.

Would it be right that the first time you met him again was actually around 1989 and one of the things he was concerned about was the involvement of the police in a camp he had been running at Loch Lomond? – I did hear about that.

Did he tell you about it? – He possibly would have told me but he knew...
when I advised him at that time to forget his boys' clubs and suchlike, he
never ever spoke about boys' clubs etc to me again, from that time on. I
wasn't interested in them in the first place.

Now, after you had come across him again, did he maintain regular contact
with you? – Not really because I retired in 1991 and although I still come
down to Stirling and I have contacts in Stirling, for the last five years I have
been mainly up north. I come down in the winter time, round about
November.

So if I had a statement that says "In the following period he would phone
my house regularly, on average once every six weeks or so", is that wrong? –
No, I never heard from John (sic) Hamilton. I saw him round about Christmas
or New Year time in the town. I never heard from him until I met him about a
fortnight before this incident.

I will come to that in a moment but back in 1989 and 1990 did he have
contact with you on a fairly regular basis? – Not fairly regularly but he would
on occasions phone all of a sudden, and then you wouldn't hear from him for
quite a while.

I take it you had regular contact with your son during that period? – Yes.
Oh, yes.

That is David MacDonald? – David.

Were you aware that Hamilton was keeping in touch with him? – Yes, he
was phoning quite often to David. Certainly more so than me.

That's fine. So you met him again in what, February of this year? – It
would have been. Yes, it would be February.

And where was it you met him? – I met him outside the Thistle Centre.

And did he seem any different at that stage from what you had known in
the past? – Not really, no.

I think you were actually doing something to the house? – Yes, my wife
and I were intending to fit a new kitchen.

Is that in the house in Stirling? – Yes.

And did Mr Hamilton give you some help? – Yes. Well, he gave me some
advice on doing it and in that particular fortnight prior he was phoning quite a
bit and his concern was kitchens and measurements and telling me the best
places to buy materials and so on.

So did that go on right up until what, the 11th of March? Up until the 12th
of March? – Yes, the 12th.

He still had contact? – Yes, indeed he had.

Did any of the conversations on the phone extend beyond kitchens at all? –
No.

Now, on the 12th of March, in the morning, did he phone you at your
home? – Yes.

And did he give you advice then about the size of units that you should be
ordering for your kitchen? – Yes, I felt it was a little bit odd because he did

mention... he was very concise and I felt very up on kitchens etc but he did suggest a 1000 unit than a 600 unit to me which would knock the whole context of the kitchen out and I thought that was a bit unusual for him. He is quite a deep thinker.

Did he say anything, though, apart from talking about the kitchen? – No, he was only on very briefly and I had a lot to do apart from the kitchen.

Was there anything in the conversation or in the fortnight or so, perhaps even a bit more than the fortnight, that you had been speaking to him again that would give you any hint that something like what he did was likely to happen? – Oh, none whatsoever. No.

Did he mention guns at all to you between February and March? – No, but he knew I wasn't fond of guns anyway and he would never mention guns to me.

Did you know he had an interest in guns? – Yes, I did.

How did you know that? – Because he mentioned it to me early in our acquaintanceship.

Your son went to a boys' club of his back in the early 1980s? – Yes, he did.

Were you ever concerned about the fact that he was at one of Mr Hamilton's clubs? – No, I wasn't concerned at that time.

Were you a Central Scotland Police Officer? – I was.

Over what period were you with Central Scotland Police? – From 1960 to 1991. 31 years.

During that period were you aware of rumours about Hamilton's behaviour towards boys? – Yes, latterly.

Roughly when did you first learn of this? – I think something developed but I can't honestly say.... Would it be in 1991? There was one incident where Strathclyde Police had something at a cinema at Balloch. I heard about that.

So you heard about something in Balloch in 1991? – That would be about then.

Was that the first that you had heard anything adverse like that about him? – Yes, I would say so. Yes, I didn't have contact with him or anything concerning him maybe from 1986 to 1990.

Let's go back to 1980. Between 1980 and 1991 where were you actually serving as a police officer? – I was in the Traffic Department.

Where is that based? – Police Headquarters.

I am trying to establish what the extent of common police knowledge might have been about his general activities. Can you tell me anything you knew prior to 1991? Let's leave that one aside *(writer's question, why?)* Anything you had heard even in the form of rumour about Hamilton's behaviour towards children? – No, not really.

No cross-examination.

And below is William MacDonald's son's evidence for the Inquiry:

STATEMENT 702/C – CIVILIAN WITNESS (Summary of original witness statement) David MacDonald – Financial Advisor.

The witness is a friend of the accused/deceased. He took a phone call from him at 9pm on 12th March 1996. The witness had known Thomas Hamilton for roughly 15 years. He got to know him when he went into the D.I.Y. shop, Woodcraft, in Cowane Street, Stirling. In 1981 when he first met Hamilton he also attended his club in Borestone Primary School for roughly 9 months. He left because the numbers started to diminish and the club disbanded. He also attended a summer camp held by Hamilton at Balmaha, Loch Lomond. The witness had heard stories about Hamilton and boys, about him being weird, but had never experienced any problems. The witness talks of favouritism towards certain boys during the camps. The witness worked in Hamilton's shop for roughly a year, finishing in August, 1982.

When the witness moved to Aberdeen in 1990 Hamilton began calling him regularly. During telephone conversations he would be on a very long time. The witness' family developed a code when phoning each other so that they knew it was not Hamilton on the phone. They would call a number, let it ring once and then dial again. Apart from talking about cameras and camera equipment, Hamilton tended on the phone to talk about his various grievances. He *would often talk about his problems with Michael Forsyth* and his problems with his clubs. The witness considers that he had almost a paranoid attitude towards the Scouts, the Police and parents in Dunblane.

Since 1987 the witness has visited Hamilton's house roughly 10 times, usually for little more than an hour. The last time the witness remembers seeing Hamilton was Christmas 1995. The witness recalls the photographs that Hamilton had on his living room wall as young boys doing press ups and other exercises. They did not disturb the witness and Hamilton never mentioned them to him. Hamilton once showed the witness videos of young boys at one of his clubs just going through exercise routines. The witness found it boring. The witness was never shown any guns by Hamilton. When the witness was in Hamilton's club, Hamilton brought in some pistols for them to see. He once brought a Rifle a Bolt action type.

The witness did not know of Hamilton having any sexual relationships with either males or females. He certainly did not think that Hamilton was homosexual.

On returning from a holiday in Hong Kong on 11th March 1996 the witness on checking his answering machine found 2 or 4 calls from Hamilton. There were no messages, Hamilton simply stated that he had called. At about 9pm on Tuesday 12th March 1996 the witness returned home and there was a message on the answering machine from Hamilton who returned the call in order to avoid persistent calling from Hamilton. In phoning Hamilton the witness was on the phone for roughly 45 minutes initially talking about cameras and then later about his business which he said was going not too well. Hamilton then stated to the witness that he was lonely and that he did not want to spend his life alone. The witness does not think that this was the most depressed he had heard Hamilton. He was not unusual about the way the conversation concluded. The witness observes that over the last six months in conversation, Hamilton's grievances had diminished and he did seem to be more depressed and lonely. When detailing the problems that he was having with his boys clubs, Hamilton would often specifically mention Dunblane. He felt that the parents of the boys in Dunblane were ganging up on him.

The witness when generally seeing magazines in Hamilton's house can remember those being photography magazines but once remembers seeing a magazine about guns. The witness describes Hamilton as being very much a loner. The witness was shocked when he discovered that Hamilton had perpetrated the act at Dunblane.

DAVID MacDONALD (Inquiry Evidence) (28), Sworn:

Examined by Mr Bonomy: Do you work as a financial adviser? – Yes.

And do you live in Aberdeen? – Yes.

Have you been in Aberdeen for about six years? – Yes, just about that.

Before living in Aberdeen did you live in this area? – Yes.

In which town in particular? – Stirling.

Was that with your own family? – Yes.

Did you know Thomas Hamilton? – Yes.

When did you first get to know him? – Round about 1980.

When was your first encounter with him? – First of all I was really with my father, and we went down to the Woodcraft shop with my Dad to buy various woodcraft.

Did he have a shop called Woodcraft? – Yes, it was Woodcraft Cowane.

That was in Cowane Street, Stirling? – Yes.

And this is about 1981 or so? – About 1980.

And you were there with your father? – Yes.

At that stage were you still – you would still be at school. Which school did you go to? – St Modan's High School.

Did you ever go to any of Mr Hamilton's boys' clubs? – Yes, I was a member.

When? – Just about that period.

Where was the club you went to? – It was a club up at Borestone.

What is the Borestone? – An area of St Ninian's, on the north side of Stirling.

When you say the Borestone – were there premises there? – It was a school actually, Borestone High School.

It was not a Primary School, it is a High School? – I'm not sure now.

For how long did you attend that club? – Maybe 18 months.

Did you go to any summer camps that were organised? – Yes.

Where did you go to camp? – It was up at Balmaha.

Roughly when was that? – It would have been in that period.

We are talking about the very beginning of the '80s? – Yes.

Summer time? – Summer.

How long were you there? – Two weeks.

Was that a tented camp? – Tented, yes. It was on the islands actually.

Off Balmaha? – Yes.

Do you know the name of the island? – No.

How did you get on at the camp? – What do you mean?

How did you get on with Mr Hamilton? – Okay, yes. There were no problems.

No problems with Mr Hamilton? – No.

Did you go to more than one camp? – Just the one camp.

Was there any particular reason why you did not go to more? – Well, I had other interests as well. I did a lot of other types of sport and so on.

Did you ever, throughout this period from then up until now, did you ever hear stories or rumours about Mr Hamilton's behaviour with boys? – Well, I know during the camp there was one child – I can't remember his name – Tom Hamilton didn't like very much, and the child left early, and I think the parents had a sort of grievance with Mr Hamilton about that.

Do you know why the child left early? – No. I think Tom maybe picked on him or he just didn't get on too well. I don't know the reason.

But going back to the question, it was really the whole period – I appreciate you referring to an actual time – but I was thinking of the whole period right up to now, did you at any stage hear stories that were really rumours about his behaviour towards youngsters? – Yes, there was a rumour that went about that he was a bit weird but it didn't seem to come to anything. No one seemed to know what that was based on.

You can be weird in a number of ways. Do you know in relation to what it was suggested he was weird? – No.

So you really never heard what may be described as firm rumours about specific types of behaviour? – No.

Did you end up for a period working with Mr Hamilton? – Yes, I worked casually in his woodcraft shop for about a year or something.

Did your father actually buy stuff from him to do his own DIY work? – Yes, along with a lot of other people.

I appreciate that, but your father would be a customer? – Yes.

Was there any particular day of the week you worked in the shop? – Yes, a Saturday morning I worked in the shop.

For how long did you do that? – Just about over a year I would say.

Why did you stop? – Mr Hamilton – he actually used to sell a lot of DIY equipment and then he started moving into kitchens, and there was a shop next door that sold kitchens, and he had no further use for me. He employed a few other people to install kitchens for him and didn't have any use for me after that.

We are talking about what, 1982 roughly? – Well, 1981 I would suppose, about August-September.

During the period you worked for him what age would you be? – About 12.

Did he do anything improper to you? – No, not at all.

Was there any hint of something that perhaps should be avoided? – No. I wouldn't have continued to work there if I thought there was something strange.

After you stopped working there did you still see him regularly or did you just never come across him for a while? – Well, there was a period when I never saw Mr Hamilton for maybe four years.

When was the next time you saw him? – I went to University in 1984 – probably didn't see him for four or five years.

When did you next see him? – Probably it would be at the University.

What was he doing at the University? – He used to get – he always used to carry this black case, and he used to get typing done.

And someone up there did it for him? – Yes.

You mean at the University? – Yes.

That would be the reason he was there? – Yes.

Did you enjoy having a conversation with him? – He was quite an intelligent man. He did seem a little eccentric in the sense that he did speak very slowly but, yes, he was interesting enough to speak to.

When was it you moved to Aberdeen? – 1990 I think it was, 1991.

Did he keep in touch with you there? – Yes.

Was there any particular reason why he did that? – Well, he was unemployed and what he used to do was sell and buy camera equipment, and he used to phone me and tell me about various deals he had done with his cameras.

Had you an interest in photography? – Yes, it was quite interesting.

Did you do any deals with him? – Deals, no.

Did he phone quite a lot? – He did phone me quite frequently, yes, and eventually it got a bit wearing having so many phone calls.

What did you do? – He used to phone usually after 9 o'clock.

In the evening? – In the evening, because that's when his clubs finished, and it got to the stage he was becoming a little bit of a pest so I actually left – I got my Mum and Dad if they were phoning me I got them to ring a couple of times and ring off and then....

You would answer it? – I would answer the phone, yes, because with Tom, when he did phone, he could be on for quite a long time.

So from 1990 right up to 1996 did he continue to keep in touch with you? – Yes.

And how frequently during that period did he speak to you on the phone? – It was maybe a couple of times a week, something like that.

What were these conversations generally about? – It was usually about cameras he was buying. He seemed to start off this business with buying and selling, and I think it was Canons or Minoltas, and eventually he moved on to Hassleblad which was a more selective type of camera and they were worth a lot more money buying and selling.

Sorry?…….. – He made quite a lot of money.

That's what he told you? – Yes.

During that time did you also see him from time to time? – Yes.

Did he appear to have money about him? – I'm not sure.

Was there any way you could judge whether he actually had any money? – No. He used to wear the same blue jacket all the time and quite a sort of crumpled sort of shirt.

Did these conversations extend from photography into other subjects? – No, it was mainly photography.

Well, did he never express grievances which he had to you? – Yes.

Was that in the context of these conversations? – Yes. He expressed a grievance about the police, and I think what happened was the police had gone to one of the camps and confiscated various equipment that he was working with.

That was photographic equipment? – Yes.

And did he have any other grievance that you talked to him about? – Well, he felt that he was being victimised.

By whom? – By the public.

The public? – The public.

Was he more specific than that? – It was really to do with his Clubs. He felt that the public, you know, had some sort of rumour about him that was stopping him from continuing his Clubs.

And did he say whether his Clubs were being adversely affected by that? – Yes.

Did he say how? – Sorry, what do you mean?

Well, did he say what was happening to his Clubs as a result? – The attendance numbers were dropping.

So that is one side. Did he ever say anything about not being able to get facilities, premises to hold them in? – He never mentioned that to me.

Just that the numbers were dropping? – The numbers were dropping.

Did that sort of feeling of victimisation take up much of the conversation? – Not really. It was quite a small part. I found it hard going. I didn't find it that useful to talk about. It was really the cameras I spoke about.

He mentioned the police and he mentioned the public? – Yes.

Did he say anything about people in Dunblane at all in any of these conversations? – Yes. It was mainly Dunblane these Clubs were, so he could have felt that is where he was being victimised.

He didn't say so in so many words, but you drew that conclusion? – Well, I drew the conclusion that was the area.

Did he ever mention the Scouting Association in that connection? – No, he did mention that he had been in the Scouts, but he didn't follow it up.

Have you ever been in his house? – Yes.

How frequently were you a visitor? – Very infrequently – maybe three or four – three times a year.

When were you last in the house? – It would have been about Christmas. 1995? – 1995.

And when you went to the house what happened generally? – Just watched TV.

And discussion of cameras and so on at the house? – Yes. He would have a collection of cameras which he would bring out.

Cheap, expensive? – Expensive.

And a lot of them? – No, not a lot of them. There were maybe three or four.

Can you give me an example of an expensive piece of equipment he would have? – He had various lenses – zoom lenses, which were quite large.

Was he specialising in any particular make? – Hassleblad, initially, I think it was.

Is Hassleblad an expensive type of equipment? – Yes.

And what are its specialist features? – Of a Hassleblad camera?

Yes. Anything particular about it? Is it lense quality or is it something else? – Well, the one feature of a Hassleblad I believe is that the lense can be more expensive than the actual body.

And apart from cameras did you see the work of his camera at all? – Yes.

And how keen a photographer was Mr Hamilton? – He seemed a very keen photographer.

Now, did he specialise in photographing anything or any people in particular? – Well, he seemed to specialise – in fact, it seemed almost all about boys in the Clubs.

Did he display these? – Yes, yes.

Whereabouts? – There was photographs all over the wall, and he also had photographs in albums.

Did these photographs have any common features in them? – They were mainly in a gym – young kids, maybe six/seven years old. All they had on was black swimming trunks.

Swimming trunks, all of them? – Yes.

Mainly, anyway? – Yes.

Did the photographs disturb you at all? – I didn't really like them. I don't think it was necessary for kids just to wear trunks – possibly if they had on shorts and T-shirts, that would have been better.

Did you ever ask him about that? – Yes.

And what was his explanation? – He just said it was natural to do it that way.

Did you ever see any video film he had shot? – Yes.

Did he actually have video equipment that he showed you, in the house? – He had a video machine, but this might have been two or three years ago.

That is a video camera? – He had a video camera, yes, and he also had a video machine, but it was about two or three years ago.

In December did he have a video camera or a video machine? – No – not that I saw anyway. I didn't see it in the room.

Do you remember if he had any video equipment by the time you saw him in December? – If he had it was very little.

Did you get the impression he was having any financial difficulties? – I would say that regarding camera equipment there was certainly a winding down, there was a lot less buying and selling.

Is there anything else you can tell the Inquiry about his interest in photography or the nature of any photographs you say that might be relevant to Lord Cullen's search for information? – No. I know that he also, apart from photography – he also did some freelance work as well, somewhere in Glasgow.

That would be on a commercial basis? – Yes.

Can I turn now to guns? Did you know he had an interest in guns? – Well, when I was in the Club he had an interest in guns then, but I didn't realise that he still had that interest now.

Back at the beginning of the 1980s did the Club have a name? – The Rovers – The Rovers Sports Club.

And how did you learn of his interest in guns at that time? – Well, the main Club was in Borestone, but occasionally he would take us to Dunblane to the gun club there and we would fire air guns.

And were these rifles or pistols? – I think there was a mixture of both.

And what did you fire at? – Just targets, round targets.

What age were you? – I must have been 12.

Was there a crowd of you? – Yes.

What was the variation in ages? – Well, they varied from very young – maybe five or six, up to 13 or 14.

And did they all go shooting? – Yes.

And so far as organisation and discipline were concerned in the shooting exercise, can you tell us something about that? – Very organised.

Did you ever feel in danger when you were shooting? – No, never.

And how was Mr Hamilton for discipline? – Very very strict.

And did that apply when he was organising shooting as well? – Yes.

Did you ever see anything, any weapon, other than an air weapon? – Yes. He had .22 guns, real guns, which were very old guns I think from the War.

.22 pistol or rifle? – Rifle.

Did he have one or more than one? – More than one, maybe half a dozen.

Were they his? – I don't know. They may have belonged to the Club.

But you have no recollection of a .22 pistol at all, just a rifle? – No, I have no recollection of a handgun, no.

Just a rifle? – Yes.

And you say up to six, do you? – Possibly, yes.

And where did you see them? – In the Club.

Did he have to take them to the Club or were they perhaps based on the Club premises? – Based on the Club premises.

Now, were they used in your presence? – Yes.

By whom? – By Mr Hamilton and the other members of the Club.

Did you fire a .22? – Yes.

How frequently were these visits to the Club when weapons other than air weapons were used? – I would say it was mainly air guns that were used – maybe once every two or three weeks – less frequently with the actual bullets.

So with weapons other than air weapons did you use them more than once? – Personally? Myself?

Yes? – Yes.

So roughly on how many occasions do you tell us that you actually used them? – Three or four times.

During the period you have known Hamilton, were you aware of him having any sexual relationship, either hetero or homosexual? – None at all.

Now, I think recently Mr Hamilton had some dealings with your father? – Yes.

What was that about? – My father was installing or looking to install a kitchen in his house, and with Tom being a previous kitchen specialist, he offered his services to help install, or select a kitchen.

Now, early in March were you out of the country? – Yes.

And when did you return? – It was on the Monday previous to the incident.

That is Monday the 11th March? – Yes.

Did you go back to Aberdeen? – Yes.

Do you have an answering machine? – I do.

Did you check it when you got back? – Yes.

Were there any calls from Mr Hamilton? – Yes.

How many were there? – I think two.

Were there any messages left? – Just to say that Tom had called, no message.

And the following evening, that is Tuesday 12th March, was there also a message on your machine? – Yes.

And what was the nature of that? – Again just to say Tom had called.

Did you do anything about that? – When I returned from work I phoned him back.

So was that in the evening after the Clubs would be over, if he had a Club? – I think it was after 8 o'clock, yes.

How long did you speak to him for? – I am not very sure, but I would think less than an hour.

A long conversation, obviously? – Fairly long.

I mean, when you say "less than an hour" do you mean approaching an hour? – Yes.

Now, what was this conversation about? – It was about the kitchen that he was installing for my father.

Did it extend beyond the kitchen? – He had said – for a while he had said that he was quite a lonely person, and that it wasn't good to be alone for all your life, which I thought was a bit strange.

Was that something he had touched on in past conversation? – He had touched on it before.

Was it different this time? – Not any different, no.

Did you react to that part of it? – Yes. I said to him, I mean that, you know, it is possible for anyone to be lonely at some point in their life, so it is not a big deal.

Did you give him any encouragement and tell him what he should do? – No.

Did you ask him about his business at all? – I did ask about the cameras.

And what did he say? – He didn't seem as interested any more in the equipment. I felt over the last few months there had been a winding-down of the cameras. He didn't seem to be selling as much.

Now, did he keep the conversation going, or was it you that....? – It just started to fizzle out.

I am sorry? – It just started to go quite flat, so I said it was getting late.

And that is when you got to the end of the conversation? – Yes.

But during most of the hour, or up to an hour that you spoke, was he fluent in his conversation? – The thought of maybe doing the kitchen work.

That was the thing he had an interest in? – Yes.

Would you say that he was noticeably different from usual on that particular conversation? – No, no.

Over the last six months or so had you noticed any change in his attitude to things in general? – He did seem – again related to the cameras, he did seem less enthusiastic about his camera business.

Was there any change in his tone or his attitude towards his grievances? – He had had these grievances for quite a long time, and when he spoke to me about them I found it quite disinteresting, and he did tend to just stop talking about it.

Over the six months before the incident did he talk at all about Dunblane? – Dunblane? Not in particular, no.

Did he talk at all about parents of boys, and any problems he felt he was having from them? – Yes.

And you have mentioned guns in the early 1980's. Did you ever see guns in his house? – No.

Did you know he had a continuing interest in guns? – I did notice – he used to have various magazines in his house, but I did notice there was one magazine which was called Sporting Life, or something, which had a shotgun on the front, so I assumed that was a gun magazine.

But in the six months before the incident how often do you reckon you were in his house? – Maybe three times.

And any sign from either conversation, or what you saw, that he had any interest in shooting? – No. Had you any reason to think he still had guns? – No.

No cross-examination.

Another acquaintance of Thomas Hamilton's within Central Scotland Police also gave evidence:

STATEMENT 50/C – CIVILIAN WITNESS
Name – John Smith Baird Wilson. Occupation – retired.

The witness was a member of Central Scotland Police and was a Firearms Instructor from 1975 until retiring in 1989. He has known Thomas Hamilton for over 20 years. The witness was suspicious of the fact that Hamilton was interested in young boys but knew that the police had no evidence against him. He knew that Hamilton was a member of a gun club. The witness met the accused around 11.30am on Thursday 7th March 1996 in the kitchen department of Debenhams in Stirling. At this meeting, Hamilton told the witness that he was now dealing in cameras and lenses and also that he was shooting at the pistol range in Callander. The two of them discussed problems that Hamilton was experiencing with range ventilation and the witness gave Hamilton some advice. Hamilton then went on to say that he would like instruction in close range instinctive shooting mentioning targets of about 10 yards and asked if the witness would go with him to the Callander range. The witness turned down the offer due to the severe tinnitus he was suffering in his left ear. The two then discussed for some time the witnesses condition. Hamilton then changed his tone informing the witness of his dislikes for the Police and saying that he believed that they had put words into young boys' statements and he complained of his treatment by Police, parents and other authorities. Hamilton proceeded to discuss the Hungerford Shootings and stated that in his opinion, the Police were slow at going in. He felt that Michael Ryan should have been shot earlier. The witness then said that situations like this were not easy for the Police and it would be better if the criminal turned the gun on himself. Hamilton then discussed the Cowie incident stating that the Police should have attended. He asked the witness how long he thought it would take for local Police response, and he said that he didn't know. The conversation lasted for approximately 15 minutes.

On the same evening at 5.30pm, Hamilton phoned the witness having spoken to a friend about his tinnitus. The witness discouraged Hamilton and said he didn't require any assistance or help. The witness then told his wife to say that he was not in if Hamilton were to phone again. The witness does not think that Hamilton was suffering from depression but believes he certainly had a persecution complex.

140

JOHN SMITH BAIRD WILSON (62), Sworn:

Examined by Mr Bonomy: I live in Stirling.

Were you formerly a police officer? – Yes.

With Central Scotland? – Yes.

Over what period? – January 1955 until July 1989.

Now, that is what – 34 years? – Yes.

That is a long time for a policeman? – Yes. I was kept on that bit extra because I was the Firearms Instructor.

And during which period were you the firearms instructor? – I qualified in 1975, although I had started in 1974, and finished some time in 1989.

Did you know Thomas Hamilton? – Yes.

How did you get to know him? – He had a shop, Woodcraft, which was in Cowane Street in Stirling, one of the DIY places. His prices were good. He used to give 10 per cent discount to the police.

So the police actually got a discount? – Well, I did, and certainly others did as well.

While you were dealing with him in the shop, and perhaps over the years after that, were you suspicious of anything? – Yes.

What? – He was unusual – effeminate. He had a tendency to sort of wring his hands. There was a bit of a feeling of discomfort.

What about his interest in Boys' Clubs, young boys? – As far as I knew he hadn't been reported for anything. I knew he was interested, because he had his back shop done out with carpet right up the wall, and he had boys' photographs on the carpet.

Can you tell me what these photos were like? – They were I think stripped to the waist like photographs – certainly nothing naked.

We have heard some evidence today of photographs with black swimming trunks and nothing else – they weren't of that type? – I can't remember that.

But nothing indecent? – No

Did you know he was interested in shooting? – Yes.

And because of your interest as the Firearms Instructor did you have something in common there, or did it never arise? – Not a great deal. I had a fair idea of what weapons he had, but I never shot along with him. On one or two occasions he asked if he could come to the Police Range, and I always managed to put him off for some reason or another.

Would you take someone else to the Police Range? – Yes

But not Thomas Hamilton? – No.

Why? – Well, I suppose because they looked normal and Tommy Hamilton definitely didn't look quite the normal person.

Were you yourself a club shooting marksman? – Well, I was an instructor.

I appreciate that, but were you also a member somewhere? – Yes. I took the class on Wednesday night, the Police Firearms Club, and so shot on a Wednesday night.

So there was a Police Firearms Club on Wednesday night? – Oh yes.

And where did that normally shoot? – Randolphfield, the Police Headquarters, Randolphfield.

Thursday, 7th March this year, did you meet Thomas Hamilton? – Now, if this is the meeting in Debenhams?

Yes? – I couldn't swear whether it was Thursday or Friday, but I did meet him.

So that is 7th or 8th March? – 7th or 8th March.

Where did you meet him? – In Debenhams, the Cook Department of Debenhams.

In Stirling? – Yes.

About what time? – I would have thought 20/25 past 11, or maybe – I was with him for about 15 minutes I think, and I do know that I left him at 20 minutes to 12.

Is that a Department where you can buy kitchens? – Yes, there is kitchen......

Or kitchen units, anyway, and fit them yourself? – No, no.

Just kitchen utensils? – I had been giving a cookery course at one of our local hotels, and I was interested in cooking – so it was utensils.

Were you speaking to him? – Yes.

Initially what was the conversation about? – Well, I heard him say "Hello, John, how are you?" I turned round, and of course it was Tom Hamilton. It was his usual, wringing of the hands, and I asked him what he was doing and he said he was dealing in camera lenses and cameras.

Did he ask you what you were doing? – Yes.

And what did you say? – That I had retired.

Were you uncomfortable in his presence? – Yes.

Was that always the case anyway? – To a certain extent. He was okay in his Woodcraft shop, because it was a customer/client relationship (sic); but in Debenhams he had put on weight – he looked different, and I felt uneasy while I was speaking to him.

When had you last seen him? – Five or six years ago I would have thought.

And this occasion on 7th or 8th March, was that the first time you had felt uneasy? – No, but I felt uneasier.

Right. Did he say anything about what he was doing in the shooting world? – Yes.

What did he tell you? – He mentioned Callander – he mentioned the range there. He said that the Linofax – the Linofax is a screen which stops spatter from bullets – was badly damaged, and the range was spattered. And he said "Much the same as you had at Police Headquarters" when our range had to be closed because there was excess lead and not enough ventilation in it.

Did you give him some advice about that problem? – I gave him advice about two or three things. The main thing I gave him advice about is I have tinnitus, a ringing in the left ear, and I told him to make sure he always had his ears covered, never to have a shot without – for a while at the Police

Range we were getting ammunition in that was pumping about a third of its content out on to the floor, so much so that when the cleaner was using the Hoover one day it blew up because it was full of gunpowder. I told him about that.

And that was the general nature of the conversation? – Yes.

Did he ask about instruction in shooting? – Yes.

What did he ask you? – He said "My conventional shooting is okay, but I am not very good at 10 yards", and he said "I could do with some instruction" – inferring that I give him it.

What was your response to that? – I said that I had tinnitus and I seldom pulled the trigger of a gun, I certainly have stopped shooting game and I have become anti blood-sports.

Did you mention the problem with your ear? – Yes. I think he knew this before – yes, I am sure he said "How did you get on with your ear?" I am sure he brought this up, although I couldn't say for certain.

And do you have some dispute going over that? – Yes, I do.

So there is a claim involved? – Yes.

And did he know that? – Yes.

When that was discussed did his attitude seek to change? – It did. For the first time ever I heard him actually speak against the police. Until then as far as I was concerned he was very very police-orientated.

And what did he say? – Regarding?

When he spoke against the police on this occasion? – Oh, yes, he said, you know, the authorities were against him, the parents of the children were against him, the police tried to get kids to say he had done things that he hadn't done – he certainly was anti-police.

Did he then go on to specific incidents involving the police? – He did.

Which was the first one he mentioned? – Hungerford.

What did he say about Hungerford? – He said that as far as he was concerned that the police, when Michael Ryan started shooting in Hungerford – that the police were scared to go in. And I said "Well, as far as I remember Michael Ryan was hidden and the police would have been going in as targets". And I finished up by saying one or two other things, but said – I was disagreeing with him, I was getting a wee bit annoyed, and I said – my actual words were – "Anyhow, these nutters normally kill themselves anyway, they don't want to be wounded by police firearms officers".

And did you also say it was better if they did that anyway? – I did.

And did he talk about one local incident as well which actually wasn't a firearms incident? – It was a firearms incident.

Well, in the sense that there were ordinary police officers there? – Yes, but this particular one had happened at Cowie just outside Stirling, where a man phoned up one night and said there was an idiot running about with a shotgun. When the first policeman went out there he found out in actual fact this was the person who had phoned, and he had the back and front of the vehicle blasted by a shotgun.

Now, you had a view about that incident, the Cowie incident? – Yes, he said that the police firearms team should have been out and taken care of it.

Did he then ask you a question about police firearm responses? – Yes.

What was the question? – I think the first one was "Are firearms kept at all police offices?" and I said "Well, there certainly wasn't while I was there. It was only places that were manned 24 hours a day". Did he ask you anything about the time that the police would take to respond to an armed incident? – Yes, he brought that out by saying "I think that there should be a permanent firearms response unit available, armed and in a car or in a van, that they can get to the scene, very, very quickly".

Can you say that again? You said.........? – He said.

That the police should.........? – That they should have an armed response vehicle like other forces do – obviously he had read quite a bit – that other forces do so that they could get to a firearms incident quickly.

Did you get the impression he was looking for information? – No, not at that time.

ENDS

The following police witness was introduced to Thomas Hamilton by William MacDonald:

DONALD COWAN (35); Sworn:

Are you a Sergeant with Central Scotland Police? – That is correct.

Based at Alloa now? – I am.

And how long in the police? – I have 17 years police service.

Did you know Thomas Hamilton? – Yes, I did.

When did you first encounter him? – It would be around 1979 or 1980 if my memory serves me correctly.

Who introduced you to him? – A gentleman by the name of Mr William MacDonald.

Was he in the police at the time? – Yes, he was.

Has he already given evidence to the Inquiry? – I am led to believe he has.

What were the circumstances in which you came to meet Hamilton? – Mr MacDonald and his son David were in the Stirling Pipe Band of which I was a member and when I used to take David home sometimes Hamilton was there.

In those days did you have any occasion to speak to him at length? – I wouldn't say speak to him at length. It would be just maybe short periods of five to 10 minutes whilst I would be in Mr MacDonald's house just passing the time before I left.

Did you form any opinion or impression of him at that stage? – Yes, I did. I formed the opinion that I would say he was strange, quietly spoken and an introvert. There was just a gut feeling I had about him, that I didn't take to him very well.

Did you know of his involvement with boys' clubs at that stage? – None whatsoever.

So you would not have any reason to be concerned about his activities with boys at that time? – At that time, no.

How well did you know Mr MacDonald who introduced you to him? – I knew Mr MacDonald fairly well, yes.

What about his son? – I knew him fairly well as well.

Were you able to work out how friendly they were with Hamilton? – I would have said they were fairly friendly, yes.

Did you ever go to Hamilton's boat on Loch Lomond? – Yes, I did. That would have been back around 1979 or 1980 if memory serves me correctly. I went up there with the MacDonald family but Mr Hamilton was not there on the once or twice that I was on the boat.

Now, I am going to ask you about your involvement in Hamilton's firearms certificate renewal in 1995. Prior to that did you have any information about him and his involvement in boys clubs or on his behaviour in general which might have caused you to be wary of him? – None whatsoever.

You hadn't picked up rumours or innuendo or tittle tattle there was about him? – None whatsoever. Although I have 17 years police service, in the main I have spent that over in Clackmannanshire and I would say I have spent maybe only four and a half years of my service in Stirling and the Stirling area and have not been party to any report or muster room or canteen tittle tattle about Hamilton.

But there is more to it than that as well. By 1995 there were a number of police complaints about him, at least complaints that the police had investigated. That is a separate chapter. Now, were you aware of any of that material? – I was not aware of that whatsoever.

So neither from the simple talk nor from the material that the police had did you know anything about him? – That is correct. I knew nothing whatsoever about him.

So what was your role in dealing with his renewal application in 1995? – I was the supervisor at that time of the Area Constables and being their supervisor, when either a grant or a renewal of firearm or shotgun certificates came through it was my duty to allocate these enquiries to individual officers.

Now, can you have D91I, please which is the 1995 application and can you have D92L and can you also have D106 which is FA63? Now, to deal with that form first of all, that is the RL3a form and your name appears on it? – On the form RL3a, my name appears on the rear of it and I have signed it underneath "Reporting Officer".

The reporting officer was Constable Anderson? – That is correct.

What was your role in the enquiry? – Again it was to supervise that the enquiry had been carried out, that the officer allocated the enquiry would go to visit Mr Hamilton, check that his guns on his certificate married up with the details of the firearms in Section 3 of the report and that everything was in order.

Now, you signed it on the 14th February 1995? – Yes, that is correct.

But you had seen it before? – Yes, I had seen his application form before.

Not the RL3a? – No, that is completed after the enquiry has been done.

So are you sure you didn't see the RL3a as well? If you look at the application you will see it is dated 15th January? – Yes, the application form came to me and because I knew Mr Hamilton I had a quick look at it and before I gave this enquiry to PC Anderson, the control docket which was attached to it, I folded it up and put a comment on it for PC Anderson. I thereafter gave the form, DNTO1, along with this control document to PC Anderson.

Now, we see your comment that you have referred to on the other document which is there which is D92. What was it you said to her? – I put at the top, and I folded it over, and I said "PC660 Anderson. With regard to pre-cons could you oblige and check that this is a definite "No" and I have underlined the "No". "I have a feeling he has or at very least is on CI". I mean by that Criminal Intelligence, and I have signed and dated that. I have initialled and dated that, sorry, 18th January 1995.

Now, what was your basis for writing that? – Again it was just on my initial meeting with Mr Hamilton. I had maybe seen him two or three times in passing in Stirling and I had thought he was a strange man. I have thought many times as to why I thought he had previous convictions or as to what type of previous convictions he might have but again it was just a feeling that I had. Nothing more than that.

Now, you got a reply along with presumably the RL3a? – Yes, that is correct.

And what was the reply? – The reply is "No trace PNC. CI intelligence on Hamilton" and it is signed A. Anderson 660. "Nothing to stop firearm application going through".

Is that last bit in the same handwriting? – Yes, it is.

So what documents came to you at the stage you signed the RL3a? – They all come to me. The application form and the RL3a along with this control docket as I call it.

You didn't have any other document like the file or the existing firearms licence? – Sorry, the existing firearms licence which was due to be renewed would be there as well.

But not the firearms file relating to Hamilton? – Not the main file, no.

And from you where did the papers go? – After I have checked it I put it into the Duty Inspector's basket.

CROSS-EXAMINED BY MR CAMPBELL: Just looking at the note that you wrote, D92L. You didn't actually say "I have a strange feeling about this man" although that was the basis for your intervention? – I have on the note "I have a feeling he has or at very least is on CI", yes.

No, I am sorry, the answer to my question I think is "No, I have not put that down" because the feeling is a reference to previous convictions. You are saying "I have a feeling he has previous convictions", not "I have a strange feeling about this man"? – Yes, it is. Yes, "Check that this is a definite No. I have a feeling he has.........", yes.

You see, it might be thought that if what lies behind your intervention at all or what lay behind your intervention in the first place was a gut feeling that you had had about this man, one might have expected that gut feeling to be recorded? – My gut feeling was back to, as I said, 1979 or 1980 and it was in purely social circumstances and it was nothing more than that.

But it was a gut feeling which prompted you to ask somebody to check out the previous convictions? – Yes.

So it is not purely social, is it? – But it is now in the police environment when as a supervisor I was wanting to carry out that check, PC Anderson to carry out that check.

What was your understanding at the time as to the reason for a firearms certificate holder requiring to apply for a periodic renewal of the certificate? – Sorry, I don't quite understand that question.

What was your understanding as to the reason for the requirement that a firearms certificate holder would require to apply from time to time for a renewal of the certificate? – Because his previous one was due to expire.

What training, if any, did you receive in the law relating to firearms regulation? – Well, going back to my probationary period, I would have received input from the Scottish Police College and I would have received input at local level, at Headquarters, and also I would be referred to local Standing Orders and obviously the experience over the years of having dealt with firearm and shotgun renewals and grants.

So it may be a difficult matter but did you receive any training in the law relating to firearms regulation? – In relation to firearms, yes, I would have in my probationary period and, as I said, at local level.

So in 1995 were you aware of the matters which required to be taken into account by those responsible for renewing Mr Hamilton's certificate? – I was aware of the role that the constables enquiring, making enquiry, had to do and I was aware of the role that I had to play in the renewal process.

What was your understanding then of the role which you were required to play? – Obviously to check that all the details on the renewal form married with the details on his certificate which was due to be renewed and that they married with the enquiry officer's report on the form RL3a.

So the instruction which you had as to your role did not go beyond that purely administrative matter? – Well, basically that would be the case, yes. I give it to the enquiry officer and with the answers that she gives me and the RL3a I can see or otherwise that the enquiry has been done.

But we can see that you have taken it upon yourself, because of the gut feeling, to do just a little bit more than that and you have written the note here of the 18th January 1995 to PC Anderson? – Yes.

Did anybody ever come to you and say to you "We have read your note here. Why did you write it?" – No, nobody.

So the only response which you received was a note received from PC Anderson relating to the CI Intelligence? – Yes, that is correct. When I put this back on the Inspector's desk – well, when I initially got that I actually folded the docket up and when I put it on the Inspector's desk it may well have been the case that was down and nobody would have reason to actually see it.

In the paperwork is there any record of a contact with the counter-signatory Mr Campbell? – In the paperwork – as I say, there isn't. I must add that it is normally something that I stress that it is done and I normally get the officer to put another part, at No 7, on the rear of form RL3a, to say that the counter-signatory has been verified, but on this occasion this has not been put on.

What do you mean verification of the counter-signatory? – By that I would expect the officer to call on the counter-signatory and confirm that he has signed the counter-signatory's section of the form, the application form.

BY LORD CULLEN: Is that all, nothing further than to ask, simply that? – Well, I can personally say that I would generally ask him to maybe write his signature so that I could personally confirm rather than just taking his word.

This is all directed to making sure the person who appears to have signed has in fact signed? – That is correct, yes.

That's the object? – Yes. Although PC Anderson hasn't signed it to that effect, knowing PC Anderson as I do as her supervisor, I would think it would be a fair chance that she would actually do that, although, as I say, I haven't actually put that on.

CROSS-EXAMINATION CONTINUED BY MR CAMPBELL: Would you expect any such visit to be recorded? – Recorded in what way?

In some shape or form? – Again, as I say, I normally record it on the rear of the form, the RL3a, but on this occasion that hasn't been done.

Would this be done by a visit or done by a telephone call? – Again, depending on the individual, speaking from my own experience I would do it from a visit.

But others may have a different approach? – Well, they may well do, yes.

RE-EXAMINED BY MR BONOMY: You were asked there about the role you played in supervising the constable. Is the extent of your check that the paperwork looks as though it has been done properly? – To my satisfaction, yes.

You don't go asking her: well, did you check this, this, this and this? – No, in general that wouldn't be the case. I would think that PC Anderson is a fairly experienced officer, a fairly mature individual, and she is an officer I could trust to do that.

ENDS.

Thomas Hamilton's connections with members of Central Scotland Police spanned a good two decades. He was friendly with both Michael Mill and John Wilson from the mid 1970s and William MacDonald and his son David from approx 1979-81. Wilson retired in 1989, MacDonald in 1991 and Mill in 1994 (or possibly 1996). Donald Cowan was introduced to Thomas Hamilton by William MacDonald. Had Hamilton's friendships – and useful contacts – within Central Scotland Police therefore come to an end by March 1996?

CHAPTER 7 :

IN THE END

Over the last few years I have had a hard lesson in politics, government and corruption. I made contact with a government lobbyist who sat through the whole of the Dunblane Inquiry. He, and another colleague, expected to hear from some of the bereaved parents within a year of the Cullen Inquiry. They believed that when the dust settled, the parents would realise the enormity of the miscarriage of justice that had happened and would make contact with them. He is as amazed today as he was then that no bereaved parents made any noises about the cover-up.

When the pruning of the hereditary peers began, he set about framing questions for the retiring peers to put to the House of Lords on controversial issues, such as the Dunblane Inquiry; for example, Lord Burton's question about DS Hughes report. This question was framed so that the reply ensured that we, the general public, became aware of the 100 year closure on the documents, something that none of us knew before Lord Burton's question in 1999. As a result of this, William Scott began his campaign to find out if this closure order was 'legal'. A few years later I got involved, and joined forces with William.

When Martin McGuiness and Sinn Fein suggested to the McCartney sisters that they should "stay out of politics" and that they would only be used by those with "their own agendas", it reminded me of comments made by one of the bereaved parents to me, when I told him I was now going to contact other "interested parties". The McCartney sisters, fighting for justice on behalf of their murdered brother, and the Deepcut families trying to find out the truth about why their children died, easily find their way onto the front pages. People fighting for the truth about the murder of their loved ones can get easy media coverage. Campaigners like myself have to work in a different way.

What concerns me about the various legislation that has been enacted since Dunblane is that it suggests that the laws prior to 1996 had not been strong enough. But they were. Let me give you another example of new legislation post-Dunblane. The Protection of Children (Scotland) Act 2003 (Pocsa). With regard to this legislation, certain areas of the Cullen Inquiry must be highlighted because the practicalities of this new law simply do not properly address the 'balance of risk'.

As the Scout Association knew only too well, Thomas Hamilton was not a 'fit' person to look after children and he was very quickly removed from their organisation. Hamilton then turned to Central Regional Council for approval of school lets for his boys clubs. The Cullen Inquiry suggested that Central

Regional Council's hands were tied and they could NOT stop Hamilton using their premises because he would simply take them to the Ombudsman yet again. As I have already detailed, this is simply not true. Central Regional Council could have stopped Hamilton using their premises for boys gymnastics clubs, because Hamilton did not have the appropriate qualifications to coach boys and the council knew this. As stated earlier, this was cleverly concealed at the Inquiry.

From the Crown Summary of Evidence No 2 (a document that was originally sealed for 100 years): "Hamilton frequently referred to himself as a "fully qualified instructor in gymnastics with the British Amateur Gymnastics Association". A number of enquiries have been made into his qualifications. In February 1993 Central Regional Council wrote to the British Amateur Gymnastics Association and made enquiry regarding his qualifications. They replied stating that Hamilton was the holder of **Women's Assistant Coach Award, Grade 5**, which would qualify him to assist in the teaching of women's artistic gymnastics while under the supervision of a Class 4 coach or above. Qualified Assistant Coaches may work under the direction of a qualified coach but must not work unsupervised".

I wrote to BAGA (now known as British Gymnastics) for confirmation of the above and received this reply: "I am able to confirm that Thomas Hamilton would obtain his coaching qualifications by attending a BG approved course and subsequently passing the theory and practical examinations. He gained the **Women's Artistic Assistant Coach (Grade 5) in 1983** and you are correct that **this would not qualify him to coach boys and he was not qualified to coach unsupervised**".

At the Cullen Inquiry, witnesses from Central Regional Council stated that Hamilton had to produce his BAGA certificate when he applied for school lets. Although it was made clear at the Inquiry that he had a Grade 5 BAGA qualification, the most important part was concealed. A Women's Artistic Assistant award did not qualify him to coach boys. 1983 is the year he made his complaint against Central Regional Council when they took action against him. The Ombudsman ultimately upheld Hamilton's complaint, Hamilton's MP Michael Forsyth encouraged Hamilton to broadcast this, and the rest is history.....

In short, the laws around the supervision of children by volunteer workers pre-1996 were strong enough. There were enough complaints about Hamilton to bring him to the attention of the authorities time-and-time again, and Central Regional Council knew only too well he did not have the appropriate qualifications to run these clubs. He could have been stopped, but Hamilton was protected by his friends – in Central Scotland Police and in Central Regional Council.

It is a tragedy that the truth was covered up at Lord Cullen's Inquiry in 1996, because the Scottish Executive (like Westminster before with its' knee-jerk gun laws) is intent on ruining the lives of children in Scotland with measures such as Pocsa. The fact that there has been a joint response from Girlguiding Scotland, The Scout Association, Youth Scotland, the Boys' Brigade Scotland, YMCA Scotland and Boys and Girls Clubs Scotland speaks volumes. Their scathing critique of this new legislation shows yet again the damage that is done to a society when governments cover up the truth. Yet more bad law has been made as a result of the Dunblane cover-up.

Given that Thomas Hamilton found people within both Central Scotland Police and Central Regional Council who supported him in his activities, he would easily have managed to manipulate a government agency like Disclosure Scotland. The Cullen Inquiry examined options for the vetting of adults in charge of children, but Lord Cullen issued warnings about how this should be done and these have been ignored.

"It is essential", he said in his report, "that if there is to be such a system it should avoid a bureaucratic approach and should be relatively easy for clubs and groups to work with, and for parents and others to understand and rely upon.... I do not consider that it would be practicable to have a system for the compulsory registration of leaders and workers in clubs and groups. It would pose difficulties of defining which individuals were affected by the requirement to register, especially those whose services were given on an informal or occasional basis. There would be a risk of creating a bureaucratic system which would deter many from volunteering their assistance and which would not provide benefits commensurate with the considerable cost involved. It would be possible for someone who was minded to evade the system to do so".

And is there any wonder that many adults are now being dissuaded from working with children at all, thus depriving children of various out-of-school activities. Why is it that the strictures in Scotland have ended up substantially tougher than those in England and Wales? Given that Lord Cullen had just overseen a massive cover-up of the truth, was he (indirectly) trying to warn us that there were exceptional circumstances that had surrounded Thomas Hamilton? And that drastic legislative change was therefore totally unnecessary? What a dilemma for the man.

The danger with this legislation is that volunteer-led organisations will find it impossible to comply with its' terms, and provision of youth activities will thus be destroyed. This will leave a vacuum, just like the vacuum Thomas Hamilton exploited in Dunblane and surrounding areas with the provision of his boys clubs. Furthermore, if, as a society, we are going to run checks on those volunteering to work with children (and obviously there have to be checks), then it is also essential to run checks on those doing the checking. Yes, where does that leave us? The cover-up of the truth at the Dunblane Inquiry has resulted in a belief that the 'law' had to be changed, when it was those in positions of influence with regard to the law who should have been vetted and changed. Hamilton's friends.

There must be a re-examination of all the evidence that was gathered for the Dunblane Inquiry and a wider search for evidence than was pulled together for the hastily convened cover-up overseen by Lord Cullen. I would argue that "the case of Thomas Hamilton" was not a strong enough case for the draconian gun laws that were brought in. Those who are involved in fighting against gun ownership need stronger evidence for their claims regarding guns and target shooting than the case of Thomas Hamilton, a man who could have been stopped on numerous occasions.

By covering up the truth about Thomas Hamilton and his associates, the Cullen Inquiry sent society down a path of further distortions and manipulations. The truth about why 16 children and their teacher lost their lives on 13 March 1996 will be lost to history if a New Inquiry is not established in the very near future.

October 2005 I've always thought it very sad that the Scottish Legal Establishment managed to orchestrate the cover-up right under the noses of the parents and all the journalists at the actual Inquiry. It is more than sad, it is tragic, that they put the finishing touches to the cover-up in such a public way.

Even without reading the material that is now available at the National Archives of Scotland, glaring inconsistencies are evident from reading the Transcript of the Inquiry, which has been available on the internet since early 2001. How many people have read and studied that? Doreen Hagger and I spent many months tearing apart all the evidence and isolating the lies and inconsistencies. We did this in the comfort of our own homes, and consulted each other by email, instant messaging and telephone repeatedly throughout the day whenever we isolated an obvious problem in all the material we were viewing. There is just no way that anyone viewing the documents at the Archives would be able to do this kind of work sitting in a library reading through reams and reams of papers on their own, with nothing to compare them with. Furthermore, it is piecing together LOTS of information that leads to the *possibility* of Hamilton being part of a paedophile network, the *possibility* that Hamilton was being tailed that morning, and the *possibility* that he was shot and killed on scene and did not commit suicide. Nothing is **stated** that makes this obvious. I'm sorry, but the documents weren't sealed for 100 years for nothing. They slapped a 100 year ban on the lot out of laziness, when there were only selected sections that actually gave the game away.

If the perpetrator of the murders at Dunblane Primary School on 13 March 1996 was still alive, he would be serving a life sentence in prison or a mental institution. There would be little doubt about his guilt and any appeal about a miscarriage of justice would undoubtedly fail. Thomas Watt Hamilton pulled the trigger 105 times, killing 16 children and one teacher, and injuring a further 12 children and 3 teachers. If Thomas Watt Hamilton was alive, we would probably not hear too much about him. He would languish in his incarceration and it is doubtful anyone would rally to his cause. As it is, he is dead, and interestingly, we still do not hear much about him... And when we do, it is a bland reference to the "lone paedophile" who carried out the "Dunblane massacre". If Hamilton was alive, he might have given us some clues as to why he did what he did.

In my correspondence with Lord Cullen and the Crown Office over the last few years, I have asked some very direct questions and received very few replies. However, in one letter dated 11 September 2003, the Clerk to the Inquiry, Glynis McKeand, replied to me on behalf of Lord Cullen, "... it was open to those representing parties to the Inquiry... to cross-examine the witnesses who were called, and also to seek leave to call witnesses. Copies of all the documents available to the Inquiry team, such as witness statements, were also available to the representatives of the parties to the Inquiry, so as to ensure that they were in a position to make informed decisions about how to cross-examine witnesses and about whether to seek to lead any further evidence". This is tantamount to saying to the bereaved families – "tough, you had your chance for justice and you blew it".

In my reply to Lord Cullen on 26 September 2003, I wrote "...I wish to clarify that I was writing on my own behalf". Further on in my letter I said, "...I appreciate that copies of all the documents were made available to the representatives of the parties to the Inquiry... and it is of great concern to me that so many questions that should have been asked by these representatives were not. However, that is a separate matter. I am writing to you again because you were the person **responsible for an independent investigation into an event which has caused considerable public concern**".

All my concerns have been repeatedly ignored. Ms McKeand again replied on behalf of Lord Cullen on 10 October 2003. Again she invited me to "make a complaint or an allegation about improper conduct on the part of any person in connection with the Inquiry". Good, I thought, I will. However, the second part of the sentence contains the sting. My complaint "should be addressed to the Crown, and in particular the Deputy Crown Agent at the Crown Office, so that it can be investigated". As I know there has been a cover-up of the truth and I know that the Crown Office masterminded it, why would I expect them to carry out an open and thorough investigation now?

CHAPTER 8 :

THE DENIAL OF DUNBLANE

"Evil isn't an army that besieges a city from outside the walls. It is a native of the city. It is the mutiny of the garrison, the poison in the water, the ashes in the bread" (Charles Morgan)

It began in Dunblane itself, inevitably. Like all other debilitating psychological conditions, it kicked in as a sort of protective device, safeguarding our numbness in the face of unspeakable horror. But in the end, it served only to cause immeasurable harm. The brave words about (eventual) 'recovery' in those days of hell in the middle of March 1996, were preparing the way for even greater denials to come. How inappropriate, looking back, that 'recovery' should have been on anybody's mind with sixteen dead children not yet buried, the injured still receiving hospital treatment. They hadn't even had an opportunity to begin their *own* personal recoveries. And for the bereaved, what hope of **real** recovery? The rest of us really didn't matter, but it was for our benefit apparently, that the deniers of Dunblane set to work in 'restoring order' and 'calm', ready for our eventual recovery. *Mutiny of the garrison.*

Is this what people really wanted and needed to hear? From the very beginning did we have absolutely no intention of actually confronting what happened at Dunblane? Who sets these agendas? As we saw all too clearly, the 'community' was not as damaged as originally portrayed by the media. One Dunblane resident only wrote about his not being traumatised by the tragedy nearly two years after the event. In a letter to *Scotland on Sunday* in November 1997, he wrote: "As a resident of Dunblane I can truthfully say that I did not suffer 'trauma' as a result of the events of March 13, 1996, and the days following. And I do not believe that other residents, who like myself had no direct involvement in the incident, did either. The media must desist from lumping us all into the same boat". If those who felt unaffected by the death of Diana were afraid to voice their heretic views, imagine how those in the "devastated little town of Dunblane" felt at the assumption this had destroyed them. There was always a lot of evidence to suggest otherwise, but the media chose to ignore it. How could one individual contradict such an assertion?

Less than six months after the death of Diana, the newspapers decided to revisit her life and death. According to Mark Lawson of the Guardian this "represented perhaps the worst example ever seen of the psychological condition of denial". He went on to say that Diana has "left behind her a nation in urgent need of a 12-step programme on bereavement". And Dunblane didn't? The public utterances of those Dunblane dignitaries who should have been defending their townspeople, their mutiny against the most vulnerable – the bereaved – was not only slanderous, but harmful to everyone living in Dunblane. Those of us who had no direct involvement but who struggled to find a way of 'accepting' that this atrocity had happened and that everything had changed now, were effectively silenced. The few who chose to speak on our behalf became the public voice of denial. Those of us not in denial would never have sanctioned their words.

Despite the immediate recognition that those directly affected will be the ones requiring long-term support, the agenda quickly changes. The myth of 'community' is created (heavily backed-up by the ministry – the potential for recruitment in the immediate aftermath of a tragedy not to be missed) and the impression of us all having been in it together is firmly cemented. Perpetuation of this myth goes some way towards disallowing any close examination of how such an obscenity ever came to happen. The 'community' inevitably wants to move on. Many are satisfied that 'it' has been swept under Cullen's carpet. And the handgun-ban is the pacifier for the bereaved, with no acknowledgement of how belated and bittersweet a ban can be.

In the first year, the endless cry of our local councillor to **leave us alone** – without any distinction made between the murder-bereaved, the injured children and their families, the injured teachers, others at the school who were physically uninjured but psychologically damaged, and the rest of us who were in no way directly affected – served the purposes of denial. If the town appeared to speak with one voice, then out of respect and reverence for a 'community in mourning', the rest of the world was satisfied to leave well alone.

Denial serves many purposes. Joan McAlpine, writing in the Sunday Times, recognised what was going on, that 'douce' Dunblane resented the publicity the families received. "Mrs Dickson gave a real insight into this side of the town when she complained about making allowances for the families for nine long months. That long? ... I wonder what it was they were tolerating in those dark days? Perhaps, as the decent people of the town sat in shock with the rest of the country, douce Dunblane was worrying about the effect of the publicity on their house prices". Well, house prices are safe again and new house-building goes on all around.

The ashes in the bread. The mal-development of those individuals who become violent might just as easily have been us. Why do I find I can relate to that – hopefully foregone – prospect more easily than to some of the behaviour that goes on after such a tragedy? The empathy-lack of a few has an almost psychopathic quality to it. Callousness and disregard for the feelings of others is a major part of the condition of psychopathic killers. It is an insult to good and true humanity that the deniers got the last word. However, as non-deniers know, there is an 'insidious side effect' to this kind of denial, writes Gavin de Becker, author of The Gift of Fear: *For all the peace of mind deniers think they get by saying it isn't so, the fall they take when victimized is far, far greater than that of those who accept the possibility.*

For the Dunblane parents to be lectured that they weren't the only ones to be bereaved that year demonstrates a total lack of understanding of murder-bereavement. To draw comparisons with other forms of grief, say bereavement following terminal illness, doesn't do justice to either group. Murder-bereavement for starters, is much more rare. It is abrupt, shocking and totally without precedent. As a society we could try to prevent it, although we are led to believe we are helpless and must trust to God. Murder is viewed as 'accidence' (one neighbour described it to me as just that: "when the accident happened" she said), or an 'oversight' on the part of God (sadly, one of the injured children believed that there were just too many of them in the class for God to save, although a minister reassured us that God's heart was the first of all our hearts to break). Nothing could be further from the truth of course. Facing up to that would involve leaving the comfortable state of denial behind, a much more frightening prospect.

Solzenhitzen has described this kind of resistance to the truth. To understand and accept 'evil' requires a splitting of the heart. Yet because we are all capable of such 'evil', yet refuse to believe it, we are not willing to give up a part of our heart. It is akin to religious faith. When the headteacher of Dunblane Primary School told the world that "evil visited our school and we do not know why", he was, in those early days of total incomprehensibility, pushing it out, 'out there', where it has nothing to do with us. It is easier to think of as 'evil-visitation', something completely out of our control. Religious faith also requires this giving up, this relinquishing, of all our heart. Yet if all of ones heart has been given over to 'faith', there is nothing left to understand evil as part of human nature. Like those who wait patiently for science, the devout wait patiently for God. Solzenitzen's 'splitting' of the heart has a double meaning then: the devout are heart-broken, but still have 'faith'; the secular are heart-intact, but in denial.

My disgust at society's complacency towards the issue of violence was rekindled by Dunblane. Disgust at the denial, disgust at all the deaths, disgust, full stop. For all the horror we felt in the immediate aftermath of Dunblane, in the long run, we are more at ease making our 'memorials' than in condemning violence. Why did Britain pull tight its blinkers, stiffen its lip, sweep under its Cullen-made-carpet, the deaths of 16 fairy-toothed children? They hadn't even been given one wish, one tooth under the pillow, one chance of hope, for a sixpence, a blessing, a fairy-tale. We had only just blessed their presence in the world. And they were gone. We have *absorbed* what happened at Dunblane now. And that is very dangerous indeed.

Mutiny. Poison. Ashes. Thereafter, the denials quickly piled one on top of the other. At the Dunblane Inquiry, the police denied that the last of the parents to hear that their child had been killed was as late as 3.30pm. They insisted that by 2.30pm, all the parents had been told. Why? It's not as if this extra hour they were trying to buy themselves added greatly to their cause (whatever that was). It brings to mind the same sort of denial surrounding the fate of the Hillsborough victims – that nobody was still alive after 3.15pm. Despite the police accounts, we now know that some Hillsborough victims were still alive up to half an hour later. Central Scotland Police maintained that they wanted to be one hundred per cent certain of the identity of the dead children, so why lie?

After this end-of-millennium massacre, we were meant to be appeased by a public inquiry. Lord Cullen drew the simple conclusion that mass murderer Thomas Hamilton suffered from a 'personality disorder', as distinct from a 'mental illness'. This distinction is a red herring. It moves us further away from understanding why some people choose to murder. And that is what it is – a choice. There is nothing inevitable about it. The resource of violence is in everyone, says Gavin de Becker, "all that changes is our view of the justification". Those who commit terrible acts of violence, choose their behaviour from among many options. What we have to do, is *second-guess* the kind of person who is likely to make that choice; and then make it difficult for them to do so, or at the very least, take precautions against them. The Cullen Report is a document that details very clearly all the reasons why Thomas Hamilton should never have had guns, but doesn't answer the question why he was allowed them. De Becker describes denial as "the powerful and cunning enemy of successful predictions."

Denial is a save-now-pay-later scheme, a contract written entirely in small print, for in the long run, the denying person knows the truth on some level, and it causes a constant low-grade anxiety. Millions of people suffer that anxiety, and denial keeps them from taking action that could reduce the risks (and the worry).

The same is true of a society in denial. One of America's leading forensic psychiatrists and experts on violence has noted that the case histories are "littered with reports, letters, memoranda, and recollections that show people felt uncomfortable, threatened, intimidated, violated and unsafe because of the very person who later committed atrocious acts of violence."

In the ultimately prescient words of Detective Sergeant Hughes, a violent act of some sort by Hamilton was predicted. In a memorandum dated 11 November 1991, he wrote: "I would contend that Mr Hamilton will be a risk to children whenever he has access to them and that he appears to me to be an unsuitable person to possess a firearm certificate in view of the number of occasions he has come to the adverse attention of the police and his apparent instability... I respectfully request that serious consideration is given to withdrawing this man's firearm certificate as a *precautionary* measure as it is my opinion that he is a scheming, devious and deceitful individual who is not to be trusted" (my emphasis). As we know all too well, no *precautions* were taken at all. Whilst the scale of Hamilton's actions could not even have been predicted by DS Hughes, the fact remains that he was acknowledged as a threat to children. By granting a gun to Thomas Hamilton, Central Scotland Police ultimately implicated themselves in his crime. The signs were all there.

But so was the denial. Hamilton's case history shows that people felt uncomfortable, threatened, intimidated, violated and unsafe. The police should be the greatest experts at "day-to-day high-stakes predictions" says de Becker, "but unchecked denial can eclipse all that knowledge". So, the deniers don't want to know. They've drawn their line underneath it. Speak of it no more.

The Cullen Inquiry explained very little of why Thomas Hamilton made the choice he did. Dr Nigel Eastman, a forensic psychiatrist, commenting on Lord Cullen's conclusions, asks, "What did he, and the experts mean? Does such a label – personality disorder – assist in understanding the offences? Would Hamilton have been treatable?" Eastman explains that a personality disorder is 'developmental' and that there is much uncertainty about their treatability. "However, what is clear is that treatment amounts to attempting to undo, or modify the effects of years of maldevelopment... the developmental origins of a patient with a personality disorder determines that the disorder is *him*". Precisely.

According to one expert at the Cullen Inquiry, there was no indication that Thomas Hamilton had at any time been subjected to anyone who confronted his paedophilia or challenged him about it. In the absence of that challenge, there was no way he would ever accept he had a problem. Hence, when police investigations were carried out into his running of the boys camps, he felt victimised. Even though the Scout Association expelled him because of their suspicions about his motives for working with boys, the reason he was given was "lack of leadership qualities".

Certainly, from what we now know about paedophiles, he wasn't likely to have recognised anything wrong with his behaviour/fantasies if confronted anyway. 'Boy-loving' (as they so quaintly call it) is indicative of emotional mal-development for the straightforward, simple reason that boys grow up to become men. There is no possibility of an enduring love relationship between a paedophile and a boy (or girl), because boys (and girls) have to be 'replaced' every few years. The paedophile is therefore demonstrating emotional retardation.

Furthermore, Hamilton's fascination with weapons (and screen violence), his militaristic approach at his boys clubs and camps, his seeming pleasure at the psychological suffering of others (the classic lack of empathy) all added to the end-justification (for him), of killing.

Coming by guns is easy in America, but as we have seen, it was also all too easy for Thomas Hamilton in Central Scotland over the last two decades of his life. The lack of an 'apology' by the Chief Constable of Central Scotland Police shows a total denial of his force's complicity with Hamilton. They were the added *complication:* the "secondary disease or condition aggravating an existing one" resulting in their *complicity* in his act. To grant a gun to a man whose "apparent instability" was observed and recorded in writing served only to aggravate the existing condition. Interestingly, neither

Chief Constable – Ian Oliver (1979-90) or William Wilson (1990-96) – was questioned at the Cullen Inquiry. Section 6.23 of the Cullen Report states that "If there was a problem the firearms file would also be passed to him" (the Chief Constable). Given the problems they obviously had with Hamilton, the firearms file must have been passed to the two Chief Constables, yet they were not questioned about their obvious failures of leadership.

The Solicitor Advocate, James Taylor, representing Central Scotland Police at the Dunblane Inquiry, submitted that the evidence presented regarding Hamilton's "personality disorder" did not provide sufficient factual support to lead to such a diagnosis. Taylor claimed that the opinions expressed by both a psychiatrist and a psychologist did not demonstrate that Hamilton had a personality disorder and argued that it was therefore unsafe to conclude that he had. Lord Cullen was "not persuaded of that". Nor was I.

Central Scotland Police were unlikely to define him as 'mentally ill' either, so we can see through their ruse. Fearing legal action by the bereaved parents perhaps, they had no choice but to claim that Hamilton was 'normal', otherwise how could they justify granting him a gun licence? However, they did grant him that licence, with tragic and devastating consequences.

Both the experts detected what they regarded as signs or traits of abnormal personality in Hamilton; their problem was simply with the categorisation of the personality disorder. From the Cullen Report: "Dr Baird pointed out every adult displayed features of personality which were particular to himself or herself. They tended to be enduring features and often, although not always, appeared to have originated from upbringing and early formative experiences. When undesirable features were prominent this could cause problems and it was in this context that the concept of personality disorder had arisen". This tells us absolutely nothing. 'Undesirable features of personality' equals 'personality disorder'. Their struggle of course was with the mental illness/behavioural disorder divide and nothing else mattered.

It would appear that Central Scotland Police want it both ways. Earlier in the Cullen Report, it is clearly stated that DCC McMurdo was exasperated with Thomas Hamilton and considered him to be bitter, petty-minded, perverting the healthy relationship between police officers and the Scout Movement into something sleazy and dishonourable. He wrote to the Scottish Office on 14 January 1992: "Both I and the two Chief Constables have tried very hard to resolve the matter but, as always when trying to reason with a zealot, each time a point appears to have been settled he re-introduces it in another guise, adjusts the facts selectively to suit his ends and it all begins again". Furthermore, as the memo of DS Hughes shows, Hamilton had come to the "adverse attention of the police" on several occasions and showed "apparent instability". Quite clearly, Central Scotland Police did not consider Hamilton to be "normal", yet they considered him "fitted" to own a gun. That would still appear to require some explanation. According to Lord Cullen, in deciding to grant and continually renew Thomas Hamilton's gun licence,

Deputy Chief Constable Douglas McMurdo: **"adopted an unduly narrow approach in which he paid not much more than lip service to the idea that a person could be "unfitted" in the absence of a conviction or pending criminal case. He undervalued the breadth of that expression"**.

Equally, the Director of Administration and Legal Services at the former Central Regional Council was not questioned as to why he decided not to pursue proceedings for defamation against Thomas Hamilton in respect of his statements about officers of Central Scotland Police (Cullen Report 4.46). The Cullen Report notes that it was considered such proceedings would not deter Hamilton and "would give him the opportunity to air his views about a conspiracy between the Scouts, the police and the Regional Council".

Typically then, no-one wanted to confront him, yet if there was no conspiracy, these proceedings would have recorded that fact. Furthermore, Hamilton's developing psychopathy would have been evident, thus demonstrating further good reason for revocation of his licence. At no point in the Cullen Report is there a hint of a suggestion that his licence be revoked. Are we really to believe that it was <u>never</u>, <u>once</u>, seriously considered?

If someone had confronted Hamilton and pursued action against him *all the way,* his abusive behaviour might just have been checked. His over-inflated, grandiose, psychopathic sense of self-worth resulted in misplaced feelings of victimisation. He felt aggrieved towards those individuals in a position of authority who, in their limited way, attempted to 'check' his wrong-doing.

After Dunblane, the ignominious removal of Deputy Chief Constable Douglas McMurdo, protesting his innocence to the bitter end – despite the comments of Lord Cullen – was meant as a reassurance. To the extent that he is no longer a serving police officer does of course offer some, for it was positively chilling to hear from McMurdo's own mouth that he would do the same again under the same set of circumstances. Positively chilling. The Cullen Report is a document that details very clearly all the reasons why Hamilton should **never** have had guns, but doesn't answer the question **why** he was allowed them.

The failure of Central Scotland Police to investigate properly Thomas Hamilton's background and their failure to take away his guns amounted to "dereliction of duty of the highest order", counsel for the families of the dead children said. Colin Campbell, QC, suggested the massacre of 16 children and their teacher in Dunblane primary school might not have happened if the police had done their duty.

In 1986, Hamilton lied that he was a top shooter who competed all over Britain, in order to gain permission to own a second 9mm pistol – the weapon he used to shoot 16 children and their teacher at Dunblane primary school. However, documents in my possession clearly indicate that a high ranking police officer in Central Scotland Police lied on behalf of Thomas Hamilton so that he obtained the second 9mm pistol. The truth about Thomas Hamilton and his associates was concealed at the Dunblane Inquiry. The Denial of Dunblane was complete.

The British Government covered up the truth about what happened and 'bought off' the bereaved parents by granting them their dearest wish – a ban on handguns. However, there is much evidence that the handgun ban has done little to reduce gun deaths. On the other hand, as a result of what happened at Dunblane, there have been "copycat" massacres (Port Arthur in Tasmania, but most notably, Columbine in the USA). And there have even been copycats of the copycats....

As a society, we could have shown the kind of outrage seen in Belgium after the abduction and murder of several young girls by a known violent paedophile. After Dunblane, our outrage was poured into the banning of handguns. Hamilton couldn't have killed so many children any other way, nor was he likely to have become a killer if his gun fetish hadn't played such a big part in shaping his identity. Even though he felt victimised by the police, the fact that his firearms certificate was always renewed, without question, and no attempt ever made to revoke his licence, gave confidence to that identity. As the Cullen Report points out, even the most weak and cowardly person could kill with guns: "Firearms and especially semi-automatic handguns had a unique ability to kill. No physical contact, strength, prowess or even bravery was required". Despite his years of apparent planning, and despite the fact that guns require no physical contact, strength, prowess or even bravery, until Hamilton fired his first shot that day, even he didn't know if he was capable of murder.

In reality, the failure of police leadership showed up all too clearly in Dunblane. So, when the deniers of Dunblane set to work 'restoring order' and 'calm' in the immediate aftermath of "the accident", they assisted the process that shuts down all attempts at understanding 'Why'. Just to mention 'Dunblane' now, brings the knee-jerk response of "we don't need to be reminded" and accusations of gratuitous reference. Only when this situation is rectified will we, as a society, begin to lift the wool from our eyes and learn, at every level, that the upholders of law and order are often an integral part of its very breakdown. And when they are part of that breakdown, they must carry the responsibility. The Denial of Dunblane will not end until then.

On 18 May 2004, I petitioned the House of Commons in the hope that they would intervene: The Petition of Sandra Uttley – Declares that the terms of the Tribunals of Inquiry Act 1921 were not met in Lord Cullen's Inquiry into the Shootings at Dunblane Primary School in 1996. A decision was taken by both Houses of Parliament that this Tribunal should carry out an investigation into the true circumstances surrounding the massacre at Dunblane Primary School on 13 March 1996 and that Lord Cullen should report back to Parliament with his findings. The truth, however, was concealed, and I therefore allege improper conduct at the Inquiry. At the time – before devolution – the Lord Advocate was a member of the British Government with a duty not only as public prosecutor for Scotland, but also as chief law officer and legal adviser to the Government. The manifest tension between the Lord Advocate's independent, impartial role as public prosecutor and his other role as law officer to Parliament was never resolved. In legal affairs, the Lord Advocate, as a member of the Scottish Executive, is equal in power with the First Minister. Neither the Lord Advocate nor the First Minister is prepared to address the problem of the Dunblane cover-up.

I respectfully request that:- 1/ the British Government censure the Lord Advocate for instigating and perpetuating a cover-up of the truth at the Dunblane Inquiry, in dereliction of his duty; 2/ There be a resolution and clarification of the Lord Advocate's powers; 3/ The Petitioner further requests that the House of Commons instigates a New Inquiry to establish the truth about why 16 schoolchildren and their teacher lost their lives on 13 March 1996.

My MP, Dr Ashok Kumar, forwarded the petition to Lord Falconer at the Department for Constitutional Affairs for his advice. Several months later we discovered that my petition had been sent up to Scotland... to the Lord Advocate! I didn't know whether to laugh or cry.

So, on 24 January 2005, I wrote to every British MP. I headed the letter: **DUNBLANE INQUIRY COVER-UP: AN ISSUE OF NATIONAL PUBLIC IMPORTANCE.** Less than one hundred MPs replied. If this is a democracy, God help the rest of the world.

"Dunblane – an issue they said was above party politics – appears to have become the latest indictment of our rather shabby system of democracy"
Graeme Wilson (The Scotsman 11 Dec 1996)

In denying us the full truth about Dunblane, the Government dishonours the dead. It is impossible to say…. that if widespread suspicion about Hamilton had been acted upon this tragedy would never have happened. Nevertheless, these questions must be asked, for only in this way will the dead be honoured with the truth……
(Editorial from The Herald, 15 March 1996)

NOTES

1. A Document Prepared for the Dunblane Inquiry

CHAPTER 'H' (1b) – <u>INVOLVEMENT IN BOY SCOUT MOVEMENT</u>

This Chapter deals with the involvement of Hamilton with the Scout Association. The extensive correspondence generated by Hamilton has shown consistent references to the Scout movement and he would appear to regard them as a rival to his own youth groups. He also makes frequent references to a perceived conspiracy against him and his youth club by the Scout movement and apparently held the view that Central Scotland Police particularly favoured the Scout movement.

Hamilton became involved with the Scout Association as an active member of the First Stirlingshire Adventure Scouts in 1973. He was known by Mr Deuchars. Hamilton approached Mr Deuchars and requested that he be considered for a position as an Assistant Scout Leader. Such appointments were at the discretion of the District Commission and subject only to a check with Scout Headquarters in London to ensure that an applicant was not registered as an unsuitable person. This check was carried out and an application form thereafter completed. The application was processed and on 11 July 1973 Hamilton was issued with his Leader Warrant and Record Book. He took up an appointment as an Assistant Scout Leader within the 4.6 Stirling Scout Group. He carried out his leadership duties under the supervision of other Scout Leaders and his progress was monitored by Mr Deuchars.

After six months Mr Deuchars considered that Hamilton was ready for more responsibility and promoted him to the position of Scout Leader. In 1974 Mr Deuchars received complaints from the parents of boys who had been taken to Aviemore on a trip. They slept in the back of the mini bus. Thomas Hamilton explained that there had been a problem with the bookings at the hostel and this account was accepted by Mr Deuchars. A warning was given regarding future conduct.

About two weeks later a similar complaint was received. Mr Hamilton complained that the hostel had been overbooked, although this was subsequently disproved and it was requested that he return his warrant. A report was prepared detailing the circumstances of the dismissal and forwarded to Scout Headquarters. The circumstances surrounding the dismissal were also communicated to Dr Fairgrieve who was the County Commissioner for Scouts in Stirlingshire. He in turn discussed the matter with the Executive Committee for Scouts in Scotland. A letter was subsequently written demanding the return of Hamilton's warrant book.

On 24 May 1974 Mr Jeffries wrote a letter to the Warrant Department Scout Headquarters advising that Hamilton had been suspected of 'improper behaviour with boys' and required to return his warrant. This document also makes reference to the medical opinion of Dr Fairgrieve who considered Hamilton to be mentally unbalanced. He thought that Hamilton displayed 'evidence of a persecution complex' and 'grandiose delusions of his abilities'. He was also suspicious of Hamilton's moral intention towards boys.

Hamilton had made an application for the post of Assistant Scout Leader with Second Clackmannanshire Scout Group. This application was not accepted and it was agreed that a confidential file would be kept on Hamilton. It was noted that Hamilton would remain ineligible for further appointment or connection with the Scout movement.

On 19 August 1974 Hamilton approached Dr Fairgrieve to discuss his dismissal. He accepted that he was wrong not to return his warrant and undertook not to approach the Scout movement unless they approached him. On 28 August 1974 Hamilton sent a letter to Dr Fairgrieve apologising for any inconvenience he had caused and requested that he be considered for any future positions in the Scout movement. On 1 February 1977 Hamilton offered his services to Denny and Bonnybridge Scouts. Contact was made with Dr Fairgrieve and Hamilton was told that they had no vacancies.

On 25 February 1977 Hamilton wrote a letter to Mr Jeffries, Scout Headquarters alleging a long campaign of victimisation by Mr Deuchars and Dr Fairgrieve. He complained that his Scout Warrant had been cancelled without any just reason and requested that a committee of inquiry be established by the Scouts to investigate his allegations.

On 28 February 1977 Mr Jeffries wrote to Mr Hamilton explaining that the issue of the Scout Warrant was entirely a matter for the area concerned and that the Scout Association was under no obligation to issue a warrant or to give any reason for not issuing one. On 2 March 1977 Hamilton again wrote to Scout Headquarters demanding a committee of inquiry. This request was again refused.

On 6 April 1977 Hamilton attended Scout Headquarters to complain. Mr Jeffries again explained that the issue and withdrawal of Warrants was discretionary and no explanation need be given. On 7 April 1977 Hamilton sent a letter to Mr Jeffries protesting at his treatment by the Scout Association. He stated that he no longer wished 'his good name' to be associated with the Scout movement in Stirling District.

On 16 August 1978, following reports concerning the activities of 'Stirling Rovers Boy's Club' Mr Jeffries was compelled to write to Scout Headquarters and report, that parents of the boys in Hamilton's club were encountering the same difficulties with Hamilton that had been experienced in 1974. At this time it was known that Hamilton had some 100 boys attending his club and wore a uniform similar to the Scout movement. The purpose of the letter was to alert Scout Commissioners from the surrounding area to the possibility that Hamilton may make approaches to the movement or start other clubs. No action was taken in respect of Hamilton or his club.

On 4 October 1982 Mr Jeffries was again made aware of the activities of Hamilton and the rover group operating in Dunblane. He advised the Scout Headquarters that the situation was being watched closely by both the Scout and Police authorities.

On 28 November 1983 the Scotsman Newspaper published an article entitled "Parents back youth leader after Council end let". The article dealt with the cancellation of lets by Central Regional Council and makes reference to Hamilton as a former Scout Leader. The cancellation of the let is dealt with fully in Chapter 'J'.

In August 1984 the Scout movement were contacted by the Commissioner for Local Administration in Scotland in relation to a complaint that Hamilton made against Central Regional Council (see Chapter 'J'). A report was given to the Commissioner to ensure that all factual accounts made with the exception of a claim by Hamilton that he had formally resigned by letter from the Scout movement in 1974. A copy of this alleged letter of resignation has been forwarded to the Commissioner. A copy letter was recovered from the file of Central Region and it is thought likely that this is a fabrication by Hamilton to support his assertion that he resigned from the Scout Association and was not dismissed.

On 7 November 1984 Hamilton attended at the Scottish Scout Headquarters and requested to know whether he was 'black listed' by the Scout Association. He said that rumours had been circulating about him and that these were affecting his business. He also mentioned that he was considering bringing the Dunblane Rovers Group to the Scout Association provided he was given a Scout Warrant.

On 21 November 1984 the Scotsman carried an article detailing maladministration by Central Regional Council regarding the let of Council premises.

In December 1984 Hamilton visited Mr Vass and accused him of passing information to a Councillor. Mr Vass formed the opinion that Hamilton was tape recording the conversation. The allegation was denied by Mr Vass.

On 17 August 1986 Hamilton called at the home of Dr Fairgrieve alleging that rumours were being circulated that he was homosexual and demanded to know why he could not be accepted as a Scout Leader. Dr Fairgrieve advised him that he was under no legal obligation to explain. He was sufficiently concerned at the demeanour of Hamilton that he immediately made a personal note of the interview. On 24 August 1986 Hamilton again contacted Dr Fairgrieve by telephone. This was also noted.

In August 1986 Hamilton called at Scout Headquarters complaining about Mr Deuchars whom he alleged advised him of his presence on a Scout 'black list' and that he was homosexual. Caution was advised by Scout officials in lieu of any legal action. Hamilton again complained by telephone on 16 September 1986 and by letter on 12 November 1986. On 7 November 1986 a letter was sent to Hamilton on behalf of the Chief Commissioner of Scouts answering his concerns.

On 12 November 1986 Hamilton again wrote to the Scout Association protesting at the content of previous correspondence and stating that the treatment by the Association was contrary to natural justice.

On 3 May 1989 Hamilton wrote to Michael Forsyth MP, complaining about the Scout Association and alleging collusion with Central Scotland Police who had given unfavourable reports about his summer camp. He also made reference to an article in the Stirling Observer where a Police Officer was pictured with Scout Officials and identified this officer, as being the fiancee of Constable Duncan who was the other officer who attended his camp in 1988. Deputy Chief Constable McMurdo replied to this letter and advised that he was not prepared to divulge personal details of personnel and that he was appalled that Hamilton would attempt to establish some tenuous link between the Police and the Scout Association. On 8 May 1989 Hamilton contacted Central Scotland Police to report that during a recent community involvement visit to the club he was not permitted to take publicity photographs, yet local press show photographs of the Police with the Scouts. On 1 April 1990 Hamilton wrote to Central Scotland Police stating confirmation that a civilian employee, James McKellar, held a senior administrative position in Central Scotland Police and was also the area commissioner for Scouts in Stirling. This information was subsequently confirmed by the Deputy Chief Constable McMurdo. On 7 April 1990 Hamilton wrote to Mr McKellar and noted that the number being used on official Scout notepaper was that of Police Headquarters, Stirling. He also wrote to the Chief Constable lodging a formal complaint re. the use of the telephone number. This complaint was replied to by the Deputy Chief Constable advising that he had no objections to the use of this number.

On 7 January 1991 Hamilton wrote to Michael Forsyth MP relative to his complaint against Central Scotland Police and the 1988 Summer Camp (details in Chapter 'I' (2)) where he states that the wife of the officer asked to investigate his complaint was a Cub Scout Leader in Dunblane.

Around 14 May 1991 Dr Fairgrieve had occasion to write to Mr McKellar requesting the return of some files he had passed over to his successor in the Scouts when he retired in 1987. In this letter Dr Fairgrieve expressed his views on Hamilton and noted that not all the organisations who had encountered Hamilton could be wrong in identifying his perceived persecution complex. While Dr Fairgrieves at no time had any evidence to suggest that Hamilton would harm children, he became progressively concerned about his mental balance. It is noted, however, that Dr Fairgrieve was not aware that Hamilton possessed a Firearms Certificate.

On 24 June 1993 Dt Constable Taylor contacted the Scout Association as part of an ongoing inquiry into allegations that Hamilton had been photographing boys (detailed in Section 'I' (2)). The Scouts Association confirmed the existence of a confidential file and advised that while nothing had been proven against Hamilton, it was felt that Hamilton should no longer be allowed to work with the Scouts. Dt Constable Taylor did not copy any documentation from the file and cannot recollect seeing any reports which would have supported his investigations nor raised any undue concern over the mental health of Hamilton.

On 30th August 1995 the Scout Association received a copy letter dated 18 August 1995 which was signed by Hamilton and addressed to 'Dear Parents'. This letter arrived in an envelope apparently written by Hamilton and had no covering letter. This letter had been circulated to Parents in Dunblane cataloguing events from the date when he joined the Scouts to leaving the Scout movement in 1974, the attempts of a Senior Scout Official to discredit him, his fight with Central Regional Council and his complaint being upheld by the Commissioner for Local Administration in Scotland in 1984.

On 31st January, 1996 the Association received another copy letter dated 26th January, 1996 which was signed by Hamilton and addressed to "Doctor Robert Ball". This letter details serious allegations by Hamilton that Teachers in both Bannockburn and Dunblane Primary Schools had been advising pupils that he was a "pervert" and mentioned "warnings given to entire schools by Head Teachers during Assembly". Hamilton identified the origins of these rumours as being from Mr Vass, whom he considered to have made malicious comments in an attempt to undermine his youth work in Dunblane.

On Wednesday 6th March, 1996 Ms Fernie, who is employed as an Administrative Assistant at the Scottish Scout Headquarters received a telephone call from a male who gave his name as Thomas Hamilton and asked who was the Patron of the Association and on being advised that it was Her Majesty The Queen the caller then went on to discuss how he had been badly treated by the Scout Association. He also said that Mr Vass and Mr Deuchars had alleged he was a pervert. Ms Fernie repeatedly offered to refer Hamilton to the Chief Executive of the Scout Association, but he declined the offer, stating that it was "too late for that". He requested details of his Senior Scout Officials. On termination of the call Ms Fernie immediately informed the Chief Executive who in turn advised that Hamilton was known to the Organisation and that they would not reply to his request for information. A report of the conversation was drafted.

On 12th March, 1996 the Scout Association received another letter from Thomas Hamilton addressed to Her Majesty The Queen. This letter again details Hamilton's version of his involvement with the Scout Movement and advised that the rumours circulated by Scout Officials had now reached epidemic proportions across Central Region. This letter was received by the Chief Executive of the Scout Association. He in turn drafted an urgent facsimile message to Scout Headquarters, London, advising them of the correspondence and of the fact that Scottish Scout Headquarters held a file on

Hamilton. As the fax was being sent on 13th March, 1996, news of the Dunblane Incident was emerging.

Around the same time Mr Vass received a copy of the same copy correspondence to Her Majesty the Queen. No action was taken in relation to this letter.

2. Document prepared for the Dunblane Inquiry

CHAPTER 'J' – HAMILTON'S DEALINGS WITH VARIOUS AUTHORITIES

J(1) – This section details Hamilton's dealings with Central Regional Council from 27th October 1981 up until 10th March 1996. In May 1983 Hamilton was granted the use of Dunblane High School for use by his Boys Club. It was decided, however, in August 1983 that any future lets should not be granted due to concerns regarding operation of the Club.

Hamilton lodged a formal complaint with the Ombudsman alleging maladministration by Central Regional Council. This official complaint was signed by a local councillor and Central Regional Council subsequently received a series of letters in support of Hamilton apparently written by parents. In November 1983 the Education Committee of Central Regional Council held the decision to terminate the let and refuse future lets.

In January 1984 Hamilton reapplied for the let of Dunblane High School and Central Regional Council Education Department decided that if he could demonstrate a new organisation and committee structure his application would be considered. The Committee decided to defer the let application pending the outcome of the Ombudsman's investigation. In November 1984 the Ombudsman published his report and found Central Regional Council guilty of maladministration in their dealings with Thomas Hamilton. In January 1985 Central Regional Council Legal Services advised the Education Department that they could resume consideration of lets by Hamilton. In September 1985 the Education Department agreed to grant Thomas Hamilton the let of Dunblane High School for his Boys Club.

During the summer of 1988 Central Regional Council became aware of the investigation by Strathclyde Police into Thomas Hamilton's Summer Camp but decided that they had no remit to intervene. In September 1988 the Council terminated its let at Graham High School in favour of their own Sports Development Scheme. Thomas Hamilton subsequently threatened them with legal action. In October 1990 Thomas Hamilton wrote to the Council Chief Executive complaining that he believed Councillors and Officials were abusing their positions in dealing with his let applications by favouring Council Groups.

In July 1991 the Council were made aware of a parental complaint concerning a child at the Summer Camp run by Hamilton. Thomas Hamilton made a formal complaint re the conduct of Social Work investigating the incident at the Summer Camp at 1991. He subsequently wrote a number of letters of complaint regarding the same incident.

169

In May 1992 he was granted the let of Dunblane High School for use by Dunblane Boys Club. From July to October 1992 Thomas Hamilton successfully applied for and was granted lets for Stirling, Bannockburn and Denny High Schools and also for Laurencehill Academy and Alloa Academy.

Following a complaint by a parent in February 1993 it was suggested that Central Regional Council check Thomas Hamilton's adult supervision requirements. Following this check the Education Department recommended an amendment of their guidelines with regard to coaching qualifications.

On 29th June 1993 the Council wrote to Thomas Hamilton advising him that his qualifications did not entitle him to teach gymnastics unless supervised by a higher qualified instructor. This, however, highlighted the problem with the Council's guidelines in that they were below those specified by the Gymnastic's Association and thereby allowed Thomas Hamilton to teach gymnastics without supervision. In November 1993 it was suggested to Central Regional Council that new standards be written into their basic Sports Coaching Guidelines, effectively raising the standards of qualification required above that held by Hamilton.

Between Nov 1994 and March 1995 some complaints were received regarding the activities at the Clubs. These complaints were considered but no further action was taken.

In June 1995 Hamilton expressed his concern that rumours were being spread by teaching staff at Bannockburn Primary School regarding his sexuality. In June or July 1995 the Council was advised that a catalogue had been found within the rear of a mini bus used by Hamilton which contained information on guns and handcuffs. This information was passed to the police.

In November 1995 the Council acknowledged Hamilton's application to hold a Summer Camp at Dunblane High School. In January 1996, as a result of leaflets distributed by Hamilton, an internal memorandum was sent regarding Thomas Hamilton. It was decided, however, that there was still no avenue for termination of any of the lets.

At the end of January 1996 Thomas Hamilton sent a letter to a Councillor alleging victimisation and damage to reputation. Around 10th March 1996 a copy letter was received by the Head Teacher at Bannockburn High School addressed to Her Majesty The Queen complaining of prejudice regarding the Scout movement.

CHAPTER 'J' – HAMILTON'S CONTACTS WITH THE COMMISSIONER FOR LOCAL ADMINISTRATION IN SCOTLAND

The main role of the Commissioner for Local Administration is the consideration of complaints of injustice arising from maladministration by, amongst others, Local Authorities. The Commissioner is more popularly known as the Local Authority Ombudsman. Included in this section are summaries of contacts Hamilton had with the Ombudsman. In five separate instances Hamilton engaged in lengthy correspondence with the Ombudsman, letters being copied to the individual authorities and individuals against whom he was complaining.

COMPLAINT AGAINST CENTRAL REGIONAL COUNCIL – 1983

On 15 August 1983, at a meeting of the Further Education & General Purposes Committee of Central Regional Council, a decision was taken to suspend Hamilton's let of Dunblane High School following complaints. During this meeting references were made to Hamilton's removal from the Scouts and suggestions that he had homosexual tendencies. The meeting also discussed complaints which had been made by parents and teachers who had assumed that the group was linked to the scouts. There had also been complaints regarding improper supervision and that Hamilton was circulating information suggesting that he was recognised by the Education Authority, which he was not.

No positive proof was admitted at the meeting regarding these allegations. It was acknowledged that the concerns raised were not new, but had been known for some time. A decision was taken to remove the let and the reasons given were the complaints from parents and teachers who had been misled, and secondly that Hamilton had claimed the support of the Education Authority which he did not have. Although these were the reasons laid down, the main line of conversation in the meeting appears to have been to discuss Hamilton's character and concern about his motives in wishing to be with the children. Hamilton was informed of the decision and he immediately appealed. He levied support from children and parents who wrote letters and a petition to Central Regional Council expressing their concern at the loss of the club.

Hamilton managed to identify the Councillors who had been in attendance at the meeting and visited four of them at their homes in order to voice his opinion in regard to the decision. He also ascertained that the main theme of this meeting had been around his character and this was an integral part of the reasons for withdrawal of the let. Three further confidential meetings were held at which concerns about Hamilton were discussed. They expressed grave reservations that Hamilton appeared to be learning fully of all comments made at those meetings. At this time Hamilton was receiving advice from **Councillor Robert Ball** and subsequently submitted a complaint to the Ombudsman about Central Regional Council. He also took legal advice and arranged for a letter to be sent from a Solicitor threatening legal action and a claim for damages. The Ombudsman decided that this complaint did fall within his remit and a formal investigation took place. The findings of this investigation were published and it was concluded that the actions taken by the Council were not justified.

In the light of the Ombudsman's decision Central Regional Council resumed correspondence with Hamilton and agreed to further lets of premises at Dunblane High School to his group which by this time had been named 'Dunblane Boy's Club'. This decision appears to have had an effect upon

171

Central Regional Council who thereafter appear to become wary of Hamilton with regard to lets and the possibility of him complaining again to the Ombudsman.

COMPLAINT AGAINST LOTHIAN REGIONAL COUNCIL – 1989

Hamilton applied for and gained access to the premises of Linlithgow Academy between 30 April 1988 until June 1989. In May 1989 Ms Hagger complained to her local councillor and informed her of her concerns about Hamilton. She was concerned about conduct towards boys in his care and the fact that a Police investigation took place regarding his 1988 summer camp at Inchmoan, Loch Lomond. (Fully documented in Chapter 'I' (1). The information was passed to the Education Department on 12 May 1989. After consideration and consultation with the Regional Solicitor it was decided that Hamilton's lets should be terminated forthwith. He was notified of this by letter on 17 May 1989.

Hamilton complained to Lothian Regional Council and the Ombudsman on 19 May 1989 regarding the withdrawal of his let and made reference to his previous complaint against Central Regional Council in 1984. The Ombudsman considered the circumstances of the complaint and called for information from Hamilton, Lothian Regional Council and Central Scotland Police. The reports made by Lothian Regional Council stated that the Council was motivated by concern for the children's welfare. It further expanded that it was not for the Region to prove or disprove allegations made and that their prime concern was for the care and wellbeing of their children. The report also stated that Hamilton made no application for further lets for the school term beginning August 1989, but that should he do so, then his application would have been given full consideration.

In response to this, with the knowledge that no further applications had been made, the Ombudsman decided not to take any action in this case and this was communicated to Hamilton in a letter dated 12 April, 1990. No further let applications were made by Hamilton in the Lothian area. This may be related to adverse publicity surrounding the termination of the lets and the creation of School Boards to review applications. It may also be related to the incident on 16 May 1989 when Ms Hagger and a friend took eggs, flour, suntan lotion, fish fertilizer, and wallpaper paste and threw it over Hamilton when he left a club. The Police were called but Hamilton refused to make a complaint.

COMPLAINT AGAINST CENTRAL REGIONAL COUNCIL SOCIAL WORKER - 1992

In 1992 a Joint Police and Social Work investigation took place into the Summer Camp organised and run by Hamilton in 1991 at Millarochy Bay, Loch Lomond. It was then alleged that Hamilton had assaulted one child, exposed others to inclement weather and obstructed the Police in the course of an investigation. This incident is fully documented in Chapter 'I' (1).

On completion of this investigation Hamilton made a formal complaint regarding two of the investigators. The complaint against Sergeant Hughes, the Police Officer concerned, was investigated through the Police Complaint & Discipline Procedure and is fully documented in Chapter 'K'.

The complaint against Ron Keilloh was investigated by the then Director of Legal & Administration. The nature of Hamilton's complaints were harassment and disruption of his summer camp and defamation of character owing to the method in which the Police and Social Work spoke to the children and to members of the public. The outcome of the investigation in relation to Ron Keilloh was that he was found to have been thorough and professional in his dealings with the children involved and there was no complaint for him to answer.

Hamilton did not accept this and made a formal complaint to the Ombudsman. This was considered and Hamilton was advised in a letter dated 2 March 1992 that there appeared to be an option for legal action to be taken by him through the Civil Courts. On receiving this advice Hamilton applied for Legal Aid via the firm Marshall Wilson Dean & Turnbull. This application was refused. He then re-contacted the Ombudsman asking him to reconsider his decision to intervene. This request was denied and the matter was brought to an end on 26 May 1992.

COMPLAINT AGAINST FIFE REGIONAL COUNCIL – 1992

In 1992 Hamilton applied for and gained lets of school premises at Queen Anne High School and Woodmill High School, both in Dunfermline. On 29 June 1992 an incident occurred at Dunblane High School where Hamilton had been holding a summer camp. About 10.15pm that evening three children from the Dunfermline area, who had been at the camp for one night only, were found by the Police having run away from the school and made their way to a telephone kiosk approximately half a mile from the school, where they telephoned for their parents to come and collect them. Two of the boys were barefoot.

As a result of this incident reports were submitted to the Procurator Fiscal in Stirling and to the Reporters to the Children's Panel in Stirling and Dunfermline. A decision was then taken to immediately suspend all lets held by Hamilton in the Dunfermline area with effect from Friday 28 August, 1992. Hamilton was notified of this decision and immediately began corresponding with Fife Regional Council giving his version of the events of that night. This included references to previous suspensions of lets and threats that if the matter was not resolved speedily with his lets returned then he would report the matter to the Ombudsman for enquiry alleging injustice. He also lodged a formal complaint with the Education Department. Hamilton was invited to a meeting with Mr Somerville of the Fife Education Department within his offices to discuss the entire incident and to allow consideration of the circumstances. This offer was declined by Hamilton.

A report was compiled dated 1 September 1992 by Edwin Liddell, an advisor in physical education within Fife Region. His report was based on a video supplied by Hamilton showing children performing exercises at the summer camps. This report was very critical of his teaching methods, discipline and general handling of the children.

Hamilton and Fife Education Department then engaged in further correspondence, all of which was copied to the Ombudsman by Hamilton. At this stage Hamilton requested a formal inquiry which the Ombudsman then declined on 7 September 1992. The reason given for this was that a formal complaint was already ongoing in relation to the Education Department and there was a possibility of them coming to a resolution. Hamilton, however, continued to refuse to attend meetings at the Education Department Offices.

On 18 November 1992 Hamilton wrote to Mr Markland, Chief Executive of Fife Regional Council and stated that he no longer wished to let premises in that area. He stated that damage caused by the let suspension was irreparable and that resources had now been allocated to clubs set up in other areas. He also stated within this letter that he was determined to pursue the complaint via the Ombudsman. The Ombudsman was kept aware of the proceedings throughout this matter and decided that he would not become involved. Hamilton was notified of this decision on 14 December 1992.

COMPLAINT AGAINST CENTRAL REGIONAL COUNCIL – 1994

On 30 May 1994, Hamilton wrote to the Ombudsman making a formal complaint in relation to Central Regional Council and arrangements which had been made relating to a summer camp to be held at Dunblane High School between 10 and 24 July 1994. The disagreement arose as a result of Hamilton's belief that he had sole use of the school premises throughout the period of his summer camp and that no other person would be in attendance at the school.

A decision was then taken by the School Council on 28 May 1994 to allow part of the kitchen area on Sunday mornings only for members of the Local 'Quaker' Group. Hamilton found this arrangement completely unacceptable and believed the entire incident to be co-ordinated by Sergeant Moir who is a member of the School Council Group. Jackie Cowan of the Community Education Department made arrangement to cater for re-allocating facilities to the Quaker Group and arranged a meeting with Hamilton on 30 May 1994. Hamilton attended this meeting but refused to allow Jackie Cowan to speak, repeatedly expressing his own concerns in relation to the matter. She subsequently sent him written notices of the changes.

Hamilton wrote to the Chief Executive of Central Region on 3 June 1994 expressing his satisfaction that the matter had been resolved and stating that his summer camp would go ahead as planned. There are no further known incidents regarding complaints being made by Hamilton to the Ombudsman.

3. Document prepared for the Dunblane Inquiry
SUMMER CAMP – JULY/AUGUST 1998 – INCHMOAN ISLAND, LOCH LOMOND

Inchmoan Island is the property of Luss Estates Company, Luss, Dumbartonshire and is within the jurisdiction of Strathclyde Police. No permission had been obtained by Hamilton to make use of the land.

30th June 1988 Hamilton with a juvenile Craig Wilson travelled to the Island to set up camp. The plan was that children would reside on the Island for blocks of one week, Sunday to Sunday, up to a maximum of six weeks. No parental visits were allowed and phone calls by children to their parents were at Hamilton's discretion.

3rd July 1988 Parents took their children to Balmaha Boat Yard where the children were taken by boat to the Island and met by Hamilton. There was only one boat available and during the period of the camp it was used to fetch supplies from the mainland. On these occasions the children left were left on the Island cut off with no means of contact with the mainland or emergency services. No arrangements were made by Hamilton with the police, local doctor or other agencies to advise them that this group was present on the Island. During this camp a number of incidents were alleged to have occurred whereby children were assaulted by Hamilton as punishment for misbehaviour or failing to perform exercises to his expectation. The camp ended on 14th August 1988.

17th July 1988 At 9pm a complaint was made to the police regarding assaults on and lack of supervision of children attending the Island. The complaint was made to Central Scotland Police.

20th July Central Scotland Police notified Strathclyde Police of the complaint and it was agreed that Central Scotland Police would dispatch officers to visit the camp. On reaching the Island officers from Central Scotland Police found the camp site on the east shore and a group of eight year old boys were playing unsupervised. The Police Officers met with Hamilton who showed them round the camp site. There were tents sited at the camp. Food had been scattered around and there was an open fire with a grill top. There was a stores tent which was also used by children for sleeping. The food available was mostly of a dried nature. There was no fresh fruit or vegetables. First Aid facilities were scant and the sleeping bags were damp. The boat was examined and found to have insufficient life jackets. Hamilton stated that "good swimmers" were not issued with life jackets. The Police interviewed the 13 children present. All were wearing black swimming trunks only with a few exceptions who were wearing only trunks and a t-shirt. All appeared extremely cold and wet. Hamilton did not allow them to wear any other clothing. All children were noted to have cuts and grazes to their legs.

Of the 13 children only three stated they were enjoying themselves and the remainder stated that they were homesick, unable to contact their parents and the food they were provided with was poor and that Hamilton was too strict.

The Police investigation revealed that Hamilton was the only supervisor at the camp.

21st July 1988 Parents of the children were contacted and informed of the circumstances found and the children were taken to Dumbarton Police Office where several were taken home by their parents but some were returned by the parents to Hamilton's care. Strathclyde Police subsequently submitted a report against Hamilton to the Procurator Fiscal at Dumbarton and after review the Procurator Fiscal decided to take no action and the case was marked "no proceedings".

4. Document prepared for the Dunblane Inquiry

September 1988 Hamilton made repeated visits to and writes numerous letters to Inspector Mill of Central Scotland Police at Dunblane expressing his dissatisfaction with regard to the Police actions and the investigation.

30th November 1988 Hamilton makes an official complaint by letter to Chief Constable Oliver of Central Scotland Police against PCs Gunn and Duncan regarding their involvement in the Inchmoan Island investigation.

December 1988 Inspector Keenan of Central Scotland Police Complaints & Discipline was appointed Investigating Officer of Hamilton's complaint. Inspector Keenan completed an investigation and submitted his findings by way of a Report to the Deputy Chief Constable, McMurdo. Mr McMurdo reviews the Report and finds the complaint against his officers to be unsubstantiated.

31st October 1989 Hamilton was interviewed by DCC McMurdo and accepts his findings in respect of the investigation. Hamilton comments he is totally satisfied with the Police Internal Complaints & Discipline investigation.

HAMILTON'S COMPLAINT TO CENTRAL SCOTLAND POLICE IN RELATION TO INCHMOAN ISLAND

28th September 1988 Hamilton wrote to the Chief Constable regarding the Inchmoan Island investigation and stated he was not making a complaint. However, during the following four weeks he wrote five letters to **Inspector Mill** of Central Scotland Police centring on the investigation. **Inspector Mill** submitted a report to the Divisional Commander and DCC McMurdo wrote to Hamilton on 28th September stating he was satisfied that Inspector Mill had answered his enquiries and also stated that since allegations had been made against the police an investigation was to follow.

24th October 1988 Hamilton wrote two letters on the same date to the Chief Constable complaining about Constables Gunn and Duncan stating they had no justification in submitting a report to Strathclyde Police about the 1988 Summer Camp.

31st October 1988 Hamilton wrote two letters to the Chief Constable and to **Michael Forsyth MP** complaining about the abuse of police powers.

2nd November 1988 Michael Forsyth MP writes to the Chief Constable enclosing a copy of Hamilton's letter.

3rd November 1988 DCC McMurdo writes to Hamilton in response to his letter of 31st October 1988 stating that no further complaint would be made.

9th November 1988 Hamilton writes to the Chief Constable stating he is dissatisfied with the response from Central Scotland Police and informs him he has written to his Member of Parliament.

18th November 1988 DCC McMurdo writes to **Michael Forsyth MP** detailing all police involvement in the Inchmoan Summer Camp investigation

30th November 1988 Hamilton writes to the Chief Constable making a formal complaint concerning Constables Gunn and Duncan's involvement in the Inchmoan Summer Camp investigation.

7th December 1988 – 9th April 1989 Numerous letters are sent to the Chief Constable and Depute Chief Constable by Hamilton complaining about the handling of his complaint and the investigating officer Inspector Keenan.

April 1989 Hamilton writes to the Chief Constable stating that he would co-operate fully with the investigation. Hamilton also complains that a Firearms Certificate is returned to him without amendment in respect of a rifle surrendered under the buy back scheme.

10th April 1989 DCC McMurdo writes to Hamilton and informs him that his complaint about the Firearms Certificate will be investigated.

5th May 1989 to 15th May 1989 Hamilton writes four letters to the DCC complaining of unnatural links between the Police and Boy Scouts movement and that Central Scotland Police have passed malicious gossip about him to Strathclyde Police.

28th August 1989 The DCC informs Hamilton that his complaint against Constables Gunn and Duncan had been fully investigated but could not be substantiated.

12th September 1989 to 20th October 1989 Hamilton sent numerous letters to the DCC still complaining he was not satisfied with the manner in which the investigation had been conducted.

31st October 1989 Hamilton attends at Police Headquarters and meets with the DCC and after a discussion declares that he is totally satisfied with the result of the Police investigation.

1st November 1989 After the meeting with the DCC, Hamilton writes a letter to the DCC concluding that he is happy to consider the entire matter as closed.

4th November 1989 Hamilton writes to **Michael Forsyth MP** thanking him for his assistance but states he was happy to consider the matter as closed. Five more letters followed to the DCC from Hamilton stating he was not satisfied with the actions of Central Scotland Police in relation to the 1988 Camp. The ending letters indicate that he would not accept the conclusions of the Police investigation.

1st April 1990 Hamilton writes to the Chief Constable making enquiries regarding the position of James McKellar who is with the Boy Scout movement and Central Scotland Police in furtherance to his belief of a Police/Scouts conspiracy.

7th April 1990 Hamilton writes to the Chief Constable in furtherance of his belief that the Police/Scout conspiracy protesting favouritism shown by the Police to the Scout movement.

April 1990 Hamilton writes to the DCC re-stating his complaint about the investigation into the 1988 Summer Camp.

7th January 1991 Hamilton writes to the Chief Constable welcoming him to his new post, states he has always been a supporter of Central Scotland Police and reiterates his grievances about the 1988 Summer Camp investigation. He also writes to Michael Forsyth MP highlighting discontent regarding Central Scotland Police asking for an independent Police Complaints Procedure.

6th January 1991 Hamilton writes to the Chief Constable in a further attempt to make the new Chief Constable aware of his grievances and has advised that the matter has been fully investigated.

28th January 1991 Hamilton writes to the Chief Constable expressing grievances and makes a number of critical remarks concerning the ability of Police Officers.

14th February 1991 Hamilton writes to **Michael Forsyth MP** summarising in his opinion the events of 1988. He states the need for an independent Police Complaints Procedure. He also writes to the CC and continues with his criticisms. He also makes reference to the Police/Scout favourtism against him.

25th February 1991 Michael Forsyth MP writes to the CC advising that he had received Hamilton's letter and requires a relevant response.

27th February 1991 The Chief Constable writes to **Michael Forsyth MP** giving a complete history of the events and pointing out the steps that have been taken in an effort to try and resolve matters.

COMPLAINT AGAINST CENTRAL SCOTLAND POLICE TO HER MAJESTY'S CHIEF INSPECTOR OF CONSTABULARY

5th January 1990 A formal complaint concerning the action of officers of Central Scotland Police is received by HMCIC.

10th January 1990 HMCIC write to DCC McMurdo requesting a case history.

12th January 1990 DCC McMurdo explains the matter has been going on for some time (19 months). HMCIC appoints Superintendent Moulson to conduct a full enquiry.

February 1990 Superintendent Moulson completes a report to HMCIC who in turn contacts DCC McMurdo and Hamilton informing them that they are satisfied the Inquiry by CSP was dealt with appropriately and satisfactorily.

7th May 1990 Hamilton writes to HMCIC expressing dissatisfaction.

SUMMER CAMP OF JULY 1991 AT MILLAROCHY BAY, LOCH LOMOND

23rd July 1991 Hamilton was interviewed by the Police and admitted assaulting (boy, RE) and handed over a video and photograph equipment but denied that he had taken photographs despite evidence from other witnesses to the contrary.

25th July 1991 Hamilton's photograph equipment was returned to him by the Police and he was asked about photographs taken but again denied that any had been. During (the time) this witness was at the camp the Police Officer observed boys playing unsupervised by a deep water jetty.

29th July 1991 Children who had attended the Camp were interviewed and stated that they had been photographed by Hamilton in compromising positions.

30th July 1991 Hamilton handed the Police a packet of photographs and six boxes of slides which he said he had "forgotten about". He also stated there was one other box of slides still being processed. Subsequent enquiry with photographic processors in Stirling revealed that they had processed eight boxes of slides for Hamilton and one being processed at the time was later recovered by the Police. The Processors also stated that they had received anonymous information from their processing laboratory with regard to the content of the photographs.

2nd August 1991 Strathclyde Police informs Central Scotland Police that Hamilton had handed 12 slides into a photographic processing shop in Glasgow to have large prints produced. They were not overtly obscene but gave cause for concern. A total of 279 slides and 72 photographs were seized by the Police in this investigation. Hamilton ultimately refused to be interviewed and in fact made a complaint to the police about a Police Officer involved and wrote to Michael Forsyth MP and to the Procurator Fiscal complaining about the situation. A Report was submitted to the Procurator Fiscal.

COMPLAINT BY HAMILTON REGARDING THE POLICE INVESTIGATION OF THE 1991 SUMMER CAMP AT MILLAROCHY BAY

There had been a joint Police and Social Work investigation of Hamilton's Summer Camp of 1991 at Millarochy Bay, Loch Lomond and as a result of this Hamilton made a complaint concerning the way in which this investigation had been conducted.

30th July 1991 Hamilton wrote to Detective Sergeant Hughes stating he was upset at the way Police Officers had broadcast malicious and libellous innuendos to parents. A similar letter was sent to the Chief Constable and copied to Michael Forsyth MP.

12th August 1991 Internal memorandum was sent from Detective Chief Inspector Holden to DCC McMurdo advising him that the investigation into the 1991 Summer Camp was likely to result in a report to the Procurator Fiscal at Stirling.

13th August 1991 DCC McMurdo advised Hamilton by letter that a Police investigation was underway and that he could not discuss matters further.

19th August 1991 Hamilton wrote to DCC McMurdo requesting the return of photographic film taken from him during the investigation. He was told that these matters would remain as productions and could not be returned to him until the matter had been reported to the Procurator Fiscal.

26th August 1991 Hamilton writes to the Procurator Fiscal at Stirling regarding the investigation attempting to put his side of the story.

29th August 1991 The Procurator Fiscal wrote to Hamilton stating he was not in receipt of the report from the Police and could not comment.

31st August 1991 Hamilton wrote to **Michael Forsyth MP** indicating he had no faith in the Police Complaints Procedure pointing out that he had been writing to him as (his) Member of Parliament for three years about the incompetence of Central Scotland Police.

1st October 1991 The Scottish Office write to the Chief Constable advising that **Michael Forsyth** had written to **Lord James Douglas Hamilton** re alleged unfair handling of Hamilton's case and had asked for a report.

3rd October 1991 A letter was sent to the Scottish Office informing them that a Report had been sent to the Procurator Fiscal and as such it would be inappropriate to comment.

28th October 1991 Hamilton sent a circular letter to parents and makes reference to the tactics he would employ in order to control children who misbehaved.

18th November 1991 The Procurator Fiscal writes to Hamilton advising him that no proceedings were to be taken against him.

2nd November 1991 DCC McMurdo writes to the Scottish Office advising that he would appoint Chief Inspector Ferguson to investigate Hamilton's complaint about the police handling of the 1991 Summer Camp investigation.

25th November 1991 Chief Inspector Ferguson arranged an appointment with Hamilton to interview him regarding his complaint but Hamilton cancelled the appointment stating he would pursue the matter through his Member of Parliament.

28th November 1991 DCC McMurdo writes to Hamilton pointing out that there was an apparent misunderstanding regarding his complaint against the Police to his MP.

He was informed that Chief Inspector Ferguson would no longer pursue his complaint given the fact that he wished to pursue the matter with his MP.

2nd December 1991 Michael Forsyth MP confirms by writing to Hamilton that it was the role of the Chief Constable and not a Member of Parliament to investigate complaints against the Police.

5th December 1991 Hamilton writes to the CC lodging a formal complaint against the Police Officers.

17th December 1991 Chief Inspector Ferguson interviewed Hamilton at home and obtained a statement from him. Nothing new emerged regarding his allegations but again Hamilton referred to the relationship between the Scouts and CSP. Hamilton's complaint was recorded by Chief Inspector Ferguson as follows: The Police investigation was not competent. Police Officers inferred Hamilton was not of good character. Camera equipment had been damaged.

14th January 1991 Hamilton wrote to **Douglas Sinclair**, the then Chief Executive of Central Regional Council making a complaint against the Social Work Department for their part in the joint investigation of the 1988 Summer Camp.

14th January 1991 DCC McMurdo sent a strongly worded letter to the Scottish Office in which he described Hamilton as an individual who was bitter and petty minded whose correspondence was vindictive and irrational.

14th February 1991 Central Region Chief Executive Mr Sinclair wrote to Hamilton advising him that his complaint against the Social Work Department was invalid.

17th February 1992 Hamilton wrote to the Scottish Office advising them that a member of staff at Dunblane High School had informed him that a Primary School Head Teacher had telephoned Dunblane High School stating that she had been informed by the police that she should not send her children to Hamilton's clubs.

19th February 1992 Hamilton wrote to Central Region Chief Executive expressing dissatisfaction regarding his complaint about the Social Work Dept stating he had been seriously defamed to the extent that it affected his ability to earn a living.

21st February 1992 Hamilton wrote again to Scottish Office advising that he had complained to the Commissioner for Local Administration in Scotland stating he was determined to pursue injustices perpetrated against him.

25th February 1992 Scottish Office wrote to Hamilton that the contents of his letter had been brought to the attention of the Chief Constable.

2nd March 1992 The Ombudsman wrote to Hamilton stating that his complaint against the Social Work Department and CSP were not matters that he could deal with.

21st April 1992 Chief Inspector Ferguson submitted a memorandum to the DCC regarding the complaint and found that Police Officers who were the subject of the complaint had conducted their duties appropriately.

6th May 1992 DCC McMurdo wrote to Hamilton advising him that Chief Inspector Ferguson had finished his investigation and that his complaint was unsubstantiated.

8th May 1992 DCC McMurdo wrote to Scottish Office advising them of the outcome of the complaint investigation.

9th May 1992 Hamilton writes to his Member of Parliament, **Michael Forsyth MP**, explaining his dissatisfaction with the outcome.

9th May 1992 Hamilton writes to the DCC notifying him of his dissatisfaction.

12th May 1992 The DCC wrote to Hamilton stating that he had attempted to show that the decisions were based on the evidence before him.

16th May 1992 Hamilton writes to the DCC still indicating his dissatisfaction.

18th May 1992 The DCC writes to Hamilton indicating that he had nothing further to add to his previous correspondence.

25th May 1992 Michael Forsyth MP forwards Hamilton's letter to **Lord Fraser** at Scottish Office.

11th August 1992 Lord Fraser writes to **Michael Forsyth** stating that he is satisfied that the investigation had been properly handled.

18th August 1992 Michael Forsyth writes to Hamilton enclosing a copy of **Lord Fraser's** correspondence. Hamilton is also written to by Scottish Office.

20th August 1992 Hamilton writes to **Michael Forsyth MP** stating that he still thinks he is the subject of serious injustice.

26th August 1992 Michael Forsyth MP writes to Hamilton advising that he could make no further representations on his behalf and that Lord Fraser's letter should conclude the matter.

14th November 1992 Hamilton writes to **Michael Forsyth MP** and requests an independent enquiry.

April 1993 Hamilton makes a 999 call to the police having witnessed a child being dragged into a nearby house. Police investigate and find it is a mother with her own child. Hamilton then writes to CSP comparing this incident with his conduct during the 1991 Summer Camp.

April 1993 Hamilton writes a circular letter to parents advertising his proposed Balfron Boys Club using prominent local officials as referees. These include Central Regional Chief Executive **Mr Sinclair**, **Councillor Ball** and **Inspector Mill** of Dunblane Police. Hamilton was told to remove the Police reference by DCC McMurdo.

26th June 1993 Parents of a child write to **Inspector Mill** and Central Region with concerns about Hamilton's Balfron Boys Club.

June 1993 Confidential correspondence exchanged between Central Regional Council and Police with regard to an investigation of Hamilton.

20th October 1993 Hamilton complains to the DCC that if complaints are made against him he should be advised so that he could respond.

15th March 1994 As a result of **Mr Robertson MP** forwarding leaflets to **Michael Forsyth MP**, **Detective Sergeant Moffat** submitted a report.

30th May 1994 Hamilton makes a complaint to the Commissioner for Local Government Administration about Central Regional Council's handling of the let for his 1994 Summer Camp at Dunblane High School. He makes an allegation that a Police Officer, **Sergeant Moir**, was restricting his access to the premises.

16th June 1994 Hamilton writes to **Councillor Ball** protesting at **Sergeant Moir's** involvement regarding Dunblane High School.

5th July 1994 Hamilton again writes to **Councillor Ball** about **Sergeant Moir** using undue influence as Chairman of the Dunblane High School Council.

27th September 1994 Hamilton writes to DCC McMurdo concerning his correspondence with **Councillor Ball** on the subject of **Sergeant Moir** complaining of inaccuracies in his complaint about Dunblane Summer Camp and the 1988 Camp.

14th November 1994 The Rector of Dunblane High School complains that Hamilton is instructing his son at Camp and making him wear swimming trunks and taking photographs. The Police initiate an investigation.

11th February 1996 Hamilton writes to **Michael Forsyth MP** recapping his complaints regarding the Scouts and the Police.

5. **Summaries of Witness Statements (the writer has redacted all addresses, dates and place of birth, except that of the accused/deceased Hamilton)**

CHAPTER C

The following relates to Chapter 'C' of the police investigation covering the events on Hamilton's behaviour during the period leading up to 13th March 1996.

Some of the statements go beyond the period immediately prior to 13th March providing general information about Hamilton's background.

Document D1C, a letter by Thomas Hamilton, 7 Kent Road, Stirling FK7 7PP dated 26th January 1996 and addressed private and confidential, to Doctor Robert Ball, Education Convenor, Central Regional Council, Stirling.

The accused/deceased addresses the recipient 'Dear Bob'. The letter is in pursuance of a letter written by Hamilton six months beforehand concerning primary staff at Bannockburn Primary School, who had warned pupils and parents that Thomas W Hamilton (accused/deceased) was a pervert. As a result all of the 26 pupils at that school who were members of his Bannockburn Boys Sports Club left.

The initial response from the Education Department to the accused/deceased was that the teachers may have been expressing personal views or opinion. The accused/deceased complains that this is unacceptable insofar as they were speaking during school time on school premises. The Education Department had warned teachers that they should not make statements which they could not substantiate. The accused/deceased complains that this is too little too late and that the Department has done nothing to rectify the situation.

The accused/deceased details that similar warnings to those given at Bannockburn Primary School have been given at schools across the region, including Dunblane Primary School. Some of these warnings apparently took place in assembly where the entire school was addressed. The accused/deceased complains that this gossip has damaged the reputation of both his clubs and of himself personally and has impaired his ability to earn a living.

He feels unable personally to rectify the situation and feels that the damage is further compounded when parents who have previously had no contact with him hear the gossip and report it to the Education Department thus confirming in the minds of the Department, gossip which the accused believes they themselves initiated. The accused/deceased states that he has no criminal record, has never been accused of child sexual abuse and is not a pervert.

He further states that his clubs have always been run in a fair, proper and competent manner but feels the defamation coming from the respective source of local primary school staff has caused him untold problems within the Region and beyond.

The accused then details the origin of this matter and the initial involvement of the schools. It dates back to 1983 when Mr W Ross of the Education Department telephoned a number of schools to warn Head Teachers that the accused/deceased was a pervert, was interfering with young boys and had been put out of the Scouts for this reason. He further stated that the accused/deceased had a long criminal record for this type of offence. Mr Ross later reported to the Council Committee in August 1983, a report which led to the termination of the accused/deceased's lets at that time. An investigation followed at which Mr Ross and his reported source David Vass, a member of a rifle group, were discredited and the lets were returned.

According to the accused/deceased at that time, Doctor Robert Ball in receipt of the letter had stated that ill-health on the part of W Ross had affected his judgment and competence. The accused/deceased states that during his long time in the Scouts, his Scout Commissioner a Mr R Deuchars, claims to have no knowledge of what Dunblane's Scout Official David Vass is talking about.

The accused/deceased concludes that this damage has resulted from maladministration of the Education Authority in the first instance and secondly, from its failure to attempt to correct the false information given to Head Teachers in 1983.

The accused/deceased concludes that this letter is for information only and is not any criticism of the recipient personally.

Copies of the letter have been sent to Primary Head Teachers.

Letter from Thomas W Hamilton, 7 Kent Road, Stirling FK7 7PP dated 18th August 1995, a letter to the parents of Dunblane which is to explain recent rumours and dispel any gossip. The details and the background to the present situation which runs as follows:-

Twenty four years previously he had been asked to help with Scouts in the Stirling area as a leader which he did for roughly one year. He claims to have been highly praised for his work but was dissatisfied with the management of the Stirling District Scouts and therefore left, claiming that this was to the apparent dismay of the local Scout Commissioner for Stirling.

He later formed an independent group with others covering similar activities, but with a stronger sporting orientation. He claims it was well run and proved very popular. He claims that several local Scout Officials were displeased at what they viewed as unfair competition. He states that the Stirling Boys Sports Club still continues as do the other clubs across the Region.

The groups in Dunblane started fifteen years previously when Stirling boys were taken weekly by minibus to the Dunblane Rifle Club as a specialist activity. He claims that several Dunblane parents who knew Stirling parents requested places for their own children to take part in the Dunblane rifle and pistol shooting and also in the Stirling Sports Club.

At that point, there was a private and confidential report of the senior Scout Official from Dunblane, to prevent the Dunblane Rifle Club being used by the boys, but his attempts failed. Membership grew to such an extent that a separate Dunblane club was formed. He claims that during those entire fifteen years, numerous rumours circulated regarding the circumstances in which the accused/deceased was forced to leave the Scouts. It appears the accused/deceased's club was then based in Dunblane High School catering for roughly 70 boys weekly.

He now understands that the same senior scout official approached the local Regional Councillor confidentially with his misinformation. As a result in 1983, use of the school was terminated without any explanation or proper investigation. The accused/deceased then complained formally to the Local Authority Ombudsman resulting in a full investigation over a two year period. Said Official refused to provide any information in writing and later denied having said anything.

Central Regional Council were, after two years, found by the Ombudsman to have acted badly and to have caused injustice by maladministration. Use of the Dunblane High School was returned to the club in 1985 after Central Regional Council carried out their own investigations. Hamilton states that the Council's investigation found that he and his leaders were qualified, experienced and of exemplary behaviour and had no criminal record.

The accused/deceased claims that at this time, a prominent Regional Councillor made certain remarks about the Scout Official involved. He was surprised that people whom he presumed to be honourable would commit such a malicious act.

The accused/deceased states that in the ten years since the disgracing of the Scout Official nothing has been done to rectify the effect of the gossip and the rumours spread. He claims them to have been unsubstantiated and motivated by a desire to prevent further competition in the area. He states that during this period he has lost out in a number of young boys joining his club but nonetheless, the club subsists.

He claims that recent events have been a great success and that the group's 1995 Summer Residential Sports Training Course at Dunblane High School, its **74th Camp** running from 2nd-16th July 1995 was attended by 25 boys and supervised by 5 instructors and was possibly the best event in the history of the group.

Hamilton concludes the letter by stating that his group is a long term commitment to supporters in Dunblane and hopes that the letter will have given parents a full understanding of the actual facts.

The following document is a leaflet circulated by the Dunblane Boys Sports Club announcing its reopening after the summer holidays on Thursday 7th Sept 1995.

It invites new members and **states a minimum age of school boys of 8 years and over.** The activities cover five-a-side football, indoor games, sports, training, gymnastics and athletics. Boys attending are requested to bring a P.E. kit and £1 weekly. The location of the meeting is the Dunblane High School gymnasium and games hall on Thursday evenings at 6 – 8pm. The leaflet states that the group has operated boys sports clubs in Central Scotland since April 1973 and gives the name, address and phone number of T W Hamilton as the President of the group. Attached at the bottom is a tear off slip which has to be completed by any parents wanting their children to join the group.

DOCUMENT D4/C

A letter from Thomas W Hamilton, 7 Kent Road, Stirling FK7 7PP dated 7th March 1996 and for the attention of her Majesty the Queen, Buckingham Palace, London.

It is stamped as having been received on 12th March 1996. It is addressed "Your Majesty" and concerns her in her capacity as Patron of the Scout Association. It details his joining of the Scouts over 20 years ago, after his time as a venture scout and his being asked to become a scout leader, explaining that he was disillusioned with the management in the District at that time.

After roughly a year, **District Commissioner J Don** offered him a position with him within his association in the nearby **District of Hillfoots** which he accepted. However his transfer was refused by Scottish Scout Headquarters without any explanation. D.C. Don approached his previous D.C. Mr R Deuchars and as a result of this, reported in confidence to Hamilton that Mr Deuchars was attempting to have him branded as a pervert. Mr Don demanded justification for this to which Mr Deuchars' only response was that Hamilton was "friendly" with the boys. Mr Don remarked that a scout leader was supposed to be friendly and reported to Hamilton that Deuchars had nothing on him but he could cause him considerable damage if unchecked. Mr Deuchars then submitted a confidential report on Hamilton in line with the Policy Organisation and rules of the Association which Hamilton considers to be a breach of natural justice.

Hamilton **claims to know** that no child has ever complained of him having behaved in a sinister or sexual nature but claims that **D.C. Deuchars** together with **A.D.C. Mr Samuels** and the **G.S.L. Mr McKenzie**, in a bid to justify his actions, visited and interviewed every child in his old group, including everyone who had been a member. Nothing sinister came to light. Mr McKenzie reported that Mr Deuchars had sought to create innuendos about Hamilton with the statement "why is he so enthusiastic – think about it?" Mr J Don thought jealousy to be the likely cause.

Hamilton was unable to acquire any information as regards the confidential report by Mr Deuchars and unable to obtain any assistance from the Scottish Scout Headquarters. He understood however, that as time passed, Mr Deuchars was continuing to spread the rumour that he was a pervert.

He complains about the damage which these rumours have caused over 20 years of his work, including council, police and social work investigations which resulted from information received in confidence from officials of the Scout Association. He feels that any subsequent investigation was unfounded. He also states that he believes that in police complaints procedures, they tend to spread innuendos in an attempt to cause maximum damage and then when their investigation fails, do nothing about retracting their accusations.

He complains that over 20 years, these rumours have been circulated, have caused him personal distress, loss of public standing and have impaired his ability to earn a living. He concludes that all of this and more has been caused by the maladministration of the Scout Association, their denial of natural justice and duty of care and considers that on the part of many Scout Officials, it was a route to oust a rival group.

Letter concludes "I turn to you as a last resort and I am appealing for some kind of intervention in the hope that I may be able to regain my self-esteem in society. I am your obedient servant. Thomas W Hamilton".

DOCUMENT D5/C

Letter dated 11ᵗʰ February 1996 from Thomas W Hamilton, 7 Kent Road, Stirling FK7 7PP to Mr Michael Forsyth, M.P. House of Commons, London.

A covering copy is sent to Mr Wilson of Central Scotland Police. The letter concerns a problem emanating from the gossip spread predominantly by Scout Officials in the Dunblane area. A list of the names involved include **Vass, Muirhead, Sharp, McFarlane and Dobbie**.

He then refers to the difficulties he experienced with Central Scotland Police and that the Ombudsman had found that an injustice had been perpetrated against him. He complains that this information was not conveyed to individual police officers and that in 1988, two police constables informed Strathclyde Police that he was a known pervert. This was not conveyed in confidence, resulting in maximum disruption to his summer camp and damaging his public standing.

He then refers to a 1991 pervert hunt by officers of Central Scotland Police, again affecting his public standing. He states that he has been unable to recover from the very serious damage caused by the Central Scotland Police. He refers to numerous detailed letters of complaint which he has sent to the addressee and adds only that the long term effects of all of these events has been a death blow to his already difficult work in providing sports and leisure activities to local children as well as to his public standing.

STATEMENT 58/C – CIVILIAN WITNESS
Name, Karen Joan McGregor or Gillies. She is a receptionist at Finlay Guy Transport Services, Stirling.

The witness attended to the accused/deceased on 11/3/96 in regard to the hire of a Ford Motor Van registration number M394 KBO. On Monday 11th March 1996 at sometime either late morning or early afternoon, the witness was at the reception desk in the office. At this point a male customer, Hamilton, entered the building. Also present in the office was John Speck, a mechanic for the company. The witness describes the speech delivery of the accused/deceased as lacking emotion and that he spoke almost like a robot. When Hamilton made his initial enquiries, the witness was on the telephone and therefore didn't hear the entire nature thereof.

On the following day, 12th March 1996, the witness was again working at the reception of Finlay Guy. At approximately 2.50pm on 12/3, the male who had been in the previous day came into the customer desk. She gives a physical description of the customer. Roughly 52-56 years of age. About 5' 7" tall, stocky build with a very round face and wearing spectacles. He was wearing a navy blue nylon or cotton hat with skip and ear protectors similar to a deerstalkers style.

The accused/deceased wanted to hire one of the small white vans. The accused/deceased, when asked, said he wanted the van for a day. The witness did not ask what purpose the van was wanted for as she felt intimidated by the customer.

The witness prepared the rental agreement form and the accused/deceased a cheque for £50, while John Speck went out to the workshop and into the courtyard to prepare one of the vans. The name signed by the customer in the rental agreement form is Mr Hamilton. The witness completed the formalities required, her only further discussions concerning Mr Hamilton was with a customer who came into the office immediately afterwards, a **Mr James Bell**, non-witness. She told Mr Bell that she had found Mr Hamilton strange and un-nerving.

STATEMENT 180/C – CIVILIAN WITNESS
Name, Cathleen Boswell Burke Kerr.

This witness speaks to knowing the accused deceased as a neighbour and to seeing him outside his home between 8am and 8.40am. She states that in all the time that Hamilton was her neighbour, which is a period which spans the entire time at which she stayed at her present address, Hamilton when she met him in the street or elsewhere would always speak to her, enquiring about her husband and his health. She states that he was always pleasant and appeared intelligent. Hamilton would often discuss his interest in photography with her – an interest which began as a hobby which he later tried unsuccessfully to make a business of.

He once asked the witness to go to his house to view his collection of photographs which she did. All of the photos were of boys involved in youth groups, football, outdoor activities etc. The witness states that they were all good photos. The witness also states that Hamilton did photos of her wedding anniversary which were very good. The witness was aware of Hamilton's involvement in youth clubs.

On the morning of 13th March 1996 between 8am and 8.40am, the witness saw Thomas Hamilton standing beside, or having just got out of a large grey saloon car parked outside his house. He waved to the driver who drove off. He was carrying a newspaper. He then went over to a white van, registration M394 KBO parked outside his house and began to clear the snow from his windscreen. The van had been parked outside his house the previous evening. She did not see Hamilton after this.

The witness states that Hamilton's manner was only odd in that when speaking to someone, he would appear to look through them not paying attention to what was being said.

STATEMENT 183/C – CIVILIAN WITNESS
Name, James Donoghue.

The witness speaks of having seen the accused deceased wiping snow off a white Ford van M394 KBO in Kent Road about 8am on the morning of the 13/3/96. The witness has stayed at his present address for 17 years and has been a neighbour of Hamilton's since he moved in roughly 8 years ago. His initial neighbours were Thomas Hamilton and his grandparents. His grandmother died roughly 5/6 years ago and 2/3 years ago the grandfather also left the house.

The witness expresses that Hamilton was a good and unproblematic neighbour. Hamilton offered to take photographs of the witness's daughter's family, which he refused. The witness states that Hamilton often went out into the back of his garden, always late at night, and burned photographs. He does not know what the photos were of. The witness states that he felt Hamilton to be weird and that he knew that Hamilton took photographs of children, although he does not explain how he knows this. Hamilton had told the witness's daughter that he was a self employed photographer specialising in children's photos and that last year he had distributed leaflets round the doors advertising the fact that he is a photographer. The witness has bad eyesight and bad hearing.

STATEMENT 185/C – CIVILIAN WITNESS
Name, John Henry Speck. Occupation – service engineer.

The witness is an employee of the car hire firm dealing with the accused deceased on 11th & 12th March 1996. The witness describes what Hamilton was wearing when he attended the depot on 12th March 1996, much in accordance with the former witness, Karen Gillies' account of his outfit. When Hamilton spoke to the witness, he never lifted his head and didn't look at him. The witness found him to be very rude. The witness had been asked by Karen Gillies to hurry up when attending to the customer because she found the man creepy and felt uneasy with him there. At no time did Hamilton state what he required the vehicle for and the witness did not ask. The witness found Hamilton to be creepy, probably due to his hat and glasses.

STATEMENT 188/C – CIVILIAN WITNESS
Name, Christopher Donald.

The witness attends the accused/deceased clubs and also speaks to seeing the accused/deceased walking across the pedestrian bridge to Dunblane Railway Station on Sunday 10th March 1996.

The witness was a member of Hamilton's club in Dunblane when he was in primary 5 or 6. The club was held at Dunblane High School on Tuesday or Thursday night. He attended for roughly one year in total and left because his mother would not let him attend the summer camp. He states that they usually had to play activities and games in just shorts and trainers with no tops on. He states that Mr Hamilton was quite strict and used to shout a lot but he never touched or hit him and that at no time did he see him photographing or taking pictures of himself or other boys. He had, however, heard that he did take photographs of some boys. He cannot remember who told him this. Nor can he remember the name or the faces of any of Mr Hamilton's assitants or helpers at these clubs.

He has often seen Mr Hamilton walking in Dunblane delivering letters or leaflets since he attended his club, but he has never spoken to him, nor has Hamilton spoken to the witness. The witness saw Hamilton on Sunday 10th March 1996 while he was out on his paper round crossing a blue metal bridge over a railway which leads to the Springfield Terrace/Doune Road side of Dunblane. The witness saw Hamilton. He remembers what he was wearing but remembers nothing else except that he was carrying a brown coloured brief case. There was no communication between the two. Nor did they nod to each other as a sign of recognition. As he passed him he did not look back to see where Hamilton went but does remember there was a train in the station waiting at the time which would have been going in the Stirling direction. He did not feel that the accused/deceased was hurrying in an attempt to catch it.

STATEMENT 193/C
Name, Gordon Stuart Crawford. Occupation Engineer.

The witness is the Club Secretary of Stirling Rifle and Pistol Club and has been since 1991. He speaks of the accused/deceased's membership of the club and his attending meetings on 4/2/96, 18/2/96 and 2/3/96. The witness has been a member of Stirling Rifle and Pistol Club since May 1986. The witness cannot remember exactly when Thomas Hamilton joined the club but knows that it was sometime in 1987. He received a Firearms Certificate when he joined but does not know what Firearm he had at this time.

He states that Hamilton kept himself to himself at the meetings. The only time Hamilton might speak to the witness was during a shoot when Hamilton might comment on how good or bad his shooting was or how he could improve it.

The witness became Club Secretary in April 1991. In joining the club, an applicant completes an application form and if he has a firearms certificate, must present this for examination. If he does not have a certificate he must declare this. The only criteria to be met by members is an annual subscription fee of £55.00. The Firearms Certificate is only checked when they join and at no other time after that.

The witness in becoming secretary, introduced a scheme whereby members were issued with badges containing a photograph of the member, the members signature and the Club Secretary's signature, i.e. that of the witness. These badges are issued on a one off basis and not annually.

He states that Hamilton's attendance at shoots was sporadic and that he would attend 2 or 3 shoots in a row and then not be seen for months. Hamilton had tended to come to meetings in the company of non-witness Clive Wood, but on 4th February 1996, came to the meeting alone. This was the first time the witness had seen him in roughly 6 months.

At this point, Hamilton was in possession of two 9mm Browning hand guns which are high powered hand guns. The witness is well versed in hand guns and is reasonably sure that these are what he had.

Hamilton also attended the next meeting at Whiteson on 18th February 1996, again alone. The witness states that similarly on this occasion he had the same three hand guns which appears to be inconsistent with his statement in the preceding paragraph that he had two 9mm Browning hand guns. He cannot recall talking to Hamilton on this date.

The last time he saw Hamilton was at the clubs last meet which was at a range in Inverclyde Sports Centre in Largs on 2nd March 1996. Hamilton was again alone but believes that he had been run to Largs by Alex Wood who stays in Hallglen, Falkirk and is a witness.

The witness talked to Hamilton at the meet explaining to him a competition shoot called the 'Police Pistol One' which was a course of fire shooting at turning targets and shooting from various distances. He believes on this occasion he had all three of his hand guns with him. He believed at the end of the meeting Hamilton was run home to Stirling by Alex Woods.

The witness believes that at the meeting Hamilton was using commercial ammunition. This is bought brand new from retailers. The majority of the members were using home made ammunition which is done by reusing the spent case and reloading the cases with powder and a bullet. The bullet itself is made of lead. The other type of available ammunition is factory reloaded ammunition which is again made by using spent cases but which is done commercially in factories. Only Hamilton and Alex Woods were using commercial ammunition as far as the witness remembers and this is considerably more expensive.

At the last meet Hamilton's score was 220 out of 300 which is very low, the average being roughly 280. He also recalls on this occasion he put fluorescent orange coloured stickers on to one of the advancing men targets, one on the nose and one on the chest which is an illegal tactic and the witness removed them. Hamilton was unperturbed by this. The witness remembers Hamilton only ever using commercial ammunition. The witness had no idea of Hamilton's background or personal life other than what he subsequently heard or read in the media.

STATEMENT 221/C
Mrs Audrey McMillan. Occupation Housewife.

This witness speaks to seeing a white van similar to the accused deceased's vehicle at 9.35am on 13th March 1996 entering the school grounds from Doune Road. Both of her children attend Dunblane Primary School, one in Primary 4 and the other in Nursery class. In the morning of 13th March 1996 her son had left the house at roughly 8.45am since he starts at 9am. The Nursery Class which her daughter attends however starts at 9.30am. The witness left her house that morning at roughly 9.27am. When she turned into Doune Road at the back of the Nursing Home on the left hand side of the road a white van was travelling in the opposite direction. It was between both entrances to the school and travelling very slowly, roughly 10 miles per hour.

After passing Baldornie House Hotel at approximately 20 yards before the school gates he put on his indicator and turned left into the school. The witness feels that he appeared to be lost at this point. He then drove into the school still driving very slowly. He seemed unsure as to where he was going. He then turned into the access road leading into the Nursery Playground where Primary 1 and 2 infants are. The witness then parked her car. She could hear the van driving. It appeared to be a diesel van. As the witness walked her daughter into the playground she could still see the van travelling adjacent to the wall very slowly. He reversed hard against the wall and the witness thinks there was a telegraph pole or lamp post which he reversed against. There was nothing parked beside him. At this point the witness's daughter remarked "What is that man doing there? He is not allowed to park there". By this point the man was out of his van and looked directly at the witness and her daughter. He walked around the side of the van and to the drivers side and opened both rear doors, then went into the van. The witness was approximately 50 yards away.

The man was inside the van for a number of seconds and then turned round laying a silver grey plastic sheet on the ground which he unfolded. The

192

witness believed it looked like a tool rack and that it had objects in it although she could not see what they were. The witness then turned to the main entrance of the school and there were no other people in the car park at this point.

The witness then briefly talked to another parent attending the Nursery, then handed her daughter over to Mrs Aisles, witness and Teacher. The witness was there for only one minute maximum. On returning to the car park she did not notice the man or the van but was looking for neither. She then drove off in her car to Tesco.

The witness offers a physical description of the man as follows: He is around middle aged, large build, if not fat and was 5 feet 10 inches in height, dark framed glasses on and the lenses were clear, like reading glasses and black in colour. He was wearing a big heavy woollen hat level with his eyebrows and it was hard to see his face. He was wearing very dark clothing and the top was zipped just about to his mouth covering his neck. Dark bottoms and black steel toecap boots like "Doc Martens" very clumpy with heavy soles.

Her description of the van is as follows: It appeared to be very new and was obviously very clean, it was a panel van and had only two doors with no markings on it. It had two back doors and the witness stated she thought it was diesel. She attempts a hazy recollection of the registration number.

STATEMENT S320/C
Civilian Witness named Greg Sinclair.

The witness attended a Club run by the accused/deceased at Thomas Muir High School, Bishopbriggs on 11.3.96. The witness talked to the accused/deceased showing him magazines and talking about bullets. When the witness went to the club it was all boys aged 8 to 11 years, from his school Woodhill Primary, St Helen Primary and West Kilgreggan Primary. He normally played football, basketball and a game like British Bull Dogs where the boys chased each other around.

The witness was one of Hamilton's favourites because he thought he was a good football player and he was always telling the witness to smile. The witness was always picked as Team Captain. The witness liked Mr Hamilton quite a lot but if he had been misbehaving Hamilton would get very angry and start shouting at them. The witness was sometimes shouted at but was never hit.

Roughly 4 weeks before the 11.3.96 the witness was going to the big gym and saw Hamilton showing a magazine to David Hicks, non witness, and Clint Conran, non witness. It was a glossy coloured magazine with a picture of 6 bullets. The witness asked Mr Hamilton if he had a gun because David Hicks had told the witness that Hamilton did. Hamilton told the witness that he had 4 guns which he used to shoot foxes, rabbits and deer. This is the only time that Hamilton had ever spoken about guns and bullets.

Statement of Andrew Cook, Aircraft Engineer (no place or date of birth given)

The witness's son Jamie has attended a boys club held at Dunblane High School for two years on Thursday night between 6 and 8pm. It was supervised by Hamilton. He had spoken with Hamilton a few times and the witness was satisfied that he was capable of running the club. Having heard some rumours the witness had made tentative enquiries but found he could not come up with any specific complaints against Hamilton. The witness monitored the club quite closely and was satisfied that it was run properly.

After the incident his son Jamie was quite subdued. Shortly after he told his father that Mr Hamilton had asked him details about the Primary School. His son said that he had asked which way to go for certain areas of the school, such as assembly and which way you turned for the Assembly Hall. When he asked questions about directions the witness's son Jamie said that he did so every week. The witness said surely it was not every week but his son said that it had been for quite a while. The son mentioned the gym but the witness did not press him further. He waited for the Police to interview him.

Jamie spoke to the Police the following day telling them that he had told Hamilton that Assembly went from 9am to 9.30am to 10am.

Statement of witness Jamie Cook (again, no place or date of birth given):

The last time the witness went to the club was the Thursday before the incident at the school. Mr Hamilton was there, with roughly 6 boys. Halfway through playing football Mr Hamilton took the witness and sat him on a bench to speak to him. He asked him the way to the gym and the way to the hall. He asked what time certain classes went to the gym and the main way into the school. He further asked directions about once he was in the main hall, how to get to the gym and where the stage was. He asked how to get to the Assembly hall and the witness told him to turn right after the main entrance. He asked what day all people go on the stage to do the play. The witness did not know and was told to ask the primary 7's to find out.

Hamilton asked if the younger children from Primary 1 to 4 went to Assembly at different time from the Primary 5 to 7. The witness told him that Assembly was on a Wednesday morning and the younger ones went after the older ones. Hamilton asked what times Assembly and gym started. The witness replied 9.30am for assembly but he did not tell him the time for gym. He thinks that Stuart Watt said that it was 9am. Hamilton wanted the witness to ask a Primary 7 but he did not.

Hamilton also asked questions concerning the gym fire exit, he thinks that it was how many fire exits there were to get out of the gym. Mr Hamilton asked these questions every week. He had been asking him for roughly 2 years. He stopped asking questions at this point and said the witness could go back to playing football.

STATEMENT 376/C
Civilian witness Richard Raymond Law. Occupation Engraver.

The witness works in the Trophy Centre of Upper Craig and speaks to the occasion of seeing the accused/deceased entering the shop at 11am on Tuesday, 12.3.96.

The witness knew Hamilton for roughly one year. He regularly came into the shop to order football trophies and medals. At 11am on Tuesday, 12th March, 1996 Hamilton entered the shop and was served by Frank Gordon, witness statement 378/C who is the shop owner. Hamilton remained in the shop for a short time before leaving. The witness did not speak to him at any time.

STATEMENT 378/C
Civilian witness Frank Alfred Gordon, Occupation – Shop Owner.

The witness is the owner of the Trophy Centre, Stirling and speaks to the accused/deceased entering the shop on Thursday 9.3.96 in the morning and at 11am on Tuesday, 12.3.96. The witness has known Hamilton for roughly 11 years and he has shopped at his shop for roughly 4 years. On Thursday, 9.3.96 Hamilton came into the shop ordering a football medal which the witness did not have in stock and he asked him to call back in a couple of days. At roughly 11am on Tuesday, 12.3.96 Hamilton returned. He appeared in good spirits and the witness gave him the football medal which he had ordered. He paid £2.25 in cash.

STATEMENT 378/C
Civilian witness Helen Drysdale Peters. Occupation unemployed.

The witness frequented the house of Hamilton in Kent Road, knows the accused/deceased and seen him (sic) on several occasions including the end of February 1996 when she saw him acting suspiciously in the grounds of Braehead Primary School, also seen him (sic) carrying a wood box in Kent Road at 9am on 11.3.96.

The witness has spent some time since June 1995 residing with her boyfriend witness statement 437/C since which time she has been aware of a male who also stays in Kent Road being Mr Hamilton. The witness had heard from her boyfriend that rumours were circulating that Hamilton was weird.

At the end of last year 1995 the witness and her boyfriend went out for a walk. The lights were on in Hamilton's house and the curtains were open. The witness looked into the house and could see photographs of people all around the room. She is unsure of who these people were, male or female but they were all individuals. The witness did not know Hamilton *(contradicts the first sentence of her statement).*

On a Friday night possibly 23.2.96 the witness was out for a walk with her boyfriend, they were walking through Braehead Primary School, Stirling, it was after 11pm at night and the school was in darkness. She was suddenly made aware of a person emerging from the shadow of the annexe. She advised it was Hamilton. He had his hood up as usual. Her boyfriend spoke to him and called him John. He replied my name is Tom. This was the first time the witness had heard his voice. His voice made her feel uncomfortable and his manner she thought to be strange.

The three of them then walked back from the school to Kent Road, the witness did not pay attention to what was being said but did hear her boyfriend asking him about a Rifle Club. At the mention of guns the witness states that he seemed to change, she states that it seemed to make him feel important and it was obvious that he was speaking about something about which he was very interested.

This was the only real contact the witness had with Hamilton although a few days later she and her boyfriend passed him in the street. The witness ignored Hamilton, her boyfriend spoke to him for a few minutes, she thinks the conversation occurred in Linden Avenue, Stirling.

At about 9am on Monday 11.3.96 the witness was in her boyfriend's house, she looked out of the window and saw Hamilton walking along Kent Road on the opposite side of the street from her house in the direction of Burroughmuir Road. She could see Hamilton carrying a wooden box in his right hand. It was light coloured natural wood about 18" – 2' square and 8" deep. It had a single handle and a raised section. The witness at this point thought that the box may be a gun box. She had only ever seen him with a brief case.

The witness stayed at Kent Road for the next couple of days but did not again see Hamilton nor did she see any vehicles parked outside his house.

STATEMENT 437/C
Robert Mark Ure. Occupation – Retired.

The witness speaks to knowing the accused/deceased over several years and speaks to the accused/deceased walking within the grounds of Braehead Primary School about 11pm at the end of February 1996.

The witness has stayed in Kent Road since December 1992. In January 1993 after winning a bowls competition in Stirling the witness was approached by Hamilton whom he had never met before and asked if he would like his photograph taken with the trophy he had won. The witness told him where to go. Consequently Hamilton ignored him for the following few months when he saw him in the street. The witness said that he immediately formed the opinion that Hamilton was weird partly based on the fact that he always had the hood of his jacket up.

Around June 1994 the witness cut hedges in the gardens of some of the older people in the street and at which point he noticed that Hamilton had not cut his hedge. After this the witness saw two young boys around 15 years of age or maybe younger cutting Hamilton's hedge and grass. He saw Hamilton standing at the door of his house watching over the boys cutting the hedge. He did not recognise the boys nor could he describe them except to say that they wore jeans and tee shirts. He heard that Hamilton was involved in some sort of boys club.

The witness had previously been informed by his now estranged wife that Hamilton was a member of the Stirling and Dunblane Rifle Club of which his estranged wife was also a member. She was in fact the Treasurer. He at this point explained that on the first occasion attending the Rifle Club Hamilton had tried to make out to other members that he had a superior knowledge of guns.

The witness also remembers an incident last summer when Mrs Ogilvie told him that Hamilton had lit a fire in the garden and had burned a quantity of photographs and film.

The witness seen (sic) Hamilton in the vicinity of Braehead Primary School around 11pm in February 1996. He maintains that from the position which he appeared he could only have been in at the school buildings. When asked what he was doing at the school Hamilton replied that he had been running a boys club. No record exists of such a club.

The witness then asked him if he was a member of the Stirling Rifle Club. At the mention of this club he appeared to become agitated. The witness asked Hamilton if he could provide him with any information about the club, like phone numbers of the Chairman. Hamilton said that he would check his house and get back to me with the information later. The witness got the impression that Hamilton was pleased that he had mentioned the Gun Club and was very pleased that the witness was aware of his involvement therein.

A few days later on a Saturday morning in early March the witness was walking home from Stirling Town Centre passing Hamilton's house and saw him washing a large mini bus. It looked like a Regional Council Van. One of the vehicles which he saw beside his house was a large blue K registration car about the size of a Granada, sometime driven by a male and other times by Hamilton. This was last year and no exact dates were remembered. There was also a van with the word "Gillespie" written on it. Witness Statement 247/L owns such a car.

On Monday 11th March 1996 witness Peters in the witness's living room pointed out Hamilton across the street. The witness was not interested in him and did not look out of the window. Witness Peters explained to the witness that Hamilton was carrying a wooden box. From the description the witness believes it sounds like a box an army officer would have to carry a revolver. The witness was in the army and has seen similarly described boxes.

STATEMENT 439/C

Allan Arthur Jeffrey. Occupation – Reference Library Unit, Stirling Library.

The witness speaks to meeting the accused/deceased between 10.30 and 11am on 11.3.96 in Stirling Library writing letters. The witness has known Hamilton for over 20 years. Initially he only knew him to see and not to speak to. Only over the last 8 or 9 years did the witness start talking to Hamilton, during which period he was a frequent visitor to the reference library. He was frequently photocopying correspondence. He tried to promote his organisations. From the way that Hamilton described these organisations the witness believed that they were much larger than he now realises they were. He remembers seeing some of the letters sent out by Hamilton.

In conversations Hamilton continually complained about his problems with Parents, the Council and other official bodies. He would sometimes boast about some scam or other that he had going. For example he would order equipment from Companies then argue with the Company that it was not up to standard and then attempted to bargain them down in the price that he had to pay.

The witness recalls Hamilton doing a letter drop in Dunblane in which there must have been about 500 letters. He can't remember what it was about but believes the letters were to Parents.

The witness describes Hamilton as being unpopular with women in the library and he personally feels that he had an arrogance or aura about him. He is aware of Hamilton having fallen out with Quakers in Dunblane about the use of a hall. The witness recalls Hamilton having trouble with the Police in Helensburgh when he with a group of youths was marched out of an afternoon matinee session in a cinema. He recalls it was a couple of years ago but cannot remember what it was about. Hamilton also once complained to the witness that he had been accused of starving children in his camps and showed the witness letters as to how he was providing nourishing meals.

The witness had been invited to come and see Hamilton for a cup of tea but he never went. He did not like Hamilton and felt that he was craving attention. The last time the witness saw Hamilton was Monday 11th March 1996 at about 10.30/11am.

The witness had broken the photocopying machine and Hamilton had come in wanting to use it. When he discovered that the photocopier was broken he sat down and wrote some letters.

STATEMENT 450/C
Civilian Witness Mr Robert Gouther – Clerical Officer British Rail, Stirling.

The witness is a British Rail Official speaking to issuing of rail ticket from Dunblane to Stirling on 12.3.96, found at the home of the accused/deceased Hamilton. Witness explains that the ticket found is a "Sportis" ticket which is a type of ticket only sold upon a train, issued from a Sportis Ticket Machine carried by the Conductor. These tickets are never issued from Platform Ticket Officers. The ticket was issued at 11.55am on 12th March 1996 and was issued by an automatic machine on a train somewhere between Dunblane and Stirling. A train leaves Dunblane at 11.54 hours. Dunblane signal box operator Frank Kane, non witness, confirms that on 12th March 1996 the train left Dunblane at 11.54 hours and was heading for Edinburgh. The train originated at Dunblane. The witness believes that the ticket was probably purchased after leaving Dunblane but before stopping at Bridge of Allan. The ticket is a day single and whoever purchased it asked for a single from Stirling to Dunblane. Ticket price £1.60 paid in cash.

STATEMENT 555/C

Mrs Grace Jones Ogilvie. Retired Shop Assistant.

This is a neighbour of Hamilton and talks of Hamilton walking in Kent Road at 8pm on 8th March 1996 carrying letters.

The witness describes Hamilton as being quite quiet and was a bit of a loner. The witness recounts the family history of people moving in and out of Hamilton's house in Kent Road. From the beginning of him being alone in the house the witness states that he started to get a lot of male visitors and that she never saw any women at the house. One of these visitors was called James Gillespie who had his own business doing gardening and landscaping. He was known as James Gillespie only because he drove up in a van with his name on the side. Over the last couple of years Gillespie visited Hamilton up to 2 or 3 times a week, sometimes more. Sometimes more than once a day. Another regular visitor to the house was a man in a Scottish Television car. The witness cannot describe the man but the car she believes to have been a blue Volvo Estate.

The witness knew that Hamilton ran a boys club but not where. He would sometimes bring the boys down to the house in a yellow Central Regional Mini Bus. The boys were all roughly 6 to 9 years old. About 2 or 3 years ago the witness discussed with Hamilton his boys clubs and the Loch Lomond camp which he described as being a very exclusive club and summer camp was £70/£80 per week.

About 3 or 4 years ago the girl Heather Morton, told the witness that Hamilton was trying to get her to send her 7 year old son Kevin to join his boys club. She told the witness that Hamilton at one point put videos through her door, the witness does not know what it was about but does know that Heather Morton's husband put the videos back through Hamilton's door.

In the summer of 1994 or possibly 1995 the witness was walking home from Bingo one night and walked past Hamilton's house, he was standing at his door at about 8.30-8.45pm. He asked the witness if she would like to come in to his house and look at a video he had of "his boys". The witness went into the house and was in the living room for roughly 40 minutes during which he played a video and fast forwarded it at bits. The boys looked between 6 and 9 years old, possibly 40 of them, all wearing black swimming trunks. All were walking in single file towards the camera and tryng to look at the camera as they walked. All the boys were slenderly built. The place the film was taken looked like a burnt grass area but the witness could not see anything in the film. She could see that it was a clear day but not sunny. He stopped the video then lifted a photograph from the floor and said that this was his "favourite boy". It was a young boy of roughly 7 years old with very blonde curly hair and the photograph was the waist from upwards. The boy was not wearing anything on top. The witness then made an excuse and left the house. She never again discussed anything about Hamilton's boys clubs with him.

During the summer of 1995 Hamilton started burning boxes in his back garden on a regular basis, about 2 to 3 times per week. The boxes varied in size from small right up to egg box size. While he was burning the boxes there was a very strong glue type smell coming from the fire. The witness never saw what was in the boxes.

The witness last saw Hamilton on Friday, 8th March 1996 at roughly 8pm at night. He walked the witness along to a neighbour's house. During the short walk he talked about staying in Upper Bridge Street, Stirling with his family when he was young and he thought that there were some kind of spooks or ghosts in the bedroom. Before parting company he said that he was going up to the Town Centre to post some letters. The witness could see at least two envelopes in his hand. It was dark and the witness could not see exactly how many envelopes there were but it looked thick enough for there to be something like a small book in one of the envelopes. The envelopes were white.

The witness spoke to some television and newspaper journalists on 13th March 1996 including some from the Sunday People newspaper and told them about Hamilton burning boxes in the back garden, saying that the smell from the burning was like paper or photographs burning.

STATEMENT 567/C – CIVILIAN WITNESS
Alexis Elizabeth Fawcett - Charge Hand.

The witness speaks to accompanying the accused/deceased to Largs on 2.3.96 in the company of witness Campbell (S630/C) and Wood (S568/C). At about 9am on Saturday 2nd March 1996 Campbell came to the witness' house in order to drive her to the shoot at the Inverclyde Sports Centre in Largs. The witness was introduced to Alex Wood and a man sitting in the back of the car who was introduced as Thomas Hamilton. The witness had never met Hamilton before but he immediately struck her as being odd. Hamilton was very quiet and rarely spoke on the journey to Largs. The witness described Hamilton as "the typical stereotype 'pervert'".

Sometime around 2pm the witness was standing back from the range when she heard loud banging, despite wearing ear protectors. The witness presumed Hamilton to have been using a very powerful handgun, judging by the noise and recall (recoil?) coming from the gun. Strangely, while everyone else was shooting at the 'body' of the targets, Hamilton was aiming for his target's head. The holes made on his target were considerably larger than anyone else's.

The witness, Campbell, Wood and Hamilton left the range at approximately 4pm. On the drive home Hamilton remained silent. When the conversation turned to guns Hamilton commented on how he used to have a semi-automatic Browning Rifle but that it had been confiscated by the police following the Hungerford incident and the subsequent change in gun law.

200

Hamilton then continued to talk about the guns he had and what bullets could do what from which gun. The witness was not really listening but she recalls thinking that Hamilton treated his guns with some affection, almost like a girlfriend which she found weird.

The witness recalls Willie asking Hamilton if he was going to the next club shoot which was scheduled for Sunday 17th March 1996 but does not recall what Hamilton's reply was. Hamilton was dropped off a few moments later at the roundabout at the bottom of the dual carriageway. This was at Kent Road. The witness always believed that Hamilton was doing something (sic) of the nature on the scale of the Dunblane incident.

STATEMENT 568/C – CIVILIAN WITNESS
Alexander Reid Wood – a Production Technician.

The witness speaks to accompanying the accused/deceased to Largs on 2nd March 1996 with witnesses, Campbell and Fawcett. The witness is a full member of Stirling Rifle and Pistol Club, of which he has been a member for 18 months prior to the Largs shoot on 2nd March 1996.

He recalls that one prior occasion ie. 21st January or 18th February 1996 he seen the person he knows now as Thomas Hamilton. He did not know him at this time and paid no attention to him on that occasion. On 2nd March 1996 the witness picked up William Campbell and Thomas Hamilton to take them to the shoot in Largs. The witness' initial impressions of Hamilton were that he was a bit odd, a bit effeminate and a stereotypical mummy's boy. They also picked up Alexis Fawcett. The only conversation the witness remembered having with Hamilton was regarding his Browning 9mm handgun. Hamilton and the witness were shooting in the same booth.

Hamilton approached the witness and asked to look at his gun which was a 'captain' model which is a top of the range model with a different sight from other Brownings and a wooden walnut grip handle. Hamilton and the witness thereafter exchanged guns and performed one detail using each other's weapons. At the end of the details they returned their guns to each other and Hamilton commented to the witness that his gun was very nice.

At roughly 2.30pm the witness recalls Hamilton entering the booth after him and firing at the target. As far as he recalls Hamilton fired the entire magazine of about 13 rounds ahead of the target with one of his Browning 9mm. The witness did not see anything sinister in this at the time.

At roughly 3pm the witness recalls Hamilton starting to use a revolver that he brought which he believes to have been a .357 revolver. The witness recalls that were terrific shock waves and sound coming from the gun when Hamilton discharged this. He believes that Hamilton was using magnum loads which are powerful rounds or bullets.

At roughly 4pm the witness recalls Hamilton still on a range shooting at the targets from about 15 yards with a 9mm Browning handgun. Throughout the rest of the day everybody, including Hamilton had been shooting from 25 yards. Both the witness and Hamilton were using commercial ammunition. At roughly 4pm the meeting stopped.

The witness recalls no conversations being led by Hamilton in the journey home in the car nor does he recall any mention of guns. Having dropped him off at his home in Stirling the witness gave Hamilton his holdall out of the boot at which point Hamilton offered the witness money for petrol which the witness declined.

On re-entering the car Alexis Fawcett commented in hearing of the witness "Thank God he is away, what a weirdo".

STATEMENT 582/C – POLICE WITNESS
Steven Connell, Police Constable, 259 Underwater Research Unit at Headquarters, Stirling – service, 16 years.

The witness is a Police Officer who recovered a rail ticket from Dunblane to Stirling on 12th March, 1996. On arrival at the scene of the incident on Wednesday, 13th March, 1996 the witness was informed by a member of the Underwater Research Unit that Unit members would have the task of removing the children's bodies from the gymnasium. He returned to the headquarters to pick up equipment and was thereafter conveyed by patrol car back to the locus. When he returned to the locus he began directing surviving children and parents away from the school.

At roughly 5.30pm on the same day upon arrival at the headquarters the witness was informed that he was required for further duties with the force search team. He had a duty to comprise searching the dwellinghouse at 7 Kent Road, Stirling. He attended with other members of the search team under the command of Inspector Huskie. The witness stated that the search was completed at roughly 9pm.

On Wednesay, 20th March, 1996 the witness was again instructed to support the full search team to return to the dwellinghouse at 7 Kent Road, Stirling to carry out a further search. At about 2pm on 20th he attended at this house where an extensive search was carried out. The only property recovered was a rail ticket valid from Stirling to Dunblane. The search was completed at about 6pm on the same day.

STATEMENT 598/C – CIVILIAN WITNESS
Mr Robert John Togneri – Retired School Teacher.

The witness met and spoke to Hamilton at 11am on 11th March, 1996 in Stirling Town Centre. The witness had previous knowledge of Hamilton by virtue of having been a member of the Stirling Chess Club for around 40 years. Hamilton had joined as a teenage boy in the mid 60s which was the only basis on which the witness was associated with Hamilton. He stayed in the Chess Club for 5 or 6 years before dropping out. There were occasions when they would bump into each other in the street, they talked casually, Hamilton generally talking about the fact that he had started up boys clubs.

The last time the witness met Hamilton was on Monday, 11th March, 1996 in Murray Place outside R S McColl in Stirling at roughly 11am. During their walk together the witness noticed that Hamilton was unusually sad and quiet. He seemed to have something on his mind and was very subdued. When asked how the numbers at the boys clubs were he said with his head lowered that they were not very good. He then offered to buy the witness a meal which the witness found strange because he hardly knew him.

STATEMENT 630/C – CIVIILIAN WITNESS
Mr William Patrick Campbell – Plant Operator.

The witness is a Competition Secretary of Stirling Rifle and Pistol Club and spoke of Hamilton attending meetings in January 1996, 18th February 1996 and 2nd March 1996. The witness describes Hamilton adapting targets. The witness attended the meeting on 27th January 1996 at the Whiteson Range in Dunblane. The only enquiry made by a witness about Hamilton at this point was to ask another what his name was.

The witness saw Hamilton on 18th February 1996 at Whiteson Range and paid little attention to him. All that the witness recalls is that he was using two Browning 9mm handguns. He noticed Hamilton because he was carrying both guns in holsters attached to a belt around his waist. The witness comments that most people only have one holster.

On Thursday, 29th February, 1996 the witness was at home and was phoned by Hamilton asking for a lift to the Largs shoot. He arranged with Hamilton for him to be at his house at 9am in the morning of Saturday 2nd March 1996 which he said he would. It was later agreed that Alex Woods, a friend of the witness would drive through to Largs. They then picked up Alexis Fawcett, the witness' cousin.

The witness recalls that at the Largs shoot, Hamilton was using two Browning 9mm handguns. The witness believes that Gordon Crawford, statement 193/C told him that Hamilton was using another gun as well but cannot recall what it was.

At around 12.30pm Hamilton came forward to the targets being used which were of the "advancing man" type and placed two fluorescent red stickers about 3 x 2 inches in size on to the target. He placed a sticker on the middle of the head of the man and the other on to the chest area. The stickers are usually fixed to the bullseye of the target but Hamilton had fixed them well above the marked target area which is in the lower stomach area of the figure. The witness found this odd but did not ask Hamilton about it nor can he recall seeing anyone else ever do this.

The witness recalls being told by Gordon Crawford, witness that Hamilton was a poor shot as regards to Police Pistol one. The witness recalls Hamilton using commercial ammunition.

On the journey home the witness asked Hamilton if he had enjoyed himself and he replied that he had. The witness found Hamilton to be very quiet and reserved but always conducting himself properly on the range. The witness recalls Alexis Fawcett to the effect of "Thank God he is gone, what a weirdo. He talks of guns as if they were babies" once Hamilton was dropped off in Stirling. The witness told her that she was being harsh and that Hamilton struck him as being okay.

On Friday 29th March 1996 a Police Officer, acting Detective Constable Harper, a non witness, called at the witness' home in relation to the Thomas Hamilton inquiry. The witness was shown production number LE33, a piece of paper with writing on it. The witness believes the writing on the top left hand corner of the page headed Stirling to Falkirk refers to train times in relation to the timetable for trains the day Hamilton came to his house for a lift to Largs but believes that the times shown are for later trains. The writing in the top of the right hand corner clearly refers to the address of the witness' home and directions to his flat.

The final part of the text and piece of paper refers to instructions of how to change and line up the sights on a handgun which the witness presumes were for one of the Browning 9mm handguns Hamilton owned. The witness does not know how he came to have the information in changing the sights of a gun.

STATEMENT 632/C – CIVILIAN WITNESS
Mr William McFadyen – schoolboy.

The witness speaks to attending Hamilton's club nights at Dunblane High School and Bannockburn High School and attending Bannockburn Club on 12th February 1996 at which he spoke to Hamilton. The witness attends Cowie Primary School and also attended the Boys Club run by Hamilton at Bannockburn High School on Tuesday nights between 6pm and 8pm run by Hamilton. He has been attending for the past 5 weeks and attends with four of his friends (non witnesses). He also attended every second Thursday at the Boys Club In Dunblane High School also run by Hamilton. On these days Hamilton picked them up in a yellow Council bus and took them to Dunblane.

On Thursday, 29th February 1996 when the witness was travelling in the bus to Dunblane, Hamilton told him that he had lots of guns and that he liked going pigeon shooting. He asked the witness what films he liked. He replied that he wasn't sure. Hamilton then told him that he like Terminator films and types like that.

On Tuesday, 12th March 1996 the witness attended the club at Bannockburn High School. He received a medal for gymnastics that night. At roughly 7.45pm he asked Mr Hamilton if football would be on at the Thursday club in Dunblane. He replied that it wouldn't as he was **going to see a man in Dunblane**. He didn't say who or what for.

STATEMENT 706/C – CIVILIAN WITNESS
Mrs Helen Fairbairn Martin MacDonald – housewife.

The witness is a friend of the accused/deceased who took a phone call from him at 9.08am on 12th March, 1996. The call was in connection with kitchen equipment.

STATEMENT 753 – CIVILIAN WITNESS
George Brown Hunter – Project Co-ordinator at Forth Valley Enterprise.

The witness works with Nigel Bell, statement 400/L. He had a conversation with him on the morning of Wednesday, 13th March, 1996 when Bell spoke of having met a man, Hamilton at his local gun club who had made him feel uneasy and had been shooting with a powerful gun at the range, Callander Rifle and Pistol Club. In conversation with Nigel Bell the witness discussed Deer stalking and poaching.

The conversation then turned to gun nuts and the witness mentioned Michael Ryan. The witness joked about how it was always the quiet unassuming member of the gun club who seemed to berserk. At this point Bell mentioned meeting someone at his gun club without mentioning his name and saying that the man had a quick powerful gun and that he felt him to be quite dangerous.

The witness only became aware of the fact that Thomas Hamilton and the person with whom Nigel Bell had been talking was the same person when mentioning to Bell that the Police were visiting him on 4th April, 1996 to talk to him about the conversation he had with Bell on the morning of Wednesday, 13 March, 1996.

STATEMENT 650/L
Geoffrey Clive Wood – Television News Cameraman.

The witness is an STV News Cameraman involved in a press news coverage events at the locus. He is also a member of Stirling and District Gun Club and an ex member of clubs in Callander and Glasgow. He speaks to being reasonably friendly with Hamilton. The witness got to know Hamilton in roughly 1981. The witness was not particularly friendly with Hamilton at any time.

In about 1987 Hamilton joined the club of Stirling District Gun Club and the witness would see him at shoots. In the late 80's, 1980-1989 Hamilton frequently phoned the witness asking for lifts in his car when going to shoots at Whitestone or Kerse Road at Stirling and District Gun Club. This was because he had recently closed down his shop premises in Stirling and had effectively become unemployed. The witness would sometimes run Hamilton to the shoots. The witness on occasion went into Hamilton's house only for a cup of coffee and from memory he never at any time saw photographs of any young boys within the house. The visits would last roughly only 20 minutes.

Hamilton did discuss taking Central Region to the Ombudsman over complaints about his boys club with the witness. The witness also remembers a lot of gossip was circulating at this time and that Hamilton had consequently stated that he was not a pervert.

In 1990 the witness bought from Hamilton a 9mm Beretta Pistol for £200.00. The transaction took place in November, 1990.

The last time the witness saw Thomas Hamilton was on 21st January 1996 when he went into his house for a coffee. The visit lasted roughly three quarters of an hour. During this visit they discussed the possibility of rejoining the Callander Rifle and Pistol Club. At sometime in the afternoon of Sunday, 9th March 1996 Thomas Hamilton telephoned the witness. The witness called back since he had visitors at the time. Hamilton wanted to let the witness know how he was getting on with the application for membership at Callander Rifle and Pistol Club. The witness felt that Hamilton was trying to persuade him to rejoin possibly so that he could give him future lifts. This was the last contact the witness had with Hamilton. The witness was not interested in rejoining the club.

In his capacity as a Television News Cameraman for STV the witness was involved in news coverage of the events on 13th March, 1996 and was surprised at the involvement of Hamilton.

He did not have any inclination at any time that Hamilton had homosexual tendencies. Nor did he ever suspect that he may have been a paedophile. During the 15 years in which the witness knew Hamilton he never noticed any changes in his behaviour or mental state. The only changes of physical change was adding weight in the last five years but as far as he is aware the witness believes that Hamilton used commercial ammunition. He is not aware of Hamilton ever having participated in close contact shooting whilst in his company. The witness believes that Hamilton was something of a loner.

STATEMENT 450/C – CIVILIAN WITNESS
Mr Robert Gouther – Clerical Officer at British Rail, Stirling.

The witness testifies to the nature of the Railway Ticket discovered by Police investigation in Hamilton's house and referred to earlier. For the journey on 12th March, 1996 from Dunblane to Stirling.

STATEMENT 51088/C – CIVILIAN WITNESS
Alexander David Robb – Joiner.

The witness first knew of Hamilton 17 years ago. His father purchased kitchen units from Hamilton's shop in Stirling. Hamilton came to take photographs of the kitchen once it had been installed and talked to the witness' father about the clubs he ran trying to encourage the witness' father to let the witness join. At this point the witness' father told him that he would not be going to any clubs run by Hamilton because of his tendencies to wee boys. At school the witness also heard of people referring to "Poofy Hamilton's Clubs".

The witness has a partner LH who has two children, S, 12 and G, 10 with whom he has lived for the past two years. G has been attending the boys club at Dunblane High School. When he first discovered this he expressed his concerns to LH based upon his previous experience of Hamilton. In late 1994 the witness' partner, LH had talked to her son G who had informed her that Hamilton had been taking pictures of him in different positions. On finding his partner LH upset the witness went with two of his friends, William

Wardlaw and Fraser Gillies to 7 Kent Road which he knew to be Hamilton's address from letters G had brought him concerning the club.

When he arrived the house was in darkness and he tried the door but it was locked. He listened at the door to see if any noise was coming from inside but he heard nothing and left. It was a Friday night. Later that night the witness returned to Hamilton's house and it was still in darkness and he could not get any response.

The witness tried with his friend William Wardlaw again the following Saturday morning, 10th December, 1994 to find out if this was Hamilton's address. Upon failing to do so he and his friend went to the Woodcraft shop formerly owned by Hamilton which was now a kitchen shop. He was informed by two boys in the shop that Hamilton was no longer involved in the shop. One of them said that he had been up to his old tricks and that other people had been looking for him.

Later in the afternoon they returned to the house to see if Hamilton was in and again got no response. On driving past the house before leaving William screamed out to the witness "there he is, there he is" and the witness saw Hamilton move the net curtains. The car was stopped and both parties jumped out. They ran towards the front door and started kicking it in. The witness screamed and shouted obscenities at Hamilton to let him in. He wanted to get back the photos that Hamilton had taken of G.

Within minutes Police arrived, the first car was a traffic Police car and the second a plain clothes car. The witness stated to the Police that Hamilton was a beast and that they had to recover photos Hamilton had taken of the child. Detective Sergeant Hamilton then entered Hamilton's house. A short time later the Officer came to the car with a photograph of G. The officer stated that Hamilton was not prepared to part with the photograph of the boy. The witness was later released by the Police saying there would be no further charges against him. The Police did say that allegations against Hamilton would be looked into and that he was already under investigation.

The witness phoned Hamilton's house at about 8.30-9pm that evening and threatened him demanding to have the photos returned to him. Hamilton reported the witness for malicious phone calls. On the Wednesday following the phone call to Hamilton's house, a small selection of photographs arrived at the address of the witness' partner, LH. The pictures had been destroyed but leaving enough of them to identify them as being pictures of G. From G's report of the photograph sessions these were not all the photos which had been taken. Included with the photographs was a receipt attached for bleach. The witness assumes that this was used to sabotage the photos.

The witness again phoned Hamilton telling him he knew that he had more photographs and threatened violence against him. The witness later was required to attend Dunblane Police Office where he was told to leave things in the hands of the Police. The witness finally saw Hamilton on 12th March 1996 in Dunblane in the High Street. They made eye contact but Hamilton ducked his head within his hood and walked away.

STATEMENT 51080/C – CIVILIAN WITNESS
William McArthur Wardlaw – Self employed Joiner.

In December, 1994 the witness was drinking in a pub with Alexander Robb on a Friday night. He left but later returned telling the witness that his girlfriend, LH said that photographs had been taken of G at a boys club. Robb stated photographs had been taken of G at a boys club. Robb stated that Thomas Hamilton had taken G into another room away from the other boys and had made him get changed in front of him. Numerous details of the events as narrated by Alexander Robb.

The photograph brought out by Police from Hamilton's house was an enlargement of about 8 inches by 5 of G wearing trunks. It was from his knees up and in an athletic stance with him standing straight up with his arms stretched out wide at his sides. The Police understood that there were a lot of photographs of wee boys which could not be considered explicit and that there wasn't much they could do.

The witness had met Hamilton years before at a Dunblane shooting club at Dunblane A.T.C. He was about 7 years of age at the time. He was with his brother James. The witness attended Dunblane Shooting Club for slightly less than a year. The Club was for boys roughly up to the age of thirteen.

STATEMENT G63A
Police Witness – Constable 631, Graham Adamson, Dumbarton Police Office, Stirling – service seven years

He speaks to incident at 12.05am on 10 December, 1994 when he and Police witness, Murphy were informed by radio from Stirling Office that there were two males attempting to break into a flat at 7 Kent Road, Stirling. Hamilton was the occupier of the flat and the complainer. The two men kicking in the door said that they were not trying to break in but were simply trying to get in to speak to Mr Hamilton against whom he believed they had a personal grievance. Hamilton explained that he believed the two persons were trying to kick the rear door in although he was aware that they wished to speak to him. The witness explained their grievance to Hamilton and checked the flat exterior for damage and found none whatsoever. Hamilton stated that he did not wish to make a complaint. Hamilton showed the witness several large poster boards approximately four feet by three feet covered in large photographs approximately ten by eight of young boys in various gymnastic poses. All the boys wore were dark shorts and nothing else.

STATEMENT 1052A
Police Witness – Constable 248 Robert Murphy, Traffic Department Police Headquarters, Stirling.

On 10 December, 1994 the witness was on uniform duty on mobile patrol accompanied by the Police witness, Adamson. The witness recounts the events of 10 December, 1994 at 12.05 am as stated earlier. He recounts all the events in the manner identical of Graham Adamson.

STATEMENT 1061

William Hamilton, Detective Sergeant 210, CI Department, Alloa – service twelve years.

He refers to having seen at about 11am on Monday, 22 April, 1996 the report from a computer print out of an incident occurring at 7 Kent Road, Stirling on 10 December, 1994. He recounts the events of that being the witness found in the house numerous photographs of varying sizes throughout the house and slides some of an indecent nature and he could find no material other than photographs. In the front bedroom of the house he found a lock fast gun cabinet which Hamilton opened for him and produced a current firearms licence. The witness verified that all of the guns in his possession were legitimately owned and noted also that there was a quantity of ammunition for handguns which he was also entitled to have possession of.

STATEMENT 651A

Police Witness, Alan Simpson, Detective Constable, CI Department, Callander – service seven years.

The witness speaks to having seen at 11am on Monday, 1 April, the computer print out of the incident on 10 December, 1994 at 7 Kent Road, Stirling. At the incident the witness took details of Alexander David Robb and William McCarthy Wardlaw. The witness waited with Mr Robb and Mr Wardlaw while D.S. Hamilton visited Thomas Hamilton. After a short time DS Hamilton returned and informed Robb that Hamilton had refused to hand over the photograph of Mr Robb.

For further information, go to http://dunblaneunburied.co.uk